Counter
Clockwise

Counter Clockwise

My Year of Hypnosis, Hormones,
Dark Chocolate, and Other Adventures
in the World of Anti-Aging

LAUREN KESSLER

RODALE.

© 2013 by Lauren Kessler

Trade hardcover first published by Rodale Inc. in April 2013.
Trade paperback first published by Rodale Inc. in April 2014.

Rodale books may be purchased for business or promotional use or for special sales. For information, please write to:
Special Markets Department, Rodale Inc., 733 Third Avenue, New York, NY 10017.

Printed in the United States of America
Rodale Inc. makes every effort to use acid-free ♾, recycled paper ♻.

Book design by Laura White

Library of Congress Cataloging-in-Publication Data is on file with the publisher.

ISBN-13: 978–1–60961–347–1 hardcover
ISBN-13: 978–1–62336–374–1 paperback

Distributed to the trade by Macmillan

2 4 6 8 10 9 7 5 3 1 paperback

We inspire and enable people to improve their lives and the world around them.
rodalebooks.com

For Nanny:

Too cool to be forgotten

contents

Introduction

Ticktock

I HAVE BEEN LYING ABOUT MY AGE SINCE I TOLD WAYNE, THE tousle-haired Atlantic City pool boy, that I was 16. (I was really 13 . . . well, I would *turn* 13 in a month.) Four years later I told the nice lady at a resort in the White Mountains that I was a college sophomore (I was a high school junior) so she would hire me for a summer job. When, fresh out of grad school, I got a university teaching job and discovered that my teaching assistants were older than I was, I suddenly aged four years to bolster my credibility. Now, of course—and for close to two decades—I've been subtracting, not adding, the years. I lie about my age all the time. I lie so often that I forget how old I really am. I'm serious. I actually have to do the math in my head when someone asks. Not that I tell the truth, but it gives me a baseline from which to fabricate. I lie to everyone except the federal government and my insurance company, and I'd lie to them if it wasn't a crime. I would lie to my husband, but unfortunately we met before I started subtracting.

Why do I lie?

It's complicated.

It's not that I want to actually *be* my younger self—as in aimless, confused, angst-ridden, a nail-biting cigarette smoker with a dud of a boyfriend and a job I hate, driving a clunker car and sleeping on 100-count muslin sheets. *Muslin.* I am not interested in going clubbing, rockin' the funky boho look, or dating a 25-year-old guy. What I am interested in, what I powerfully and passionately want, is to be all those good things we associate with "young." Because, despite my independence of spirit and my modest successes and a strong streak of feminism, I am part of a culture that labels "old" bad (weak, sickly, sexless, boring, crabby) and "young" good (healthy, vibrant, sexy, creative, adventurous). And I want to be good. I don't mean just looking good—which is a given. I mean deep-down, from-the-inside-out *feeling* good.

Sadly, our negative and sometimes downright nasty stereotypes about age are entrenched, pervasive, and very difficult to escape or ignore. Forget about mining sociological treatises on the subject. Just stand in front of the birthday card section at your local store, and here's what you'll see: On the front of one card are two older ladies blowing on party favors. The text reads, "At our age, we don't call it a 'party favor' anymore." Inside: "We call it a work-out." Or this one: An overdressed older woman in a fur coat is standing outside a bathroom stall looking confused. Inside the card, the text reads, "At your age it all comes down to one question. What was it I came in here for?" Really? Late middle age is about not having the breath to blow on a party favor and forgetting why you walked into the bathroom?

How old do you have to be for the greeting card industry to assault you with insults masquerading as humor? Not as old as you think. Maybe, in fact, as old as you are *right now*. On one card, a cross-eyed cartoon vulture is perched on a branch. The text reads, "So, you're 50. Hey, look on the bright side." Inside: "Okay, so there is no bright side. There's a bright light, but you're gonna want to stay away from that." At 50 there is no "bright side"? At 50 you're eyeing death? The card next to it proclaims in big bubble letters, "40 isn't old!" Inside: "Cover isn't true!" Forty is old? What about "40 is the new 30"? Aren't magazines targeted to women "of a certain age" (now seemingly defined as the first day after your 35th birthday) proclaiming just this in upbeat stories accompanied by airbrushed, studio-lit photos of gorgeous women who are 40 but look 25? The message—and I'm not convinced it is a positive one—doesn't seem to be moving the culture in an age-friendly direction. The stereotypes are alive and well.

Unlike, apparently, the people being stereotyped.

Consider that on a Web page looking for answers to the question "Could you give me some examples of stereotypes of older people?" you will find links to sites about fall prevention and dementia and paid ads for an assisting living facility and an online store selling wheelchairs. No need, really, to cite any examples of stereotypes in order to answer the question. The examples are right there, in front of you. "Older" means fragile, sickly, and dependent. "Older" is no fun. Not for you, and certainly not for those around you. And "older" is . . . 40? Is it any wonder that I—any of us—want to distance ourselves from the (ever increasing) number that announces our (ever increasing) age? Is it any wonder that I lie about my age, what with midlife lampooned as the end of anything interesting about you or happening to you and the beginning of a night table stocked with meds?

I know it is horribly unenlightened of me to buy into our youth-obsessed culture. I should be seeking wisdom, not toned abs. I should be thinking great and significant thoughts, not worrying about the slowdown in my metabolic rate. I am smart and educated. I know why—and how—youth is sold in the marketplace. And I know, as 1 of 50 million or so baby-boom women in America, that I am in the commercial crosshairs. I have a target pinned on my back. But, although I can prevent myself from falling for some of the products aimed at my lucrative demographic, I can't seem to prevent myself from being captive to the ideology. I wish I were like those 40- or 50-something "comfortable with everything about myself" women quoted in magazines. You know, the self-accepting, "I've earned every wrinkle and gray hair and I'm proud of it" women? I've earned a lot of things I am proud of, but incipient jowls is not one of them. No, I am more of a "rage, rage against the dying of the light" kind of woman.

I love what Woody Allen had to say to the *New York Times* reporter who asked him how he felt about aging. (Allen was then in his mid-70s.) "Well, I'm against it," he said—and then laughed. But he wasn't joking. "It has nothing to recommend it," he continued. "You fall apart, is what happens." Later in the interview he said he would trade any wisdom or understanding of life that might come with age for "being 35 again." Woody Allen may be the iconic American neurotic, but if he's being neurotic about aging here, it's a neurosis millions, even tens of millions, of us share.

Fearing aging is about fearing death, or infirmity, or a progressive lack of independence. And maybe it's about vanity. Of course it's about vanity. But it is also about control—about how much of it we have over our own bodies, our own lives, our futures. In other words, this whole aging thing is loaded. So when I lie about my age I'm not just fiddling with numbers. I'm giving expression to my own fears of illness and dependence, of someday not being the boss. I'm grabbing hold of the hands of my biological (analog) clock and trying to slow down the entire mechanism. Or reverse it. What I really want is not to *say* I am younger than I am. I want to *be* younger than I am. And by "be" I mean feel, act, think, and, yes, I admit, look younger than the number on my driver's license would indicate.

I think it's fair to question what that number actually means, the number that marks our years on earth, the number I've been adding to and subtracting from since I was 12. Is that number really how old I am? Here's one way of looking at it: My DNA and my eggs are the only parts of me that date back to the day of my birth. My skin cells are sloughing off and replacing themselves every moment. Over about a month, my entire epidermis is replaced. So, going by that measurement, I am one month old. The entire lining of my stomach and intestine is continually re-created, with a turnover time of a week or less. Inside my gut I am practically a newborn! My red blood cells are never more than four months old. My liver cells are perhaps a year old. My skeleton rebuilds itself too, with estimates ranging from a two-year to a seven-year regeneration process. The body is not a permanent structure, like a building with an etched bronze plaque: "Erected 1961." It is in a constant state of renewal.

Forgive the biology lesson. I love learning (and sharing) snippets of information like this. It's one of the joys of turning life's challenges into first-person journalistic investigations—which is what I do. When my mother died of Alzheimer's, and I was struggling to come to terms with that, I turned my confusion and grief into a three-year project (that became a book) exploring, from the trenches, the world inhabited by people with this disease. When my about-to-be-teenaged daughter was driving me crazy, when I was struggling to navigate the stormy seas of the mother-daughter relationship (and sinking), I turned it into a journalistic project (and a book). I would understand teen girl culture. I would plumb the depths of the mother-daughter bond. The project kept me sane and, to my great surprise, elevated, enriched, and greatly improved our relationship. Now I find myself facing (or refusing to face), scared of, angry about, and generally locked in a psychological battle with the idea—not to mention the reality—of aging. I hate the stereotypes. I fear the losses those stereotypes tell me are just around the corner. I am so not ready to fade away. So what do I do? I channel my angst. I turn it into a project. I make a story out of it.

I am immediately comforted when I discover that those who study aging question the relevance and veracity of the number of candles lit on your birthday cake. Chronological age is meaningless, say the experts at Tufts University's Human Nutrition Research Center on Aging. It's the age of the body that's important, the true biological ages of the heart, lungs, arteries, brain, muscles—everything inside. The Baltimore Longitudinal Study of Aging, a massive effort that tracked 3,000 people from their 20s to their 90s, concluded that people age at such vastly different rates that by the time they reach 80 or 90, the differences are so marked that birth dates are entirely irrelevant. In fact, there seems to be widespread agreement that after age 35 or 40, the date on your birth certificate is one of the least accurate indications of how old you are. Yes: Every day you *get* older. But the pace at which you *grow* older varies enormously. We don't have control over the former. We do have far more control than we think over the latter.

WHY DO WE AGE? "SENESCENCE," AS THE PROGRESSIVE deterioration of bodily functions over time is called, is one of the least understood biological processes. Back in the mid-1970s, when the National Institute on Aging was established, gerontologists were looking for a single, all-encompassing theory of aging. But we are dauntingly complex organisms, and it is highly unlikely that one single theory is going to explain our passage through time. Instead, for the past almost 40 years, scientists have been postulating, researching, and debating a number of ideas. One notion is that we are genetically programmed to age (and die), that each of us is born with our own unique internal biological clock—a self-destruct program that resides in our DNA—that controls how many times our cells can replicate. When our cells hit that limit, they die. When cells die, the organism dies.

Other schools of thought suggest that aging is the result of wear and tear on the body or the destructive work of free radicals or the slow buildup of errors as cells go about the business of replicating themselves. Or maybe these hardworking machines that are our bodies are being gunked up by the accumulation of molecular garbage. Related to this is a newer idea—recently bolstered by the findings of a Mayo Clinic study—that damaged, dying, or dead cells actively harm the cells around them. It's a sort of aging-is-contagious approach.

Researchers may have differing ideas about why we age, but they do agree that there are two distinct (but overlapping) aging processes: primary aging and secondary aging. Primary aging is the body aging itself, whether by self-destruct instructions or free radical damage or nasty dead-cell damage or the accumulation of errors and random mistakes. Secondary aging is the result of the accumulation over time of everything we do or do not do to ourselves, the choices we make every day about how we live. Secondary aging speeds up the biological clock, resulting in everything from plaque in our arteries to wrinkles on our faces. Many experts now think that lifestyle accounts for close to 70 percent of how and how quickly (or slowly) we age. That means, to a great extent, secondary aging is within our control. Control. I like that word.

In a way, this is revolutionary. For so long, the standard (and unhelpful) response to "How do I age well?" or "How do I stay healthy?" has been "Choose your parents carefully." But if heredity is only 30 percent of our future, then vibrant—or sickly—parents will only take us so far. In another way, though, this relatively recent revelation about the power of secondary aging and the control it gives us is just par for the course. Those of us in the midst of or fast approaching midlife are accustomed to exerting power over our health in ways unimaginable to past generations. Polio vaccines, organ transplants, birth control, Prozac: We've grown up in an age where health and well-being have come more and more under our control. So why not control aging?

That's a rhetorical question, really. From Harvard researchers to Internet scammers, from Big Pharma to the holistic practitioner down the block, controlling aging is, without a doubt, the next big thing. "Anti-aging" is simultaneously important science and a valuable brand. It is, according to the AARP, an $88 billion business. The *Global Strategic Business Report* on anti-aging products—an almost 200-page-long, statistic-laden study that tracks 799 companies involved in making or marketing anti-aging pharmaceuticals, supplements, and products (and costs $4,450 to download)—projects a $292 billion international marketplace by 2015. Much of this money is being or will be spent by the baby-boom generation. This much ballyhooed (by themselves), much stereotyped (by others) generation—my generation—is now turning 60 at the rate of 330 people an hour. That's a compelling way to state a statistic. It comes from an aggressively promotional brochure directed at doctors who may want to "develop a lucrative new revenue stream" and "earn excellent income without the need to take insurance."

In fact, the field of anti-aging medicine is the most rapidly growing medical specialty today, with as many as 30,000 physicians (mostly MDs, but also doctors of osteopathy and others) in more than 100 countries. The practitioners are encouraged, supported, and, in many cases, accredited by the American Academy of Anti-Aging Medicine and the World Anti-Aging Academy of Medicine. Medical-practice entrepreneurs have flocked to this new and expanding marketplace, offering "turn-key packages," "custom private-label supplements," and "effective national and local marketing programs" for medical professionals looking to jump on the anti-aging bandwagon. This is not to say that some anti-aging docs aren't sincerely interested in preventive and restorative medicine, in helping people maintain and enhance vitality, not merely deal with disease. Given the way health care is delivered in our country, a "provider" can be simultaneously Hippocratic and entrepreneurial. It is probably the norm.

I have to say: I hate the word (or brand) "anti-aging." It's associated with $200-an-ounce wrinkle crèmes and surgeries that transform faces into masks and kooks who arrange to freeze their bodies in cryogenically controlled coffins. There's a desperation about it, a failure to ground oneself in what it means to be alive. I hate the word because it's silly—and meaningless. You can't be *anti* aging—against aging—the way you can be anti capital punishment or anti animal testing. If you stand against aging, if you say "No!" to aging, what exactly are you in favor of? What are your options? Death or the deep freeze?

Those in the scientific and medical communities who are most serious and thoughtful about controlling the speed and trajectory of aging look at the whole thing differently. They are not against aging; they are in favor of increased and prolonged health and vitality. True, there is a minority, mostly on the fringes (although often no less serious and thoughtful), who focus their attention on longevity, the extension of the human life span. But the pushback there—and it is significant—is that simply living longer, assuming that this is possible, may not be particularly desirable—for the individual or for society. Recently, researchers at the University of Southern California found that while life expectancy increased by 1 year during the past decade, people also faced an additional 1.2 years of serious illness and an extra 2 years of disability. By some estimates, nearly 85 percent of people over 65 suffer from one or more degenerative disorders. Who would want to live to be 120 or 150 if that meant 40 or 50 years of failing health and decreasing independence, of disease and medication? What society would want to—and could afford to—support such a population?

Most of those interested in untangling the mysteries of aging for our benefit think instead about how to extend that healthy middle of life that so many of us enjoy. Someone cleverly coined the word "middlescense" (like adolescence only much older, and with no acne) to capture those generally vital years between, say, 40 and 60. Prolonging middlescense is about preserving the (relatively) youthful function, attitude, and even appearance of midlife into the years—and hopefully the decades—beyond. Others talk about "extending the health span," which is basically the same idea. It's not about stretching out the total number of years lived (life span); it's about extending the total number of years lived with energy, vitality, and health. Or, as a very long bumper sticker might put it: "It's not about adding years to life. It's about adding life to years."

If you prefer geek-speak to bumper-sticker-ese, the phrase you're looking for is "compression of morbidity"—that is, reducing the time spent suffering from illness, which is another way of saying extending the healthy period. There's also the unnecessarily clunky expression "rectangularization of life." Imagine your life as a line graph with a slow climb from birth through youth to mid-adulthood, an apex at 35 or 40, and then a long decline (in the absence of something catastrophic) until death. Now take away the long decline. Imagine instead a prolonged plateau at the top with a brief sayonara at the end. The line graph now looks more like three (unequal) sides of a rectangle rather than the peak of a mountain.

What exactly is possible in this brave new (scientific, medical, and commercial) world full of tantalizing research, bold promises, controversial therapies, and perhaps a bit too much wishful thinking? What is possible if we get serious about that 70 percent of secondary aging that is within our control? Vitality and resilience into old age, according to groundbreaking MacArthur Foundation research on successful aging undertaken almost 20 years ago. A health span and a life span that match, or come as close as possible to it, according to researchers at the Human Nutrition Research Center on Aging at Tufts. A biological age that is younger than your chronological age, says a top Johns Hopkins gerontologist.

Or, to escape the box of Western medicine and thought for a moment, consider this notion, which I'm calling the Tao of aging. It's derived from the concept of the Three Jewels (or Treasures) of traditional Chinese medicine, the essential energies that sustain human life. We are all born with these three treasures: *jing*, our physical essence; *qi*, our energy and life force; and *shen*, our spirit and soul. The Guatemala-born, California-educated Chinese herbalist who explained this to me said she thinks we are like candles. Jing is the wax; qi is the flame; shen is the candle's light put out into the world. Is it possible to keep our flames burning bright? Can we burn as brightly, put as much light (and heat) into the world, at 65 or 70 as we did at 35 or 40?

That's what my quest will be about. I intend to look at the best research and the worst scams, to go to conferences and clinics, to spend time in cutting-edge laboratories and on big-promise Web sites, to ask questions, to observe, and to use myself—within reason—as a guinea pig. This is, after all, far more than a journalistic exercise for me. It is a personal mission. It's my way of facing the ticking clock. Can I halt or turn back its hands?

A detox cleanse promises a rejuvenated gut? I'll try it. Caloric restriction is the answer to a more youthful me? Bring it on. Supplements and herbal concoctions? Metabolic boosters? Human chorionic gonadotropin? Superfoods? Creative visualization? Hot yoga? A self-compassion workout (probably needed after hot yoga)? Yes. And yes again. At the end of this journey, at the end of this book, I want to be able to report to you that I am younger than I am right now.

one

Viva Las Vegas

I AM SITTING ON ONE OF SEVERAL THOUSAND CHAIRS SET up in long, neat rows in a room roughly the size of a football field located deep in the bowels of the 1-million-square-foot Mandalay Bay Convention Center. There is no bay. And Mandalay (a city in Upper Burma) is a good 8,000 miles away. Much closer—next door, in fact— is the 30-story Luxor pyramid (a mere 100 feet shorter than the Great Pyramid of Giza), and just down the street is a two-thirds-scale Arc de Triomphe.

You have guessed that I am in Las Vegas.

I am here for the 18th Annual International Congress on Anti-Aging Medicine and Regenerative Biomedical Technologies. I mention the locale, this ersatz landscape, this topography of illusion and pretend, because it is more than venue. It is theme and subtext. Vegas is both a working city and a fantasy playground, a place for dreamers and risk takers run by eagle-eyed entrepreneurs and hardheaded businessmen. Which is, in many ways, how I come to think of this conference during my three days in attendance: an almost seamless blend of fantasy and reality, of science and hucksterism, of life-changing research and unadulterated opportunism.

The twice-yearly conference (the other venue is, predictably, Orlando, home of that *other* commercial fantasy-scape, Disney World) is sponsored by, and the public face of, the American Academy of Anti-Aging Medicine, known as A4M. It is an interesting—and controversial—organization, an upstart in the world of mainstream medicine, a group that, like the specialty it represents, has attracted both true believers and harsh critics. A nonprofit organization that trains and certifies physicians in anti-aging medicine, it began with 30 like-minded doctors in the early 1990s and has grown to include more than 22,000 members in 100-plus countries. A4M's conventions got off to an unconventional start in 1993, when a small group of physicians gathered for the opening of an anti-aging clinic in Mexico. The founder of the clinic, a 59-year-old businessman, was an early adopter of and proselytizer for the use of human growth hormone. He'd been flying down to Mexico to get injections and, after reporting miraculous anti-aging results, decided to start a clinic of his own.

Today, although A4M "board certifies" physicians in anti-aging medicine, the specialty itself is not recognized by established medical organizations like the American Medical Association and the American Board of Medical Specialties. Some physicians, intrigued by functional or regenerative medicine (the other terms used for the anti-aging approach), have embraced the new specialty. Others call it a "sham" and a "racket" because of both its powerful entrepreneurial bent—the clinics and therapies and treatments and supplements that can directly enrich a specialist's practice—and the less-than-gold-standard science that supports it. Much (not all, but much) of the science behind commercial anti-aging therapies does not come from large-scale, placebo-controlled, double-blind human studies. Although that approach is not without its critics, its carefully constructed scientific investigations are designed to be as objective as possible, removing the chance for the investigators themselves to influence the outcome, controlling for factors that might affect the results, and including a (human) test group large enough to generalize from. Studies like this are phenomenally expensive. They are undertaken with an eye toward FDA approval of a drug or treatment and the subsequent bonanza that approval can mean for a drug company. But many anti-aging treatments are supplement based. Supplements are classified as food, not drugs, so FDA approval is not needed, and that means large-scale human studies are not required—and, because of their prohibitive cost, not undertaken. Thus reports on the successes of various therapies come from small studies, animal studies, and that bane of every scientist's existence, anecdotal evidence.

The organization doesn't do itself any favors with its stance of aggressive self-promotion. And it probably doesn't help the cause of mainstream acceptance that the founders of A4M, Ronald Klatz, MD, and Robert Goldman, MD, are not shy. And by "not shy" I mean: They are showmen. Klatz, credited with coining the term "anti-aging" and hailed by *BusinessWeek* as its "guru," is the author of 32 books with, as his Web site will tell you, "over 2 million copies in print." He was an early and enthusiastic proponent of using human growth hormone to purportedly reverse aging, and his *Grow Young with HGH* was a national bestseller in the late 1990s. He is an enthusiastic producer of podcasts and a tireless self-marketer.

Klatz's A4M partner and friend, Robert Goldman, calls himself "anti-aging's global ambassador." And he is. The man travels the world, consulting and teaching at universities from Central America to South Asia. He sits on boards, creates companies, gets handed keys to Italian cities, and actively—and I do mean actively—promotes physical fitness. He holds 20 world strength records, including one for 13,500 consecutive situps and another for 321 consecutive handstand pushups. You will find him in *Guinness World Records*. You will also find him at this A4M convention, waiting in the wings as his colleague, Dr. Klatz, opens the show.

The convention center's main ballroom is so cavernous that, even though I am sitting only a third of the way back from the stage, I can hardly make out Klatz's face. Happily, there is a movie-theater-size screen on each side of the dais that projects the image to me and the 5,000 or so other people from 60 countries who have gathered here to learn the latest about anti-aging research from more than 100 presenters.

Klatz, 10 feet tall on screen, is not, alas, the best advertisement for his specialty. He is thick-necked, a little portly, and a little out of breath, all of which I find oddly comforting. His message this morning is upbeat and inspirational—in both medical and commercial terms. He is a coach speaking to his players, players who love and believe in the game. And want to win.

"Anti-aging medicine is transforming the practice of medicine and transforming the world," he tells us. "It is a new intelligence for the entire planet." Klatz says that anti-aging medicine is the world's fastest-growing medical specialty, the "hottest trend" in health care. In case there's any doubt as to what this means to the audience gathered in the convention hall, he ends his welcome with this statistic: By the year 2015, revenue in the global anti-aging market will exceed $200 billion.

Dr. Goldman is next up. I was hoping he would do a few handstand pushups, but instead he delivers a brief, passionate message about wellness that positions anti-aging medicine at the forefront of best practices. "It is about health, not illness," he says. "Conventional medicine waits until something breaks to fix it. Anti-aging medicine intervenes before that happens. It is about prevention." I find the message powerful and convincing. The two doctors, in less than five minutes, have managed to get me on their team. And they're just getting warmed up.

Third at bat, and apparently a regular at these conventions, is Ken Dychtwald, PhD, a psychologist, gerontologist, author of 15 books, filmmaker, and, as he later tells us, "old hippie" and friend of spiritual figure Ram Dass. He is 60 with a full head of curly hair, the posture and stance of a 30-year-old, and the energy and excitement of a revivalist preacher. He says that 65 was selected as the marker of old age back in the mid-1800s. Up on the screen flashes a slide of the iconic painting Whistler's Mother, painted when she was 65. Her back is curved. She's got jowls and a turkey neck. Then he clicks the remote in his hand and next to Whistler's Mother there appears a photo of Sophia Loren at 65. Let me just say that Whistler's mother suffers somewhat by comparison. The audience laughs, then claps.

He clicks through a slide show featuring active, adventurous, tech-savvy, vibrant older people. He shows a picture of John Glenn suited up for his final space journey at age 77. Glenn looks clear-eyed and resolute, strong and vital, ready for the challenge. "People want to be healthy so they can continue to dream and create and do meaningful things," he says. I can't help myself: I clap.

Dychtwald says he wants to do away with the term "retirement." Me too. I think of stewed prunes and All-Bran for breakfast, fishing trips, knitting projects, those special recliners with the lever that tips the seat forward so you can get your aging ass out of the chair. As Dychtwald talks, I look up "retirement" on my smartphone. "The act of retreating," says the entry. "The act of withdrawing into seclusion." That's not what I have in mind for the latter part of my life. Whatever else happens at this convention, I tell myself, I will keep Ken Dychtwald's message in mind. Staying youthful, vital, and healthy can have a purpose.

Before the opening speeches this morning, I spent a solid hour studying the convention booklet with the goal of plotting my own schedule for the next two and a half days. The booklet, a hefty, magazine-size publication larded with advertising, lists every paper presentation, speech, and seminar, from the marquee presenters who will address thousands in the ballroom to the unknowns assigned to one of the dozens of small seminar rooms. With four or five presentations scheduled for every hour, it's a challenge to figure out a plan. I want to see what doctors and researchers in this yet-to-be-recognized specialty of anti-aging think is most important, where they are pinning their hopes, what they see on the horizon. If anti-aging is, as Klatz says, the "hottest new trend," I want to know what the hottest new trend is within the hottest new trend.

Once upon a time, in the mid-1700s, the biggest thing in anti-aging involved placing five virgins in a small airtight room, piercing a hole through the wall of the chamber, and inserting the long neck of a flask used for distilling. The warm breath of the young girls would flow into the flask and condense into a "clear water, which is a tincture of admirable efficacy," a few drops of which could make the old young again. Dr. Johann Cohausen, whose theory this was, was only half kidding. Both a physician and a medical satirist (did you know that was a job category?), he lived to be 105.

Alas, I'm not expecting any presentations on virgin's breath today. I head out to my first session, the focus of which is inflammation— not the puffy-sprained-ankle kind of inflammation but internal inflammation, along the walls of arteries, in the brain, the kind that leads to cardiovascular disease and Alzheimer's, the kind that ages you from the inside out. This researcher, a fast-talker with a PowerPoint slide show only a biochemist could love, says that 90 percent of all chronic disease has an inflammation component—and that half of us suffer from at least one of those diseases. Chronic illness is both a marker for and an accelerator of aging.

Now she launches into the villains in this story: the unhealthy lifestyles of so many of us. She cites research suggesting a direct link between food—particularly sugary foods and foods rich in omega-6 fatty acids, like cottonseed oil and tub margarine. Her slides, with lipoprotein, CRP, IL-6, and TNF-alpha flowcharts, are simultaneously incomprehensible and utterly convincing. She talks about chronic stress and the stress hormone cortisol, about the evils of cigarettes and obesity, known for doing so much other damage to the body and now also indicted in the body's inflammatory response. She's not thrilled about EMFs and cell phones. I scribble notes about taking CoQ_{10}, vitamin D, and bioflavonoid supplements, which she says are powerful antiinflammatories, and wonder if I should get my cortisol level checked . . . especially right now, as I try to process all this information, copy down as many citations as I can, eavesdrop on a heated, albeit whispered, conversation behind me (the cell phone controversy), and check my schedule for the next session. I wonder: Can attending an anti-aging conference age you?

I'm off to Hyaluronic Acid: The Anti-Aging Answer for the Whole Body. I've never heard of hyaluronic acid, and my knowledge is not greatly enhanced by learning, in the presenter's introduction, that hyaluronic acid is an anionic, nonsulfated glycosaminoglycan distributed widely throughout connective, epithelial, and neural tissues. Whatever it is, we used to have a lot more of it when we were younger. Its presence accounted for our soft skin, vibrant circulatory system, healthy connective tissue, and limber joints. It appears to be a lubricant and repairer of tissues, the sort of molecule you want on your side. I'm not keeping up with the steady stream of slides, but I am understanding the basic idea: The plum-to-prune or grape-to-raisin phenomenon that is an unhappy external hallmark of aging occurs not only at the skin level, but also throughout the body. And it occurs, at least in part—this guy says in large part—because of decreasing levels of hyaluronic acid. The stuff is integral to our 50 to 100 trillion cells, our 60,000 miles of blood vessels (stats courtesy of one of the few slides I could actually comprehend), our ocular and oral health, our everything. As levels decrease as we age, we prune up from the inside.

I learn that medical use of hyaluronic acid has been around since the 1970s. It's been used in various eye surgeries, in the treatment of osteo-arthritis, to help alleviate eczema, and, since 2003, as a wrinkle-plumping injectable. (Restylane and Juvéderm are the brands you might recognize.) But this presentation is not about topical applications or injectable substances. It is about biochemically altering the body, which is really what much of this pioneering anti-aging research is about. In this case, it is about giving the body the hyaluronic acid it no longer makes or helping it make more so that we can be, inside and out, more plum than prune. It's one of those "this is the key to anti-aging" ideas— and there are many being forwarded at this conference—that sound too good to be true.

One of the overlooked benefits of aging is that your too-good-to-be-true antennae become increasingly sensitive to too-good-to-be-true ideas. My first thought is: Isn't the body far, far more complicated than this? It can't be that you tweak one chemical and fix everything. My next thought is that tagline from a long-ago margarine commercial: *It's not nice to fool Mother Nature.* That night, doing follow-up research back in my hotel room, it doesn't take me long to discover that hyaluronic acid, for all its wonderful actions in the body, is also an integral part of cancer metastases and angiogenesis (the growth of new blood vessels to nourish a tumor). So if I trick my body into producing more hyaluronic acid in an effort to stay plum- and grape-like, could I also be setting the stage for big problems? This is when one of those non-existent large-scale, double-blind, placebo-controlled studies would come in handy.

The last session I go to that afternoon is New Insights into Redox Signaling. I come with no insights, new or old, nor with any clue about what redox signaling is. The man who will enlighten me and the 50 or so others in the room has a PhD in atomic/medical physics (uh-oh) and has written and self-published a book on redox signaling. He is also, as are a number of the presenters, involved in the marketing of a product related to his talk. The signals he's talking about are the messages cells send to other cells. A cell needs to be able to identify when it's in trouble and then send out an SOS to get help. This internal communication system is apparently how the body manages and controls the healing process, how it keeps itself alive. We're not talking healing like knitting a wound, but rather the second-by-second repairs needed within cells. I learn that there's an everyday cleanup crew that needs to be signaled as cells make energy—and produce toxic wastes (oxidants, free radicals). Then there are the distress calls that go out when a cell is compromised by our poor choices (tobacco or alcohol use, poor nutrition, lack of exercise).

These *"Quick! Do something!"* messengers are called redox signaling molecules, and the presenter says they can help power up the cell's antioxidant shields, keep cellular communication channels clear, optimize immune function, and even enhance aerobic performance. Here's the catch: As cells age—that is, as we age—the number and the efficiency of these messenger molecules decrease. Signaling becomes less efficient and so our cells don't get the repair and rejuvenation they need, which leads to further aging, which leads to even less efficient signaling. You get the picture.

There is, of course, a cure: the world's first and only redox signaling molecule supplement. Like the fix-it for decreasing hyaluronic acid levels, this involves giving the body a version of what it naturally makes but is not, as it ages, making as much of. The testimonials from folks who take this supplement are remarkable. I read them later that night on a commercial Web site that features a prominent YouTube endorsement by the presenter. The folks who drink this special formulation ("redox signaling molecules suspended in a pristine saline solution") report that the product has ramped up their energy, taken away their ills, made them feel young again, and changed their lives. I don't doubt the sincerity and passion in the testimonials. But I also know the placebo effect can be extraordinarily powerful (and absolutely real). And who knows what other good and healthy things these folks were doing (or the bad habits they shed) while they were drinking the supplement. That's what, once again, a controlled, double-blind study would tell us.

The next morning begins with what is billed as the highlight of the convention, the must-see presentation: Suzanne Somers. Whether having Somers as the marquee attraction for A4M and its conventions—she has headlined more than a few of them—is a brilliant public relations move or a stunning (not to mention repetitive) error in judgment, I have no idea. But it is, for me, disconcerting to go to a medical convention and find a '70s sitcom star and ThighMaster spokesperson at the podium. On the other hand, she is the author of a string of best-selling self-help books aimed at the anti-aging crowd (*Sexy Forever, Ageless, Breakthrough, Bombshell*) and one of the country's most passionate and vocal adopters of alternative anti-aging therapies. And, at age 66, she is, at a distance, a walking advertisement for the industry: trim and toned with sculpted shoulders, a dancer's posture, and energy to burn. But her face—projected five feet high on the screens—looks like it's been worked over pretty hard. She has no nasolabial lines (those etchings that go from the nose to the sides of the mouth) and no fore-head wrinkles. Her skin looks stretched so tight that it might be painful. Her lips are, well, more generous than one would expect. Or find believable. She says she has had no plastic surgery and attributes her appearance to her daily "age management" regimen: injections of human growth hormone, a glutathione patch, a "designer" mix of estrogen, progesterone, testosterone, DHEA, and pregnenolone, and 80 to 90 different supplements. A few months after the convention, I read that she is conducting what appears to be a one-person clinical trial, attempting to regrow her breasts using stem cells. "Many people write Suzanne off as a quackadoo," Oprah Winfrey said when Somers appeared on her show a few years back. "But she just might be a pioneer." Or, I think as she takes the stage, both.

Whatever else she is, or isn't, Suzanne Somers is a great speaker. She is engaging and upbeat, articulate, organized, passionate, and—no small feat—conversational and friendly in front of a crowd of several thousand. She is both slick and sincere. She even borders on being authoritative. She speaks for more than 40 minutes without notes. And she says many of the "right" things: that good health is a choice we have to make for ourselves, that "eating crap and sitting on the couch" is not the path to a long and happy life, that to do good you have to feel good. But she also says that using bioidentical hormones is the key to optimum health (widely controversial) and that we all should be using Life-Wave glutathione patches for whatever ails us. (She is, I discover later, an "ambassador" for LifeWave. The patch, according to testimonials, erases sun damage, sharpens vision, increases strength, softens skin, and "almost within hours" turned one user into "a younger and more vibrant me.")

Somers is passionately insistent about the wonders of hormone replacement therapy (HRT), possibly the single most popular topic at this convention. What I have heard and read about HRT is so scary that

I haven't for a moment considered it for myself. The big news—shocking news, really—back in 2002 came from the discontinued Women's Health Initiative (WHI), a huge National Institutes of Health study that was in part designed to assess the benefits and risks of HRT. HRT was supposed to turn back the clock for women. Since the 1960s, pharmaceutical companies had been promoting hormone replacement as a way for women to be "feminine forever." (Both my aunt and my mother were true believers.) From smooth skin and shiny hair to healthy libidos and lubricated "parts," hormones were the answer—the cure for that life passage that had become a disease. You know: menopause. Results from the WHI included findings that a common combination of estrogen and progestin increased a woman's risk of heart problems and breast cancer; that those who took only estrogen had a heightened risk of endometrial cancer plus increased density of the breasts that interfered with interpretation of mammograms; that risks from prolonged use included pulmonary embolism, increased blood pressure, and cardiovascular disease. Other side effects included nausea, headache, cramped or bloated stomach, anxiety, mood swings, acne breakouts, and swelling of hands and feet due to fluid retention. Really, they had me at "cancer."

Since that first bombshell in 2002, the news about HRT has been confusing and contradictory. The risks—and benefits—are quite different depending on the combination of hormones taken, how old the woman is, and how long she has taken whatever it is that she takes. But one finding is, and remains, very clear from the study: It is risky for an older, postmenopausal woman to use hormone replacement therapy. "Older" meaning, say, like the 66-year-old Suzanne Somers.

So why is she so unabashedly enthusiastic about it? Why does she take daily injections of five hormones? And it's not just Somers. I sit through four different sessions later that morning and into the afternoon during which doctors sing the praises of HRT. (For "man-o-pause" too.) The difference—and those in the world of alternative medicine believe it is a huge difference—is that the hormones they're talking about, the hormones they are prescribing to their patients, are "bioidentical." That means they are identical, on the molecular level, with the hormones inside the body—not, for example, like the estrogens isolated from the urine of pregnant horses that is marketed as Premarin. And there are other important differences, insist those who believe in, prescribe, and take bioidenticals. Each person's therapy is individually determined based on the results of blood or saliva tests that pinpoint her (or his) unique hormone levels. The mix is created just for that person by a compounding pharmacy. I must admit, this carefully formulated hormone therapy does sound much different from the maligned HRT.

The afternoon presenters, including a wildly popular (and stunning) young doctor who runs an anti-aging clinic in Florida, insist that bioidentical hormone replacement therapy (BHRT), perhaps beginning as early as age 35, can do wonders. Those wonders include everything that HRT is reputed to do, like reducing the symptoms that can be associated with hormonal decline before, during, and after menopause (hot flashes, vaginal dryness, skin thinning, memory loss, concentration loss, anxiety, depression, weight gain, irritability, fatigue, insomnia, decreased sex drive, urine leakage, muscle weakness, and joint pain). In addition to symptom relief, bioidentical hormone advocates say the therapy protects the brain, heart, blood vessels, bones, skin, hair follicles, and muscles from decline. Most patients who start on bioidentical hormones, according to the Florida doctor's Web site, feel "emotionally and physically better within two weeks."

But mainstream doctors and researchers are not fans of BHRT. In fact, I discover that the American Medical Association, American Cancer Society, Mayo Clinic, International Menopause Society, American Congress of Obstetricians and Gynecologists, Endocrine Society, North

American Menopause Society, American Association of Clinical Endocrinologists, and FDA have all released statements saying there is a lack of evidence that the benefits and risks of bioidentical hormones are any different from their non-bioidentical counterparts. They also warn that compounded hormone products may have additional risks related to the compounding itself. On top of that, there is widespread controversy about the accuracy of blood and saliva testing in determining hormone levels in the first place. Counter that with the unbridled enthusiasm of alternative-friendly MDs and the extraordinary testimonials from their patients. It's a battle royale—one of many—between the worlds of conventional and alternative health care.

As I sit through the fourth and last of the sessions on bioidenticals that I attend, I make my personal peace with the controversy. Here it is: Conventional medicine has hit some home runs. Antibiotics? HIV antivirals? Pain meds? Nanosurgery? You bet. But, like so many people today, I see the limits of conventional medicine, and I am open to other approaches. I've taken classes in holistic health and in nutrition. I've had "energy work" done. I have prepared for surgery with creative visualization. But I am also not a person who wants to unwittingly participate in potentially risky experimental therapies. My aunt and my mother did that when they bought into HRT in the 1960s, when it was presented to them as a cure-all. Forty years later, they, along with millions of other women in their generation, learned about the risks. With no large-scale study of bioidenticals to review, no proof that they do anything different than the hormones my mother took, why would I potentially make the same mistake? I wouldn't. I won't.

I'm happy to have figured this out for myself, but my head is exploding. I look at my dog-eared convention schedule and see I have circled five sessions for tomorrow, several of which focus on something called adrenal fatigue. I can't attest to the state of my adrenals, but I can tell you that I am in the throes of self-diagnosed conference fatigue. I'm interested and engaged in the conference, but this is grueling work. And, although I doubt my head is in danger of actually exploding, I do have a crushing headache and the kind of full-body ache you get from doing nothing but sitting all day. If I have to look at another PowerPoint slide depicting nonenzymatic glycosylation, oxidative pathways for brain lactate metabolism, or the Krebs cycle, I'll scream. What should I do? The conference goes on for another day.

I call my husband, who is a veteran of medical conferences, having covered the West Coast for the *Journal of the American Medical Association* early in his career. He tells me to stop going to sessions and head to the exhibit hall. The exhibit hall, he says, is where the action is.

It turns out he's right. I spend the third and final day of the conference cruising a 45,000-square-foot space populated by more than 500 exhibitors. Here I find booths displaying supplements, nutraceuticals, electroceuticals, bioidentical hormones, homeopathic tinctures, weight-loss plans, face serums, hair rejuvenation products, body scanners—even shapeware. There are reps from dozens of compounding pharmacies and diagnostic labs and anti-aging clinics and medical spas, scores of booths displaying detox powders and protein bars and various elixirs made from berry seeds and mushroom dust and royal jelly. There are high-tech medical equipment companies. There are fitness equipment companies. There are aesthetic medical treatment facilities. There are doctors hawking self-published books. At the entrance to the exhibit hall is a shiny new BMW that is being raffled off. Whoever wins it, I suspect, will have its twin already in the garage. This is a well-heeled crowd.

I wander the aisles munching on samples of low-glycemic energy bars and washing down my free-sample omega-3s with vibrational water that promises to "re-establish the harmonics of [my] body's living systems." I stand on a several-thousand-dollar bioimpedance scale. A few booths away, a pleasant, white-lab-coated young woman puts some sort of device on my finger. A minute later, we get a computer readout that tells me—I don't know how—something about the state of my arteries. Apparently, it's pretty good. But what it's testing is a mystery to me, and, it seems, to the nice young woman as well.

I make my way to a large corner booth (the priciest real estate) filled with impressive equipment that "interrogates the body's communication systems and introduces specific signals that stimulate the natural healing process." Another pleasant, white-lab-coated young woman sits me down, holds my hand, and passes an instrument that looks like a 1980s cordless phone up and down my arms and across my shoulders. If I were in pain, which I am not, this would supposedly help alleviate it. It's also good, I am told, for cell function, circulation, improving sleeping patterns, and relaxation. It is being sold to docs and medical clinics to create new revenue streams. That's what another woman is telling a very interested convention-goer sitting at the station next to me.

At another booth a woman offers me a reclining chair (nice), slathers my face with a cooling gel (very nice), turns dials and presses buttons on an impressive-looking machine, and then uses two metal prongs to massage my face. I try to relax as, according to the product literature, the "microcurrent systems use Specific Bioelectric Signatures with advanced Nano technology to communicate at a cellular level via the neurological pathways using ultra high definition signals to improve and return a youthful appearance" to my face. Medical spa clients love the results, the technician–saleswoman tells me, and sign up for packages of five treatments at a time. What I feel as the prongs travel the contours of my face is an uncomfortable warmth accompanied by tiny zaps of electricity. At the end of the sample treatment, my skin does feel softer to the touch, but when I look in the mirror, I see a red mask across my cheeks and nose. I think the prongs have awoken a long-dormant case of rosacea.

I gather a few more protein bar samples, sip a jigger of pomegranate-açai juice, and then find another equipment-packed booth. Here I mount a contraption that shakes as I lift light weights, thereby throwing me off balance. In order to stay on the vibrating platform, I have to engage my core muscles, a seriously buff middle-aged rep tells me. I'll work harder without even knowing it, he says. Sounds good. I do some biceps curls and triceps kickbacks while managing not to fall off the platform. A small group gathers to watch.

But the 15 protein bar samples and the shot of pomegranate juice—not to mention earlier drinks of wheatgrass and lychee fruit concentrate and mangosteen extract—plus three bottles of vibrational water are announcing their presence in my gut. I do enjoy an audience, but it's time to find a quiet place to recover.

I find it a few aisles over at the Earthing booth. Earthing ("the most important health discovery ever") is based in part on what I'd consider simple, self-evident truths: People need to feel a connection to the earth, and when they do, they feel better. Walking barefoot on soft grass elevates the mood—and I'm betting lowers blood pressure and stress levels—more than, say, walking in four-inch heels across an expanse of chemically treated carpet in a Las Vegas convention center ballroom. But Earthing takes that idea a few furlongs further, positing that the "primordial natural energy emanating from the earth" is the "ultimate anti-aging medicine." Tapping into that energy, say Earthing's believers, can dramatically improve insomnia, chronic pain, exhaustion, stress, anxiety, and premature aging. It has something to do with the earth's boundless store of free electrons and our own electron deficiency.

If you're wondering where the revenue stream is in advising people to take a nice long walk in the woods, wonder no longer. Many people will not or cannot take that barefoot stroll, nor are they likely to spend an afternoon lying on their backs in a meadow. Twenty-first-century life does not abound with those opportunities. And so the Earthing folks offer for sale special conductive sheets or pads connected to a metal rod stuck in the ground outside your bedroom window. You sleep on the pad, and you derive the same healing energy benefits you would if you were sleeping on Mother Earth. They say.

The booth has a cordoned-off area with three massage tables, each of which has been fitted with one of these pads. I have been walking the aisles of this 1.03-acre ballroom for hours. I would love to lie down, with or without the promise of primordial energy. A smiling woman leads me to one of the tables, gives me noise-canceling headphones, and covers me with a thin blanket. I want to ask her hand in marriage. I stretch out and close my eyes. Through the earphones I hear a babbling brook, birdsong, the wind. I forget where I am. My breath slows. I guess I fall asleep because it seems like just seconds later, the smiling woman gently taps my shoulder to tell me my 15 minutes are up. I feel great. If the pad and sheet sellers had asked me for a testimonial, I would have given them a glowing one.

So many of the alternative anti-aging treatments and therapies are like this: They work. They seem to work. They work or they seem to work for people who believe in them and want them to work. They have some kind of a scientific basis, enough to make you stop and think, but they are not what is called "evidence-based medicine." They emerge from enlightened beliefs about health and wellness and are infused with the worthy goals of keeping people strong and vital and not waiting until they are sick to care about or for them. They are based on honoring the body. And yet, these treatments and therapies, these products and devices, are also the basis of an aggressively commercial multibillion-dollar anti-aging industry.

I have heard and seen a lot these past three days. I've traveled to the frontier of anti-aging, and it is truly a frontier, a wild Wild West of theories and ideas and products. I want to learn more about what I've seen and heard here, the studies behind the abstracts I've skimmed: mitochondria and telomeres, supplements and superfoods, detoxification, calorie restriction. I will try to make sense of it as I figure out how—not if, but how—I can turn back my clock.

two

Mirror, Mirror, on the Wall

KARL RICANEK JR. HAS POSSIBLY THE MOST INTERESTING face I've ever seen, which is only fitting because the man studies faces for a living. Dr. Ricanek—he is an associate professor with a doctorate in electrical engineering—heads the Face Aging Group at the University of North Carolina in Wilmington, where I've come to find out about the latest research on how and why our faces age. I figure this is a good place to start my counterclockwise inquiry. Of course, slowing the biological clock involves far more than tinkering with appearance. It is about increasing vitality and energy, boosting stamina and resilience, about feeling and acting—not merely looking—youthful. But appearance does announce our age, to ourselves in the mirror every morning and to the rest of the world every day.

Yes, appearance is more than face. It is hair, body, clothing, affect, style, and, so very important, posture and movement. But the face is our personal poster, our declaration of who we are, our calling card. The commercial side of anti-aging (the products and treatments, the serums and surgeries) is more often focused on how we look than how we feel— and on the face in particular. I am not sure where the line is between looking good and feeling good. It's clear that one often is a reflection of the other—and that it goes both ways. And I don't know where the line is between self-esteem and vanity. Perhaps it isn't a line but a Venn diagram, overlapping circles. That's it: I am traveling to North Carolina to meet Ricanek and his crew to explore that overlapping space.

And now to Karl Ricanek's face. It is a bold, animated, overtly friendly and welcoming face, but that's not what makes it so interesting. What is fascinating and stare-worthy is the unusual, unreadable combination of ethnicities.

"What are you?" kids would ask Karl when he was growing up in Washington, DC. They'd squint hard at his face. Was he Hispanic? Maybe East Indian? Possibly African American? His skin was neither dark nor light, but rather the color of strong coffee with a good splash of milk. His hair was black and curly, but not coarse or kinky. There was a hint of something in the slant of his eyes, a mystery to the open, high-cheekboned cast of his face, something impossible to classify about his generous mouth and big, powerful jaw. (For the record: His mother is African American; his father is Czech. He looks like both of them, and neither.) Not surprisingly, Karl was fascinated by faces, his own included, from an early age. He was a people watcher, a personality trait that became a hobby that morphed into a field of study that has become his life's work.

Karl's Face Aging Group is a loose consortium of colleagues from computer science, anthropology, mathematics, and statistics, along with a research associate, a postdoc, a research assistant, and a handful of student workers. Together they are teaching computers how to recognize and distinguish faces, and, based on complex algorithms, how to digitally age and de-age images of faces. Their techniques, aimed at catching criminals, not advancing the art of plastic surgery, are grounded in the science of craniofacial morphology (that is, the structure and form of the head and face) and built on a sophisticated understanding of the principles and processes of aging. Since 2003, Karl and his team have fed 1.7 million images of faces into a database they have used to create a 252-point grid that plots how a face changes over time. If anyone knows how the face ages, it's Karl and his crew.

About that crew: It is a kind of United Nations of Face. As I meet one after another of his colleagues, I wonder if maybe "possess a particularly interesting face" is part of the job description. There's Midori Albert, PhD, a forensic anthropologist, a self-described "bone person" whose expertise is in the scaffolding of the face and how it changes as we age. Her face, like Karl's, is a hard-to-read amalgam: exotic yet entirely familiar, multicultural, mysterious, yet completely American. (Her mother is Japanese. Her father is a Russian Jew.) Amrutha Sethuram, the crackerjack code writer from India, has a face both youthful—gorgeous, velvety skin—and old—big, wise eyes. Karl's computer science colleague, Eric Patterson, PhD, has long red hair and the unlined, uncomplicated face of an undergrad. (He's in his late 30s.) He looks like a guy who skateboards to work. On his personal Web site, he quotes John Locke, the Bhagavad Gita, and Sting. I'm thinking someone should pitch a TV show about these guys, a kind of *Criminal Minds, CSI* drama. Oh, and did I mention that Karl, in addition to his research, speaking, teaching, and grant writing, is a competitive, trophy-winning, professional bodybuilder? You can't make this stuff up.

To prepare for my visit to the Face Aging lab I delve into the mysteries of the youthful face. We are awash in these images: the micropored, dewy-eyed, pouty-lipped, unlined faces of Hollywood and TV stars, of magazine models, even—maybe especially—of models in ads for anti-aging crèmes and serums. I have a pile of these ads, all torn from magazines targeted to midlife women. And by "torn," I'm afraid I mean ripped, angrily, with an excess of attitude. (Men's magazines are catching up quickly with their images of perfectly chiseled, flinty-eyed, iron-jawed models with sexy three-day beards and mysteriously hairless but oh-so-sculpted chests. Welcome to our world, guys.) I study these ads that promise to make my skin firm, elastic, and wrinkle free, and for a moment I am caught up in the fantasy: This is what I can look like if I slather my face with product X made with secret ingredient Y! But of course that's not true. The only people who look like that are genetically blessed, exquisitely featured 22-year-old models, and even they don't look like that without expert makeup, great lighting, and the magic touches of Photoshop. But my pre-trip preparation is not about revisiting (and railing against) these impossible-to-achieve young face images that we see in the media. It is about mining the scientific data.

There is, I discover, an entire field of inquiry populated equally by anthropologists, psychologists, and animal behaviorists that focuses its attention on the construction and features of the youthful face. These are not scientists working to provide data to cosmetic surgeons. They are, instead, interested in what people, across cultures, perceive as youthful. They are interested in the links between perceptions of youth and perceptions of attractiveness and fecundity, and how all this plays into evolutionary biology. Most of the studies focus on the female face for reasons that seem both disturbing and obvious: Women are evaluated and judged more on physical appearance than men are. Youth is a more important standard for women than for men (from an evolutionary biology standpoint) because of women's shorter period of reproductive activity.

These researchers study what I learn is called the "neotenic" face, the youthful "baby" face. Across cultures, races, ethnicities, ages, and genders, people appear to agree on the hallmarks of a youthful female face: a high forehead; thin, highly set eyebrows; large, widely spaced eyes; a small nose; a small chin; full lips; small ears. Ask North American college students or Venezuelan Indians, Brazilians or Russians, 20-somethings or 60-somethings, women or men. The responses are the same. Remarkably—some anthropologists would say oddly—the same.

Not only is there widespread agreement on what a youthful face looks like, there is also widespread agreement that—not that this is news to any of us—youthful faces are consistently deemed more attractive than older faces. "Neotenous features on the face are decisive in attractiveness judgments about females" is how one (clumsily written) cross-cultural study put it. Or, as a team of anthropologists reported, perhaps too bluntly: "In no culture to our knowledge are the physical markers of reproductive senility . . . considered attractive." "Reproductive senility." That's the slap-in-the-face way of saying menopause, in case you didn't get it. Apparently, youthful facial features matter more than other physical cues (waist to hip ratio, for example, or perkiness of breasts) in people's ranking of youth, health, and beauty.

Okay, I get it. The face is all-important. That's why I travel across the country to visit the Face Aging Group. Anthropologists may be experts on what constitutes a youthful face, but Karl and his crew are the experts on how—and why—the face ages. If I aim to go back in time, to travel counterclockwise, I need to find out everything there is to know about the face.

KARL AND I ARE EATING BREAKFAST AT ONE OF HIS hangouts, a diner where the waitress knows his name, sweet tea is the drink of choice, and grits come with everything, even when you request otherwise. He is sitting across from me in a Naugahyde booth, studying my face. I ask him what he sees. I don't want to put him on the spot by asking him to guess my age based on my face. I'll let the computer do that when we get over to the university lab. Right now, I'm just interested in what he notices, what my face announces to him.

"Greek?" he says. I shake my head. "Well, Mediterranean, somewhere . . . that olive skin. Thick. You're lucky." I smile. "You're not a smoker," he says. "That's so easy to tell on a face." I ask him to continue. "Well," he says, "I'm cheating here because I know where you live, but I can tell from your face that you're not from the Southwest, or the desert, or anyplace hot and dry." That—speaking as an Oregonian for most of my adult life—is an understatement.

With little prompting, Karl launches into just what I came for: a minilecture on face aging. First he wants me to know that facial aging, like the process of aging everywhere in the body, is both innate and environmental, which is just another way of saying primary and secondary. The innate changes are sequential and progressive and hold true for everyone, although exactly how and when they show up is highly individual. So for all of us, Karl says, the bony support structure of the face as well as the musculature change over time. There is, those who have measured hundreds of skulls tell us, an "appreciable reduction of facial height" as we age, plus a modest increase in facial width and greater "craniofacial convexity." Are you picturing this? Our faces get shorter and wider and protrude more. However, the upper jaw moves backward slightly (which is one of the reasons, in addition to smiling, that we get those deeply etched nose-to-mouth lines called nasolabial folds).

Meanwhile, cartilage grows. Yes, that's right: The nose and the ears get bigger as you age. It's cold comfort to know that they don't actually get as big as they end up looking. Their modestly increased size is exaggerated by the fact that the head itself is shorter and the face protrudes more. That's a relief, huh? As cartilage is busy growing, the connective tissue, the upholstery of the face, begins to atrophy. There is lessening volume, a progression from plump (in a good way) to gaunt, and the tissue itself loses elasticity. Also, for mysterious reasons, the upper lip thins. And did I mention gravity? One does not defy it.

This general sequence of aging is predictable, although the timing varies from person to person. What is less predictable, which is a backward way of saying more under our control, is environmental aging—the things we consciously do or don't do. Karl goes ballistic over photoaging—aka sun damage—which he, and every dermatologist you will ever talk to, sees as the number one enemy of healthy, youthful skin. Sun is not merely a superficial ager, a drying agent, a creator of lines and wrinkles and age spots, but also a beneath-the-surface ager, contributing to the loss of elasticity in collagen. Add to that wind and arid air and you've got a great start on the leather-bag look. Smoking? No good for so many reasons more important than what it does to the face that it seems trivial to mention the dry skin and telltale vertical lines in that space between the nose and the upper lip. The lines are what Karl was referring to when he said you can recognize a smoker's face. Drugs, yo-yo dieting, poor nutrition, stress, and sleep deprivation are other powerful environmental agers.

Facial changes begin in our 20s, accelerate a bit in our 30s, gain momentum in our 40s, and, well, you can guess the rest. Typically the period of greatest change is from 40 to 50, according to the research Karl cites (and has published in collaboration with his Face Aging Group colleagues Midori, Eric, and Amrutha). This is when those expressions that have played across your face for decades become imprinted. But it is also when ancestry (dark skin stays younger longer), geography (gloomy, gray skies may be depressing—but not for your skin), and the accumulated merits or demerits of your life kick in. "Your face and how it ages is as individual as your fingerprint," Karl says. One person's 40 can be another person's 60.

Here's how it all plays out—at some point—from top to bottom:

Horizontal creases across the forehead. Lowering of the eyebrows. Vertical lines between the eyebrows. Drooping eyelids. Increasing transparency and lack of elasticity of under-eye skin, causing bags, rings, and dark shadows. Crow's-feet. Rougher skin texture. Larger pores. Age spots. Hollowed-out cheeks. Larger nose. Nasolabial lines. Thinner lips. Larger ears. Jowls. Neck creases and wrinkles. Karl doesn't mention thinning hair, receding gums, and yellowing teeth, but they are part of the picture too.

On this happy note, our breakfast concludes. We'll reconnoiter in a few hours at the lab. I walk slowly to my car as I consider, on the one hand, the unlined, big-eyed, small-nosed, round-cheeked "neotenous" face—the cute, attractive face, the one we'd like to keep for as long as possible—and the face that will be our future. It's that future face, my future face, I will see this afternoon when the computer program has its way with me, aging an image of my face into my dotage. I don't want to see it. But I do. Forewarned is forearmed, right? Know the enemy. Stare it in the face. Only in this case, it's *my* face. I'm a little scared about what I'll see. But I am also intensely curious. In fact, I am so curious that back in my hotel room, I log on to a semi-cheesy Internet site (there are several) that promises to "magically transform your youthful face into an old, haggard-looking and wrinkled face." That's hardly magic, I think, or at least not the kind dispensed by a fairy godmother. I learn that I can choose to age my image 20 years or "the ultra depressing 30 years." I'll do it. I feel I must prepare myself before I go to Karl's lab.

As instructed, I download a recent photo to my computer. I use a studio portrait, an author photo, figuring to stack the deck a bit in my favor. After all, I wore makeup for that photo. And the photographer used kind lighting. How bad can it be? I must answer only three questions: gender, age (+20 or +30 are the only choices—I love this site!), and whether I am a drug addict. Then I upload the image and wait. While I wait for the "magic," I note that 34,873,126 other people have been here before me. The image appears. I have crow's-feet, crepey eyelids, sunken eyes, and a thin, nasty-looking upper lip. This is a "fun" Web site, according to its creators. I'm struggling with this definition of "fun." (Later, at home, I show one of my sons the aged photo. "Are you really going to look like that someday?" he asks. I hear fear in his voice. "You look like an evil wizard or something.")

That afternoon, I drive over to the campus. The Face Aging Group is located in the spanking new computer science building, but first Karl takes me to the math building to meet the team of Chinese statisticians who figured out the algorithms and models for face-age estimation and classification. I start out at a deficit here, not having taken a math class since 11th-grade trig and not actually knowing what an algorithm is. But Yishi, Yaw, and Tracy are teachers as well as researchers. They are accustomed to clueless, intimidated students, of whom, this afternoon, I am clearly one. They spend two hours with me, writing equations on a huge whiteboard, showing me videos, talking data sets and variations and means, writing more equations. They explain in great detail and are patient with my deeply ignorant questions. And for a moment, I almost understand. Comprehension is so tantalizingly close, like that word you almost but don't quite remember, the one on the tip of your tongue. I am sweating with the effort. What I do understand is that their model takes into account both the changing shape (bones, cartilage) and changing texture (skin) of the face. And it's been tweaked and tested and tweaked again, made increasingly sophisticated as they incorporate more and more diverse facial images into their database. They tell me that the program can accurately estimate the age of a face within four years and can de-age a face to age 20 and fast-forward it to 75.

The software they're working on is being developed for law enforcement and surveillance purposes, to help the cops and the FBI and the intelligence community recognize and apprehend bad guys, especially bad guys for whom a recent photograph does not exist. Let's say you've got a bad guy on the loose and what you have to go on is a 20-year-old passport photo. What description, what image can you give your people out in the field? With this sophisticated program, you have a shot at being able to identify a person who looks significantly different today than in the image you have. Karl imagines other uses for the technology, like accurately aging those heartbreaking milk carton images of long-ago-abducted children or, on a lighter note, realistically aging characters in animated movies or your personal avatar. Karl tells me that a kind of age-estimation software is already in commercial use in Japan. In a mall, for example, a person walks past a machine. A camera captures an image of that person's face. Software recognizes the gender, estimates the age, and flashes demographically specific advertising on the screen. There's so little fiction in science fiction these days.

From the statistician's lair, I go to lunch with Midori, who walks me through the research behind the math as we chow down on Indian food. I spend most of the afternoon with Karl, first in his office and then in his lab, where I am introduced to a half-dozen students, young men with the paler-than-pale complexions of computer geeks, who guzzle Big Gulps, call me ma'am, and clearly idolize their professor. They talk to me about the work they're doing as Karl checks their data, teases them about an open box of pizza on one of the desks, and laughs easily with them, a big, booming guffaw that can be heard up and down the hallways. His laugh is apparently notorious. When Karl deposits me for my last appointment with his research associate and chief coder, Amrutha, I discover that she's been expecting us. It's not because Karl told her we were coming. It's because she heard his laugh. Her office is near—but not all *that* near—the lab.

Amrutha sits facing a 27-inch computer screen, her back to the window out of which, if the blinds were not permanently drawn to create a darkened, glare-free space, you could see a lovely green meadow and a pretty neo-Georgian brick building and camellias still in bloom in mid-November. She moves a pile of books and a sloppy stack of papers from a chair, pulls it close to her big screen, and motions for me to sit. This is the moment I've been waiting for, the highlight (and finale) of my visit. Amrutha has the face-aging software on her computer, and she can write a program just for me. We're going to find out how old the computer thinks my face is. And then Amrutha is going to ask the computer to create images of my face beginning at age 20 and then every five years thereafter until age 75.

I sit and, as directed, stare straight ahead with no smile as the camera on her computer captures an image of my face. I am wearing no makeup but wishing fervently that I was. I also wish I wasn't sitting under glaring, greenish fluorescent lights. I say this to Amrutha. She thinks I'm being funny. I'm not. Her fingers fly across the keyboard as she codes my image and gives instructions to the computer. She shows me the image the computer is working with—I've looked better, and I've looked worse—and then superimposes a green-lined grid, a kind of mask that covers my face from midbrow to chin. It's the 252-point grid they've created to recognize and track face shape and texture changes. Amrutha needs to do some additional coding so that my face can be compared to other female Caucasian faces in the database. I wait. I walk to the window that Amrutha never looks out of and peek through the blinds.

"Okay," she says after a few minutes. "Do you want to know how old the computer thinks your face is?"

"Should I be sitting down when I hear this?" I ask. She smiles. Amrutha doesn't know how old I am.

"You're 44," she says, tilting her head slightly as if to gauge whether this is good or bad news.

This is good news. I haven't been 44 for a while. I really like this computer. Amrutha looks relieved. Now she is busy doing more coding, typing in the instructions that will de-age and forward-age my face. It takes just a few minutes.

"What do you want to see first," she asks, "old or young?"

"Old," I say. Better to get it over with. Amrutha clicks on Lauren75.jpg. I see a haggard face, all the features pulled downward by three-quarters of a century of gravity. My eyebrows crowd the tops of my eyes, which look hooded and squinty. My nose—never my best feature—is now my most prominent. It is longer. The tip droops. I have deeply etched nasolabial lines—more like pleats, really. My philtrum—the vertical groove at the center of my upper lip—is flat. My upper lip is so narrow that it seems to have vanished. On the plus side, the computer doesn't yet know how to age necks, so mine looks pretty damn good for a 75-year-old. And the program does nothing with hair. So the 75-year-old me still has long, thick brown locks. The hair makes me look a little younger, I think. But it also makes me look like a bag lady. I stare at the picture. I can't seem to tear my eyes away from the screen. Is this my future face?

Maybe. Or maybe not. My genetics are my own; the speed at which I age is my own. My lifestyle will make a difference. That said, it's clear that many of these changes are inevitable. It's just a question of exactly how and when they will manifest themselves. I take another long look. Beyond an immediate urge for surgical intervention, I make this note: When I get this old, I have to remember to smile. A smile would really help that face. A smile is an antigravity move. Also: Should I ever, *ever* think about how good I'd look with a tan, I must call up and stare hard at this photo. I don't need any extra aging help from the sun, that's clear.

Amrutha is ready to move on, even if I am not. In quick succession, she opens the files showing me at 70, 65, 60, 55, 50, 45 years old. I see myself go backward in time. My eyes get bigger and my nose gets smaller. My upper lip returns. I begin to look as if I've gotten a full night's sleep. Like maybe I've taken a walk outside. At 35, 30, 25, and 20 my face is increasingly smooth, decreasingly lined. My complexion brightens. My cheeks soften; my jaw firms. There's a high arch to my eyebrows that gives my eyes an innocent look—almost, I have to say, a vacant look. Is that what I looked like at age 20? I pull out an old snapshot of myself that Karl suggested I bring along. I am standing next to a row of tomato plants—my first garden—wearing dirty overalls, squinting into the sun, and grinning. I am 23. I hold it next to Amrutha's computer screen, the real Lauren shoulder-to-shoulder with Lauren20.jpg. The digitally de-aged Lauren looks a bit personality-less, but there's no mistaking that the two images are of the same person at about the same age. All of a sudden, I have an overwhelming desire to look like her. Like either of them. A plastic surgeon could lift what needed to be lifted. Injections could flatten lines. Fillers could plump up creases and make my lips all sweet and pouty. My current "44-year-old" face, my projected 75-year-old face, could look a lot different if I did any or all of this.

I'm not saying I'm not tempted.

three

Face It

IF YOU WANTED TO PHYSICALLY RECAST YOURSELF, TURN back the pages, transform into an earlier edition, and if you had more money than sense—make that *a lot more money*—and if you had no aversion to elective surgery, needles, cannulas, drains, silicone bags, autologous fat transfers, compression garments, scars, keloids, and the unhappy knowledge that you let vanity win a battle that can never be won, then there is a lot you can do to erase not years, but decades from your face and body. I have at various times—and, I am ashamed to say, not just for the purpose of this book—considered many of them.

I know that youthful vitality comes from inside, that counterclockwise movement has far more to do with the elasticity of arteries than the elasticity of neck skin. I know that in the end (or even in the middle), gravity trumps all. And yet, the smooth-faced, firm-jawed image of Lauren20.jpg is now deeply implanted in my brain. And just yesterday, when I looked at an impromptu photo my daughter took of me doing water aerobics, I was compelled to Google "brachioplasty," which is surgery that combines sucking out fat from the backs of your arms with skin tightening. It gets rid of bat wings, which is a slightly less awful way of saying arm flab.

Yes, I'd like to have sleek, toned, unjiggly arms. But when I'm really blue-skying it, I think: full body lift. This is the mother of all plastic surgeries, up to nine hours in the operating room with four or five surgeons, more than a dozen incisions, and, depending on whether it's performed at a doctor's surgical facility or in a hospital, an $18,000 to $40,000 price tag. The procedure removes extra skin and fat from the belly, hips, butt, back, arms, and outer and inner thighs. I watched two doctors demonstrate the procedure on a mannequin, using Magic Markers to show where the incisions are made. Their banter was unnervingly lighthearted as they recounted the one square *yard* of skin they had removed from a recent patient and the *10 feet* of sutures that were necessary to sew the lady back together again. The most dramatic incision circumnavigates the waist. The surgery involves—how shall I phrase this?—cutting you in half and then hiking up your skin from the waist as if pulling up a pair of droopy pants. Then there are the incisions under the butt, along the bikini line and at the groin. For the tummy tuck part of the surgery, a surgeon has to scoop out the belly button and hold on to it until the abdominal skin (lifted and snipped) is repositioned. Otherwise, the navel would be right around the rib cage.

That's just the lower-body lift. The upper-body procedures include attending to saggy back skin (who knew?) and bra bulge, a breast lift, and my personal favorite, the aforementioned brachioplasty. The docs don't talk about sag and flab and droop. They say "body laxity." And they don't talk about cutting, vacuuming, and stitching. They say "body contouring." I love the language of these surgeons. I am seduced by this language. I can imagine my body being contoured. I hear another compare young skin to spandex that snaps back, middle-aged skin to cotton, and older-adult skin to linen. Have you ever made the mistake of wearing linen slacks on a cross-country plane trip? When you arrive, the pants are two sizes bigger, sag at the butt, bubble at the knees, and have more wrinkles than a shar-pei puppy.

The full body lift was originally created for *The Biggest Loser* types who dropped so much weight that they were left with drapes and folds—apparently totaling square yards—of excess skin. But the language of the über-surgeons who perform the complex procedure is becoming more inclusive.

"Do you wish your body was tighter and firmer?" one surgeon's Web site asks. (If ever there was a rhetorical question, that's it.) "You aren't alone," continues the text reassuringly. "Many women and men experience problems from sagging skin for one reason or another." One of those reasons is—you guessed it—age. The more years we spend on earth, the more years gravity tugs and pulls at us. We defy it for a while with our young, supportive connective tissue and our toned muscles and super-elastic skin, but by midlife, the underlying tissues are not as resilient as they once were, the skin is thinner, and we are beginning to lose the battle. Everything that can sag begins to, from eyelids to the tip of the nose to the skin on the backs of the (okay, the backs of *my*) arms. Enter the full body lift. It provides a way, say the surgeons, to "sculpt and perfect the body." Why, it's almost irresistible.

Almost. But not quite. While "firm," "toned," and "perfect" sound really good to me, nine hours of elective surgery does not. Nor does the fact that I'd have to max out several credit cards to afford the procedure. And then there's the karma. Such vanity does not go unpunished. Add to this the likelihood that my husband would divorce me and the message I'd be sending to my teenage daughter about body image and acceptance, and it looks as if I won't be going under the knife—make that "knives"—anytime soon. But that doesn't mean I have decided against all age-defying interventions.

A PAIR OF THREE-FOOT-TALL IMPORTED CHINESE IMPERIAL guardian lions flanks the heavy glass entry door. The room they guard, with its soft lighting, original art, bold sculpture, and black-and-white Euro-sleek furniture, looks and feels like the lobby of a boutique hotel. In fact, it is a doctor's waiting room, the portal to plastic and cosmetic surgeon Dr. Mark Jewell's domain, which he has dubbed—make that branded—the Jewell District. The expansive suite of exam, treatment, spa, and conference rooms is tastefully designed and decorated (with the exception of the OR, which looks like what it is: a fully functional, self-contained operating room). The place is lovely: understated, elegant, whispery, like an art gallery. The message is clear: If the guy in charge exhibits this kind of taste, if he appreciates color and texture and form and the blessings of soft lighting, then this is the guy you want working on your face. Or whatever part of you announces an age you don't wish to announce.

Dr. Jewell is, as you'd expect given his line of work and his mostly female clientele, personable and charming—but, it is important to note, not in a smarmy way. He is also handsome enough to play a guy like him on TV, but not so handsome (or youthful appearing) that you would suspect he's had major work done. If there has been work—"rejuvenation," as the doctor would say—it's subtle, just like you'd want yours to be. More to the point, though, he is a 30-year veteran of the plastic surgery world; a past president of the American Society for Aesthetic Plastic Surgery; the current United States national secretary for the International Society for Aesthetic Plastic Surgery; a clinical researcher who has published more than 60 peer-reviewed scientific papers, books, and book chapters; and an international lecturer and educator. In other words, the guy's a player.

I am here to interview Dr. Jewell. I am here to do research, which is both true and an excuse simultaneously. This project gives me legitimacy—in my own mind and with my family. I'm not some vain, midlife woman angsting over wrinkles. I am a vain, aging midlife journalist researching the world of plastic surgery. Ha! I am ushered into one of the lovely exam rooms by one of Dr. Jewell's lovely assistants. His all-female staff wears stylish fitted black lab coats embroidered with "Jewell District" in red and looks like who you want to look like after Dr. Jewell gets finished with you. I have tried to dress up at least a little, meaning I am not wearing sweatpants. I'm not here for a consult—not *yet*, that is—but rather to get the plastic surgeon–eye view of the way the body shows its age. I think I know what he will say, at least about the face. After all, I just spent two days with the North Carolina researchers who plotted and graphed and coded every inch of the aging face. But I want something more. I want a head-to-toe recounting of the midlife woman's body. I want to be educated about the visible markers of age and learn about the best ways to address them.

Before the good doctor begins, he spends a full five minutes railing against the sun—just like Karl Ricanek did. *The sun is evil. The sun is the enemy of youthful skin. Tanned skin is damaged skin.* How I wish someone had told me this when I was 15 and at summer camp slathering myself with baby oil and holding a reflective foil collar around my face to maximize the tan. I mean the *damage*. Lucky for me I have Mediterranean coloring so the damage wasn't as bad as what accrued to those porcelain-skinned blondes I used to envy in high school. And lucky for me I have spent most of my adult life under the gray, moody, sodden skies of the Pacific Northwest.

Dr. Jewell can't say enough about the sun and the havoc it wreaks on face, neck, décolletage, and hands: the drying, the wrinkling, the mottling, the hyperpigmentation. Like Karl, he decries the damage to the underlying layers, the structure that holds up everything. Or would hold up everything if the sun hadn't gotten to it first. He shakes his head and sighs.

His guided tour of the aging face is not for the faint of heart. Happily, I am inured to the worst of the news because of my time at the North Carolina lab, not to mention the long moments I've whiled away staring at that series of computer-aged photos of my own face. Echoing what I've learned, Dr. Jewell begins the litany: The forehead wrinkles. The brow droops (and don't forget the eyelids). The midface thins. Lips flatten. Jowls appear. The jaw squares. The neck "bands." There are corner-of-the-eye wrinkles and bags under the eyes and sunken temples and nose-to-lip furrows and corner-of-the-mouth–to-jaw creases that make you look like a marionette. And age spots.

Okay, so that's the bad (and hardly unexpected) news: The face, all of it, stem to stern, takes a beating as we age. But, if you have some extra cash and are imbued with the spirit of self-improvement and, like me, are vain enough to want to look better than nature intended, Dr. Jewell has good news for you. For me. There are treatments and procedures, from clinically tested skin-care products that may actually work to full-on facelifts that do not have to make you look like Joan Rivers—and everything in between: lasers to zap age spots, injectable fillers to erase deep lines and plump thinning lips, neurotoxins (like Botox) to smooth out the forehead, serums to make scanty eyelashes grow thick and lush.

In preparation for my visit to the Jewell District, I did a bit of homework on the plastic surgery industry. Americans—mostly women and at younger and younger ages—spent almost $11 billion on cosmetic procedures last year. Although actual scalpel-and-suture surgery remains very big business, much of the growth in the industry (and it *is* growing) comes from "noninvasive" techniques—if the doctor sticking a needle in your face can be considered noninvasive. The use of neurotoxins, for example, has gone up 3,500 percent in the last decade and a half. Yes, you read that right. Botox injection is the number one cosmetic procedure today. Fillers and plumpers are not far behind.

The list of what can be done to alter a face is longer than it has ever been. In a high-end magazine called *New You*, I read a plastic surgeon's menu of procedures that could, he says, turn mere mortals like you and me into fresh-faced, raving beauties like Salma Hayek (whose gorgeous photo accompanies the story): facelift, liquid facelift with fillers, neurotoxin injections, eyelid surgery, nose job, chin implant, liposculpture, chemical peel, and neck lift. I may be leaving out something. Perhaps a total head transplant. When anything is possible, it is almost impossible to decide what to do. This power to turn back the clock, albeit superficially, is so great that it is almost as paralyzing as I hear Botox is to the forehead.

Part of me is trying to make sense of this—What should I do? Can I really look like Salma Hayek, even a little bit?—while another part of me is awash in that recurrent tide of guilt triggered by my own vanity. Part of me wants to look like Lauren35.jpg. Part of me wants to fight the superficiality of wanting to look like Lauren35.jpg. I ask the doctor to explain why undergoing these "rejuvenating" procedures is anything more than an unadulterated act of narcissism, the misguided action of a shallow, self-obsessed, and unevolved person (aka me). Yes, I phrase my question with a bit more subtlety. The doctor immediately references a colleague, David Sarwer, PhD, a clinical psychologist who also does research at the University of Pennsylvania's Center for Human Appearance. The center is dedicated to the study and treatment of appearance-related disorders like body dysmorphia and anorexia and their effect on quality of life.

But when I take a look at the Web site later that afternoon, a statement Dr. Sarwer makes speaks directly to my mild appearance-related neurosis (i.e., my desire to look younger than I am). Dr. Sarwer writes: "Whether we admit it or not, appearance matters in our culture. Our society often idealizes attractive people." Often? How about always. Then he goes on to reference research that shows what most of us probably already know: "Those who are attractive typically receive preferential treatment across their life span." And, because our youth-obsessed culture conflates attractiveness with youthful appearance (remember the neotenic face?)—especially when it comes to women—it's no surprise to learn that those who continue to look young as they accrue experience and expertise (that is, as they age) are preferentially treated in the workplace.

I recently read that cosmetic surgery and other less invasive but often spendy "rejuvenating" procedures have actually increased even as the United States has experienced hard times and high unemployment. That seems counterintuitive. After all, if people have less money to spend and find themselves in a world of job and market insecurities, wouldn't that make them more cautious about spending it on such expensive frivolities as blepharoplasty (eyelid surgery)? But just the opposite has happened. One of the most-cited reasons for undergoing the knife? To look young and fresh and vital in a tough job market. A great résumé is apparently not sufficient. One must be experienced— but then undergo procedures so as to not look *too* experienced.

"It's not surprising that the way we look has a great deal to do with our own confidence and self-esteem," Sarwer writes. "Our appearance can shape our self-image and affect the way we deal with others." And the way others deal with us.

This is, essentially, Dr. Jewell's answer to my question. He sees real benefits to the self-esteem of the people he treats. The treatments and procedures are not window dressing. They are serious confidence boosters than can affect relationships, the decisions people make, their jobs, their lives, their quality of life. I think about the realities of midlife that can make us feel less than what we are. The important ones have little to do with crow's-feet and incipient jowls. They have to do with loving, caring for, and letting go of aging parents, with yearning for and then grieving over the empty nest, with confronting the weight of choices made, of paths not taken. These are big issues, issues that cannot and should not be nipped and tucked. But who is to say that paying some attention to appearance interferes with paying far more attention to important life issues? Who is to say that having "work" done on your face (or some other body part) means you won't do the work necessary to grow into the last third of your life? Who is to say that glowing skin or a firm belly could not invigorate the journey? Not me.

DR. JEWELL DISCREETLY GLANCES AT HIS WATCH, BUT NOT so discreetly that I don't notice. "Okay," I say. "Let's be done with face and move on."

Hands are next, and, unlike the face, there's less opportunity for cosmetic cover-up. Hands are hands, and old hands are old hands: rough and gnarled and spotted, with papery skin, visible veins, and ropey tendons—"dermal atrophy," says Dr. Jewell, by which he means thinning of the skin due to the loss of underlying tissue and subcutaneous fat. (Yes, sometimes fat loss is a bad thing.) Hands take a beating in everyday life, from diapering to dishwashing, cooking to cross-country skiing. And few people protect their hands the way they might protect their faces, with sunscreens and moisturizers. I sneak a look at my hands. I think I can discern a few of what I'd like to call "freckles" but are, undoubtedly, the pale beginnings of age spots.

Next stop: breasts. Breasts are Dr. Jewell's bread and butter, so to speak. Like plastic surgeons nationwide, he performs more breast surgeries—augmentations, to be exact—than any other surgery. (Breast reduction ranks number four in his practice.) I'm not much interested in this topic, as graduating from a B to a D—or whatever size bag one wants slipped under the pectoral muscle—doesn't seem to have much to do with aging. But there is also a breast lift surgery, which is more to the point. Like many women, I know up close and personal what pregnancy and breastfeeding and gravity do to otherwise perfectly adequate breasts. But, I figure that unless one is talking about parading around naked—which few midlife women are—then the unpleasant result of years of carrying around breasts can be ameliorated by a good bra. I am ready to move on.

Dr. Jewell wants to talk tummy, as in stretched-out skin (pregnancies, the weight loss–weight gain merry-go-round), as in "thickening of the waist," as in menopause paunch, as in . . . tummy tuck. A tummy tuck (the third most common surgery performed in the Jewell District) combined with liposuction (number two) can transform a flabby, pooched-out abdomen into a taut midsection that might not earn you dinars on the belly-dancing circuit but would allow you to dress like your 13-year-old daughter. I apologize for being snarky about this. I have seen the before-and-after pictures posted on some surgeon's Web sites, and the results can be remarkable. (Although only slightly less remarkable than the fact that all these women, and a few men, allowed the pictures to be posted.) If a midlife pooch is your problem and Spanx is not doing the job for you, the tummy tuck can be mighty tempting. I, however, am not tempted. I am, and continue to be, pear shaped. Which is to say: My midsection is okay. Yes, I have been pregnant—with a first child so enormous that all the nurses on the obstetrics floor came in to ogle—and no, my skin didn't snap back like a new rubber band. But I am hoping that ab work in the gym rather than surgery will take off a few years. Besides, I have bigger (literally) areas of concern.

When Dr. Jewell starts talking about lumpy, saggy thighs and glutes that have given in to gravity, my ears (which, need I remind you, are growing bigger as I age) perk up. This was never a stellar part of my anatomy, and aging has done me no favors. I am wondering what could be accomplished with some serious vacuuming and recontouring. The doctor warms to the subject, telling me about a new generation of ultrasonically powered liposuction tools that apparently offer improved (and safer) results. But he is even more excited about an even newer noninvasive technique for sculpting and contouring. No incisions, no little hollow rod poking around under your skin, slurping up fat deposits. No hoses; no Hoovers. This new technique manages to deliver focused ultrasound to deep layers (that is, fat deposits) while leaving the skin intact. It basically liquefies the fat, which the body then absorbs. I learn that Dr. Jewell has been conducting clinical trials on the technique, melting fat from the abdomens of dozens of (lucky) patients for the past year and a half. Now the FDA has approved the device, and he's offering the procedure in his practice. I ask if this is something he can use for thigh, hip, or butt "sculpting," as in my thighs, hips and butt. I am ready to sign on the dotted line right now.

His response speaks directly to why I am beginning to seriously trust this guy. Although he is clearly excited about this new tool, he does not launch into a sales pitch. I don't see dollar signs in his eyes. He leads with the negatives: The fat-melting procedure works when there is a certain amount of fat, not too much, not too little. It can't be used when the fatty area is right near a bone (thus, inner thighs are not, forgive the pun, on the table). I'm nodding, still very much interested. Then comes the spoiler: extra skin. Although there wouldn't be yards of it, as happens with the 200-pound-weight-loss folks, there would be some, and, given my midlife body, it would be of the "linen" rather than the "spandex" variety. Not likely to snap back. Likely to hang there, flapping. In explaining what is to be done about this, he uses the same imagery, actually pretty much the same words, as the docs I watched on YouTube discussing the full body lift: pulling up a baggy pair of pants. That means a post–fat removal procedure that involves making an incision all around the waist, hiking up the skin, snipping off the excess, and resewing. No thanks.

Except for a few words about varicose veins and how weird (my word, not the doctor's) old toenails get—yellowed, thick, corrugated—we are finished with our tour of the aging body. It's been a harrowing journey. Although I care far more about feeling youthful than I do about looking youthful, that doesn't mean I don't care about how I look. I do. A lot. And now that I know how many ways those looks can be enhanced, rejuvenated, and otherwise artfully manipulated without inviting the "boy, has she had work done" look, I am ready to switch roles from curious reporter to hopeful patient. I am ready to do . . . something. I schedule an appointment.

Back home, I scour magazines, books, and Web sites for popular wisdom on the subject of what makes a person look older or younger than her birth date. I note an article in *Redbook* that says large pores add three years to the face and receding gums make you look 10 years older. Veiny, mottled hands? Add seven years. A beauty Web site lists two unfortunate choices, each of which presumably adds 10 years: wearing too much makeup (dark lipstick, thick foundation) and sporting "old lady" hair (helmet-head hairstyles, mom bobs, dark, monochromatic dye jobs). Another women's magazine lists sunken cheeks, bags under the eyes, and yellow teeth, but doesn't do the math. Finally, I come across some good news: "Voluminous hair" (as distinguished from helmet-head and undoubtedly different from Texas-style "big hair") and lush eyelashes can subtract three years! Full lips turn back the clock five years. And there's excellent news about smiling: According to a study published in the journal *Psychology and Aging*, subjects shown more than 1,000 photographs of people displaying a variety of facial expressions tended to underestimate—by more than two years!—the ages of women and men who were smiling in their photographs. But wait a second: Doesn't smiling, like any facial expression, create lines that over time deepen into creases and folds? What a predicament. I better not frown about it.

Perhaps the best anti-aging appearance news I come across is this: Good posture and a strong, steady gait can make you look up to 10 years younger. The shoulders-back, abdomen-tucked, head-lifted position is said to also have other rejuvenating effects, like improving circulation and digestion, making breathing easier and deeper, and keeping muscles and joints in proper alignment. Just ask any yoga teacher. In fact, if you've ever seen, or taken a class from, an octogenarian yoga teacher (as I have), you know the power of posture.

A WEEK LATER, SITTING TALL WITH SHOULDERS NICELY squared, I wait for Dr. Jewell in an exam room that manages to look stylish and clinical at the same time. He takes a seat across from me, our knees almost touching, and stares at my face. He asks me to put my (voluminous!) hair behind my ears. He asks me to smile, to frown, to look left and right. I've told him that, although I would dearly love to be vacuumed, contoured, sculpted, shifted, lifted, and amended back to my, say, late 30s, realistically I am interested only in what he can do to rejuvenate my face. I am hoping that some yet-to-be-devised combination of exercise, ultrahealthy eating, shapeware, and a really good pair of black pants will help reinvigorate the rest.

Dr. Jewell tells me I have good bone structure and nice thick skin. My brows have not seriously migrated downward; my eyelids aren't drooping; my jawline is passable (for another few years). I do not have sunken cheeks that need to be plumped. So much for the good news. He sees much room for improvement in the texture and tone of my skin. He'd like to get rid of some hyperpigmentation (which, mercifully, he does not call age spots) along the sides of my face. He'd like to "smooth out" my forehead. He'd like to soften the lines that go from my nose to the corners of my mouth. And my upper lip looks a bit thin to him. And my eyelashes could be, well, lashier.

"A man's face is his autobiography," Oscar Wilde once wrote. "A woman's face is her work of fiction." Just how big a book am I willing to write? I decide to start with the most conservative (and inexpensive) of options: upgrading my skin-care regimen. Except for moisturizing at night and protecting my skin from the sun during the day, I don't actually have a regimen. I've thought about how I should have one. I've been alternately tempted and badgered by late-night infomercials and magazine ads and Web site come-ons that promise to "dramatically reduce the appearance of lines," "strengthen skin's density," "plump and hydrate," "visibly lift, firm and restore deep luminosity," and, my favorite for its combination of brevity and overarching sweep, "brighten dullness."

Dr. Jewell's skin-care specialist counsels me to ignore all advertising. "Skin-care products can only do so much," she says. "But some can do more than you think." She wants to make sure I am using a good moisturizer with SPF every day, even during the long, sunless Oregon winters. I assure her that I am. She wants me to start using Retin-A at night. It's a vitamin A derivative that's been much studied and seems to do what it claims to do: help the skin renew itself by hastening the sloughing off of surface cells. These dead cells clog pores, dull the complexion, and obscure that "deep luminosity" we hope we still have, somewhere. In our teenage years, the skin on our faces naturally exfoliates every 14 days. At age 25, the process slows to every 28 days. And it's all uphill from there. Retin-A also promises to increase blood supply to the skin and to stimulate the growth of collagen under the skin, that connective tissue that, when strong and elastic, can keep us from sagging and bagging. Sounds good.

And she wants me to add a niacin-based "rapid depigmentation serum" to what has now evolved into a nightly "regimen": cleanse, moisturize, apply serum, wait a half an hour, apply Retin-A. It may take months to see any difference. The difference may be subtler than I would hope. But it turns out I have another option, one with significant research behind it and hundreds of persuasive before-and-after photos. It's a combination of something called IPL (intense pulsed light) and Laser Genesis (LG). IPL, another of Dr. Jewell's skin specialists tells me, treats brown spots, sun damage, tiny veins, and redness. She has seen amazing results and thinks the treatment will work for me. She pairs IPL with a noninvasive laser "facial" that treats large pores, uneven skin tone, and fine lines. Her name is Sherrie, and I have to say, with her clear, bright, velvety (midlife) skin, she is a walking advertisement for these treatments. I sign up for a series of five, delivered in a combination to be determined by Sherrie when she examines my skin at each session.

About the IPL, which I have three times: It works. Almost immediately after the treatment, the spots on the sides of my face darken (this is good). I hide them with my youthful and voluminous hair. A day or so later, the spots look like coffee grounds. Then the coffee grounds flake off. Voilà, no more spots. Seriously.

Another thing about IPL: It hurts. For the treatment, I lie on a comfortable massage table with a silky pillow under my neck, a light blanket over my legs, and soft New Agey music playing. Then Sherrie comes at me with a wand attached to an impressive beeping machine. "Here's the first one," she says, her voice calm. The literature for this treatment reads, "When the pulse of light is delivered, patients will experience a mild pinching or stinging sensation." How about an electric zap that raises the hair on the back of your neck? How about a sharp sting like being jabbed by a needle?

"Do you hate me?" Sherrie asks, pausing before delivering the next "mild pinching." Kinda.

The treatment, zap by zap across both cheeks, along the jawline, across the forehead, along both sides of the nose (the worst) lasts for close to an hour. But time goes quickly when you're having fun. Sherrie soothes my face with gel. She cools me with a special refrigerated roller. She lets me take breaks. She spurs me on with remarks about how quickly and well my spots are responding. I decide I don't really hate her. After this, the laser "facial" is a breeze—warm, painless, and relaxing. Sherrie moves a handpiece back and forth about half an inch above my skin. The laser is gently heating tissue below the surface, supposedly stimulating collagen regrowth. This treatment is far more understated than IPL. I have a hard time seeing results until Sherrie shows me the before-treatment photos she took of me. My skin does look more even toned, more vibrant, healthier. And, as the dishwashing liquid commercial used to say, virtually spotless. So Retin-A is brightening my complexion, IPL has removed age spots (which the niacin serum is reinforcing), LG has made my skin feel (and look) creamy. I want more!

I consider an injectable filler to soften, or maybe even erase, the lines that go from my nose to the corners of my mouth. I see the full-page ads for Restylane and Juvéderm, the go-to brands, with the happy, age-free faces of the models. I learn about a new tissue filler made from components found in your own blood and ponder the wonders of autologous fat transfer. I look at a brochure touting a drinkable nutritional supplement said to provide "bioavailable building blocks" used to "rebuild the dermal matrix from the inside." In the end, I do nothing, my decision based on my memory of a midlife woman who was sitting next to me on the plane back from North Carolina. Her face was smooth, plumped up, unlined—and weird. I hadn't thought before that moment about how some lines—like the nasolabial ones—look natural on adult faces. The absence of those lines was disconcerting. Looking at this woman was like looking at an airbrushed photo. Her face actually gave me the creeps.

I do decide to go for another needle-in-the-face procedure, though. I have Dr. Jewell smooth the lines on my forehead by injecting Dysport. It's a lot like Botox. It blocks the signal from the nerve to the muscles that cause frown lines. Note that I say "blocks the signal," not "paralyzes." It's probably about the same, but sometimes a euphemism is just what the doctor ordered. I choose Dysport rather than Botox on Dr. Jewell's recommendation. He believes it lasts longer and gives a softer appearance. I like it because it doesn't have "tox" in the name and—extra bonus—if someone ever asks me whether I've gotten Botox, I can say no.

A few days after the injections (far less painful and a lot quicker than the IPL), I see, and really like, the result. My forehead is smooth but, unlike the awful pictures you sometimes see of celebs, it is not tight and shiny, like it's encased in plastic wrap. My forehead is not "frozen." My face is as expressive as it ever was. The change is subtle, like good lighting. So subtle, in fact, that my teenage daughter, who notices (and comments on) almost everything about me, doesn't notice. Neither does my husband. But I didn't expect him to. One time I cut my hair six inches and changed my part from left to right, and he didn't notice.

Dr. Jewell uses the word "refreshed" a lot when he talks about the look he is after, and that's what I see in the mirror. Between the skin-care regimen, and the intense light and laser treatments, and the forehead injections, my face looks, yes, refreshed. It doesn't look weird. It doesn't look worked on. It doesn't look like Lauren25.jpg or, for that matter, Lauren35.jpg. But I don't want it to. Instead, it looks brighter, more alive, like I've been sleeping really well or have just come back from a vacation. Another thing: I don't feel guilty. I haven't spent an outrageous amount of money. I haven't let vanity trump good sense. I haven't gone down the rabbit hole. I'm done. For now.

One thing Dr. Jewell says during our first meeting sticks with me. He tells me that typically women come to him and say, "I want to look as young as I feel." I've been thinking about this as I've delved into the world of plastic surgery, and I think the opposite might be true. Maybe they come to Dr. Jewell because they feel tired and stressed and sluggish, enervated, out of sorts—and look like it. Inside, their bodies are aging, but they see only the obvious, outward signs. So they mask those signs. That's not turning back the clock in any meaningful way. It's not what I want to do. Yes, I want to *look* refreshed. But really what I want is to *be* refreshed. To do that, to actually turn back the clock, I need to find out how old I am, inside, and how I might be able to fiddle with the clock's mechanism, not merely move the hands.

CHAPTER
four

What the Numbers Say

I AM FOUR SCREENS INTO A SEEMINGLY ENDLESS HOW OLD Are You Really? online self-test, struggling to answer questions about the shape of my bowel movements (what exactly constitutes "well formed"? I wonder), just how many friends I could call midcrisis at 3:00 a.m., and if my carpets are synthetic. I am devoting the entire day to taking every calculate-your-biological-age test I can find on the Internet—and there are way more than you might imagine. So many, in fact, that the act of taking them all may be aging me. Here I am sitting all day (sedentary lifestyle: add three years) in front of "electronic equipment" (more than six hours: add two years), skipping lunch (add one year), and experiencing moderate stress (add two years) while I drink liters of untested well water (I could be dead tomorrow). I better hurry up and find out how old I am before I get any older.

It's either good news or bad news—depending on how we've chosen to live our lives thus far (and, to a lesser extent, the cards we've been dealt)—that at midlife, the age of our bodies and the number of candles on our birthday cakes may be quite different. It's easy to know one number: Just glance (and wince) at your driver's license. It's not so easy to determine the other one. That's what these self-tests are trying to do. Many of the questions are based on "biomarkers of age," the quantifiable specifics of how our bodies work (or don't), statistical snapshots based on solid research and long-term population studies.

Biomarkers can help us figure out how old we are inside and—if we decide to actively intervene in the aging process, as I am going to—can track counterclockwise movement. The logic here is that if population studies show that a particular biomarker tends to go up (say, cholesterol level) or down (muscle strength) with chronological age, then determining your own biomarker will give you an indication of your biological age. So a by-birth-certificate 55-year-old with biomarkers consistent with a by-birth-certificate 40-year-old is, biologically speaking, far closer to being 40 than 55. Biomarkers are signposts on a guided tour through the aging body. They also pinpoint what's going on inside so we can focus anti-aging efforts where they belong.

Just about everyone who writes "grow younger" self-help books has something to say about biomarkers, whether they call them that or not. And just about all of them owe their understanding of the subject to studies conducted at the USDA Human Nutrition Research Center on Aging at Tufts and to *Biomarkers*, the 1991 book that came out of that work. In it, two world-class researchers from the center—a physiologist and a medical doctor—outline 10 quantifiable indications that they believe predict health and vitality (and thus biological age).

Four of the 10 biomarkers are closely related—intertwined, really: lean body mass, strength, basal metabolic rate, and body fat percentage. First, consider lean body mass (the amount of your total weight that is not fat). The less lean you are, the older you are. The Tufts researchers say that the average American loses 6.6 pounds of muscle every 10 years starting right after young adulthood. After age 45, the rate accelerates. Maybe. With every one of these biomarkers, there is the bad news—the decline or worsening or progressive inefficiency that comes with age— and the good news: The biomarkers are, to a great extent, under our control. One of the main reasons lean body mass decreases as we age is that the older we get, the more sedentary we are. We stop taxing our muscles, they decrease in size (and weight), and our lean body mass plummets. It is a pretty straightforward use-it-or-lose-it proposition. Which is good—albeit sweaty—news for you and me.

Strength, the next biomarker, is directly related to this. Older people are "weaker" than younger people because they have less muscle mass, and the muscle they do have is less dense and works less efficiently. The Tufts folks say that between the ages of 30 and 70, the average person loses 20 percent of the motor units (the bundles of muscle fibers and their associated nerves that together make up a muscle) in the large and small muscle groups and 30 percent of total muscle cells. And the cells that remain get smaller. Not a pretty picture. And speaking of not-pretty pictures: In the Tufts biomarkers book I find a photograph of a cross-section of a thigh muscle from a 20-year-old female athlete next to one of a 64-year-old sedentary woman. Picture two circles. The young thigh circle is surrounded by a very thin perimeter of fat. Inside is a large, dense section of muscle and, in the middle, a sturdy bull's-eye of bone. The old thigh circle is surrounded by a layer of fat so thick that it makes up a good third of the circle. The muscle section is marbled with fat, so marbled that it looks to be about half fat, half muscle. But does it have to look like that? Could the woman who is chronologically 64 be—strength-wise—biologically 54 or 40? It's a possibility.

As for basal metabolism: That's how many calories the body uses to maintain itself. It's not how many calories you burn walking or skiing, or even reading a book. It's how many calories it takes to pump blood and breathe air and digest food and do all those wondrous things bodies do without us paying attention or putting forth conscious effort. The higher the metabolism, the more calories burned, the fewer calories stored as fat. So here's the bad news: Basal metabolism declines by 2 percent every decade after age 20. But now the very, very good news, direct from the Tufts researchers: "We feel that older people's reduced muscle mass is almost wholly responsible for the gradual reduction of their basal metabolic rate." So, to express this in the positive: Increased muscle mass leads to increased strength, which is directly related to a quicker, more youthful metabolism.

Which brings us to body fat, possibly my least favorite subject ever, which—no surprise, given what's going on with muscle mass—increases as we age. In fact, between voting age and retirement age, the average person doubles his or her ratio of fat to muscle. And, although the ratio is worse for confirmed couch potatoes and overeaters, it doesn't matter if you are (miraculously) the same weight at 50 as you were at 20: More of your body is fat and less is muscle. It's kinder to look at this in the reverse: The more you can lower your percentage of body fat (within reason), the younger, biologically, you'll be. How does that happen? More muscle, more strength, higher metabolism, less fat.

It's the next biomarker, if youthful, that will get you there: aerobic capacity, your body's ability to use oxygen efficiently. If you have good aerobic capacity, you can exercise vigorously, which helps with the fat-to-muscle ratio, muscle mass, strength, and metabolism. Because aerobic efficiency depends on strong lungs, a powerful heart, and a healthy vascular system, many researchers believe it is the single most important indication of biological age. Population studies show that by age 65 the average American has lost 30 to 40 percent of his or her youthful aerobic capacity. Maximum breathing capacity (how much air you can get into your lungs) decreases by as much as 40 percent between ages 20 and 70 because the lung tissue loses elasticity and the muscles of the rib cage shrink. Meanwhile, the heart muscle thickens with age, and blood vessels accumulate fatty deposits and lose flexibility. These changes—aided and abetted by obesity, a fatty and/or salty diet, smoking, and lack of exercise—contribute to the steady increase in the average American's blood pressure, which is another of the biomarkers.

How much of all this is due to the passage of time, and how much of it do we make happen with how we choose to live? No study has been able to determine an exact percentage, but pretty much everyone doing the studying believes that the mere passage of time has far less to do with it than we used to think. It's really interesting that the best, most reputable studies of octogenarians and nonagenarians in the world's healthiest cultures show that they maintain most of their youthful aerobic capacity and low blood pressure into old (chronological) age. These are cultures where vigorous physical activity is a part of daily life, and where people eat mostly plant-based diets. Obvious lessons there.

One of the most devastating of the so-called age-related changes, according to the Tufts team, is reduced blood sugar tolerance, the body's ability to use glucose in the bloodstream. By age 70, they say, 20 percent of men and 30 percent of women have abnormal glucose tolerance levels. The change is symptomless, but it can lead to type 2 diabetes and contribute to elevated cholesterol, higher blood pressure, and heart disease. The use of the term "so-called" by the Tufts team raises this question: Does glucose tolerance have to decline with chronological age? Is it a result of chronological age? Or is it, at least in part, a result of overtaxing our systems with diets loaded with sugar and simple carbs? And then there's the cholesterol LDL-to-HDL ratio, another important biomarker. Total cholesterol level tends to rise with age in both men and women, but the important number is not the total, it's the amount of "good" protective cholesterol (HDL) and the ratio between that and the artery-clogging stuff (LDL). Low LDL and high HDL is a measure of biological youth.

Bone density, or rather the lack thereof, is also a biomarker. Biologically younger bones are dense and strong. But by age 70, women may lose 15 to 20 percent of their bone mass. The result? Honeycombed, weaker, more brittle bones. That's osteoporosis. But what age takes away, weight-bearing exercise may help you keep. That's what a number of studies are suggesting.

Have you noticed that physical activity—or its lack—plays a part in just about all these biomarkers? That includes the final one as well, the body's ability to regulate its own internal temperature. I'd actually never thought about this as a marker of age, although I've probably read scores of news reports about elderly people succumbing during heat waves or hard freezes. Apparently, the body's ability to maintain a steady 98.6°F, plus or minus, declines with age, the result of a number of other declines like metabolic rate, fitness level, and aerobic capacity. Plus, oddly, older people have a reduced sensation of thirst so they drink less, become dehydrated more often, and don't easily break a sweat.

I'm now approaching four hours of self-testing. I started with RealAge.com, probably the most popular online test, part of an extensive educational—and commercial—Web site developed by media heavy hitters Dr. Oz, of *Oprah* fame, and his best-selling buddy, Michael Roizen, MD, whose online bio states that he is "65 calendar years old, but his RealAge is only 43.8." The test asks many questions about lifestyle, habits, personality, relationships, diet, fitness, medical history, and family history. I answer each question carefully and usually honestly. (Okay, I lie about the weight. I just can't bring myself to type in the

RealNumber.) I want to do well! Dr. Roizen is more than 20 years younger than his chronological age. The bar is high.

I click the button and wait. My habits aren't perfect, but I know I have better-than-average nutrition and my activity level is good. Like everyone else, I bring both pluses and minuses to the equation of aging. I have always had low blood pressure, for example. On the other hand, my father gifted me with high cholesterol. I'm still waiting. Finally, the results: I am 4.1 years younger than my birthday says I am. That's better than being older, but not as good as I had hoped. Perhaps another test will give me a better score. Yes, I can be competitive about anything.

I click to the PainAge: JointAge test on the RealAge site. (*Note:* This test is no longer online.) I'm active and pain free, so I ought to ace this one. The results come back that I have the hip, knee, and hand joints of someone under 30. That's great. I go to Yourmedicaldetective.com and take that test. According to it, I am six years younger than RealAge says I am and 10 years younger than my chronological age. I would have been an additional year younger if I could have truthfully reported that I move my bowels more than two times every day. This test is quite interested in toxicities and adds three years to my biological age because I have a mouthful of amalgam fillings. But still . . . 10 years.

I find another test on an elegant Web site for an über-upscale anti-aging medical and health spa. The facility is located in Atlanta, in an antebellum mansion that perhaps too closely resembles Tara. This test delves deep, asking about my house, my occupation, my educational and income levels, as well as every good and bad habit imaginable. I get slammed for my constant dieting and yo-yoing weight. My sedentary work life robs me of some youthful years. But still, according to this test, I am almost 16 years younger than my birthday. Growyouthful.com thinks I am even more youthful. After 140 questions, I discover that I am now 18 years younger—and, if it weren't for the fluoridated water I grew up with and the fact that the creators of this test think I am too hard on myself, I might be even younger. But my happiest moment comes when I take a bio-age test I find on a site from India. There, I finally achieve a 20.3-year age regression! I feel downright adolescent. On the feedback I get from the site about a perfect anti-aging diet, it is suggested that I eat ½ katori of scrambled egg white along with 2 nos of mooli paratha. I'll get right on that.

I COULD SPEND ANOTHER ENTIRE DAY TAKING TESTS LIKE this, but I've learned all I am going to: First, that these tests have very little—probably no—validity if you're looking to determine your bio age. The fact that the very same person walking around in the very same body (me) could get such different results makes that pretty obvious. Second, that there is some value in taking these tests. The questions alerted me to personal and environmental issues I had not considered to be possible influences on how (and how quickly) we age.

So, if online questionnaires are not the way to determine a person's bio age, what is?

Welcome to the wide (and very lucrative) world of anti-aging diagnostic labs, facilities that offer a dizzying array of tests with names like Comprehensive Wellness Panel and Anti-Aging Bundle Levels I through III that look at your blood, urine, and/or saliva (and occasionally hair) for age and health indicators. Want to know how well your liver functions? The status of your adrenal glands? How much (or how little) of various hormones you have circulating? There's a lab—scores of labs—that will tell you. The aforementioned wellness panel, for example, costs $1,275. That's what the lab charges the doctor, not what the doctor would end up charging you. These lab results might or might not be accurate. A naturopath friend of mine says there are several labs he just doesn't trust. And the extensive results—one lab promises a 38-page color printout with graphs and graphics—may or may not be entirely relevant to biological aging. They just test for absolutely everything, including, for example, Lyme disease. I am not tempted.

But what does tempt me is an Executive Health Evaluation offered by the world's largest "age management medicine practice." You might have seen their ads in health magazines or alongside Google search results. The ad features a photograph of a seriously buff man—a seriously buff older man, as in 70-some-odd years old. The image is actually pretty creepy. The guy has the face of a man his age and the body a 25-year-old man only wishes he had. It looks Photoshopped by someone who was playing a joke. But it's no joke. The guy has successfully remade his body, inside and out. His secret, the ad claims, is the age-management program offered by this company, the first step of which is a complete evaluation. This is a hands-on, all-day event arranged at one of the company's 20 medical centers throughout the United States. I go online and read all about it, send a "contact me" note to the Web site, and within hours get an e-mail back from a New York doctor affiliated with the company. We talk for almost an hour on the phone. He's smart and asks good questions. I have to say that I like the idea of a complete head-to-toe workup, an "extremely thorough set of diagnostics," as the literature promises. I would know more about my biological self than I could ever discover short of an autopsy. And by then, of course, it's a bit too late.

But I don't do it. I can't do it. I can't do it because it costs $3,995 (plus travel expenses—the nearest facility is almost 900 miles away). And even if I could scrape together the money, I'd be doing something that very few other people (like all of you reading this) could afford or choose to do. Instead, I am on a mission to find out what I can about my biological age in a way accessible to almost everyone. So, what's free, or almost free?

My bathroom scale, for one. Several years ago I bought a Tanita, a scale that uses what's called bioelectrical impedance to measure body composition, or proportion of fat to muscle. You step on (with bare feet) and a small electrical current is sent through your body. Sounds Franken-steinian. Isn't. The scale measures resistance to the electrical signal as it travels through the water found in muscle and fat. The more muscle a person has, the more water. The more water, the easier it is for the current to pass through it. The more fat, the more resistance to the current.

On the scale I go, not without trepidation. I have a love–hate relationship with scales that is mostly hate. I don't expect good news. And I don't get it: One-third of my body is fat. That puts me right on the border of "overfat" for a 40- to 59-year-old woman. Where I want to be is 25 percent to 30 percent fat, which would be in the "healthy" range for not just a 40- to 59-year-old woman, but—see those clock hands moving backward—for an 18- to 39-year-old as well. As for muscle mass, I earn a disappointing 2 rating, which translates into "high body fat, average muscle mass." What I want is a solid 6—average body fat, higher than normal muscle mass, although I yearn for a super-athlete-level 9 (low fat, high muscle). Much work to be done here. Cardio, strength training, nutrition. Check, check, check. Yes, I exercise—a run that's more of a jog, time spent on treadmills and stationary bikes—but I don't push myself. And I don't do any strength training. And yes, I try to eat well, but mostly that translates into avoiding foods I know are bad (stacks of onion rings), not actively seeking out what might rejuvenate me from the inside.

A few days after the great scale debacle, an interesting (and free) diagnostic opportunity suddenly presents itself. My local hospital is promoting women's heart health by offering a special, free heart health screening. I go to the clinic, fill out a long questionnaire about family history, personal health history, and lifestyle. A nurse weighs and measures me, listens to my heart, takes my blood pressure, does an EKG, and draws blood for a cholesterol screen. All the information is input, and, at the end of the visit, I get a three-page printout and a 10-minute consultation with a cardiac nurse. My blood pressure—my ace in the hole—is, as it has been my whole life, nice and low (100/60). Don't hate me. It's unearned, really. With that blood pressure I could live forever. Or I could faint every time I stand up. The nurse tells me I have "borderline brady-cardia," which scares me. But it turns out this is good. It means my resting heart rate is low. I mean low. As low as that of a 26- to 35-year-old athlete, according to the chart she shows me. I'm loving this. There's more good news: My fasting glucose level is low and my "good" cholesterol is high. But there's bad news too: My "bad" cholesterol is also high, as in close-to-scary, and my weight, she says kindly, "needs improving." I am "doing well," she says. But I could be "excellent" if I lost 15 pounds and lowered my bad cholesterol by 10 percent. Does "excellent" mean younger? Sort of, she says. It means far less likely to develop diseases related to aging, far more likely to remain active and vital. She hears what she's just said and smiles. "Yes," she tells me, "younger."

At my annual medical checkup a few weeks later, I ask my doctor to order all the blood panels he thinks my insurance company is likely to cover. I show him the three-page list of items from the super-expensive anti-aging diagnostic test, with its measurements of vitamins and minerals, hormones and antiinflammatory factors, metabolites and lipids, and more. He checks boxes on the order slip I take to the lab. Later in the week, he faxes me a copy of the results. I don't learn anything new from the cholesterol panel. All the numbers, the good ones and the bad ones, are within a point or two of the test I had done at the hospital clinic. Most of the rest of the results are what doctors call "unremarkable," which is the opposite of "worrisome" in doc-speak. Unremarkable is good. But I do learn that my C-reactive protein level is above normal. My doctor has starred this result and handwritten "call me" in the margin. Worrisome. CRP, I learn, is a protein that circulates in the blood, but at a higher level when there's inflammation in the body, including inflammation of the coronary arteries. Doctors are finding that it's a far more accurate indicator of a future problem with heart disease than cholesterol levels alone. And inflammation in general has been impli-cated in many of the serious diseases associated with age, like cancer and Alzheimer's. I need to get on this.

My doctor says that the simplest way to lower my CRP level is to reduce the inflammation that is apparently in my body, and that the best way to do this is through diet and nutrition. He is most insistent about adding foods rich in omega-3 fats, like cold-water fish and flax-seeds. He gives me a little lecture on the difference between omega-6 fats, which we get plenty of, and omega-3s, which we need more of. The optimum ratio of omega-6s to omega-3s for heart health should be 4 or 3 to 1. But Western diets typically have ratios of 10 to 1 or even, some research shows, as high as 30 to 1. I don't know what my ratio is, but I am going to start paying attention. Clearly, nutrition will be a big part of my anti-aging plan.

THIS MEASURING AGE FROM THE INSIDE OUT IS COMPLICATED business. Just when I think I'm making headway, I hear about some metric of aging I had not yet considered that just might be the be-all and end-all. The man bearing this latest news is a soft-spoken, youthful-appearing University of Colorado physiologist named Douglas Seals, PhD, one of the country's top researchers in the field of vascular aging. A colleague of his at the University of Oregon, the school in my own backyard, had alerted me that Dr. Seals was coming to town for a conference. It turns out that he's the keynoter and star of the confer-ence, but he agrees to break away to meet with me. It's an opportu-nity for him to preach the gospel of arteries. This guy is all about arteries. Flexible, unclogged arteries are *the* key to successful aging, he says. (Later, I find a quote from a 17th-century British physician: "A man is as old as his arteries.") Dr. Seals manages to be simultane-ously passionate and wonky about the subject. He tells me about oxidative proteins and velocities of pulse waves and flow-mediated dilation. He tells me about LPWs and HPWs. He's a great explainer, but I'm still struggling.

"Listen," he says, perhaps noting my furrowed brow, "there are all these tests we do in the lab as part of our research, but there is a 'poor man's' index of arterial health." It's easy, he says, just track blood pressure. If, over time, systolic pressure (the top number) goes up, and there's a widening gap between it and the diastolic (bottom) number, your arteries are aging. You are aging from the inside out. Behind that BP number lurks inflammation in the artery walls, inelasticity, and impaired dilation. My blood pressure has been the same since I was a kid. I am about to breathe a big sigh of relief when he adds that high LDL—the "bad" cholesterol—is also related to arterial health. He won't say which is more important, only that both are and that they are often interrelated. His research, as well as that of others in the field, shows that exercise, sodium and saturated fat restriction, and a diet rich in omega-3s is the way to go.

THE MORE I READ ABOUT BIOLOGICAL VERSUS CHRONO-logical age, the more convinced I am becoming that fitness is the key. You can answer hundreds of questions; you can spend time and money measuring everything that could possibly be measured. But it seems to come down to the basics of being in shape: aerobic fitness, recovery time, strength, and flexibility. It makes sense, as these measures depend on a number, maybe even all, of the generally accepted biomarkers and have much to do with the health of the heart and arteries. Fitness seems like a good body-wide measure. I can self-test for this, or I can have someone else do it. I decide to do both.

The self-tests are straightforward and require nothing more than a stopwatch and a good pair of walking or running shoes. First is aerobic fitness. I find variations of this test in many places, from the Tufts biomarkers book to RealAge.com to Oprah's magazine. I am to walk, going as fast as I can, for exactly one mile while timing myself with a stopwatch. It's important to walk, not jog, and it's important to do this on a perfectly flat surface. When I cross the finish line, I will take my pulse. I drive over to my daughter's high school track for the test. Let me say that it is hard not to look funny when you're walking as fast as you can, especially when everyone else is running. And 16 years old. This is all pointed out to me, in detail, by my daughter, who, she says, just happens to be passing by. I clock a mile at 13.4 minutes. My pulse is 140. In the graph I find in the Tufts book, that puts me on the low end of "good" for a 50- to 59-year-old woman. Not the decade I'm interested in. A cardio exercise plan is in the future.

Rate of recovery—that is, how quickly heart rate returns to a resting level after tough, taxing exercise—is another fitness marker. This test is harder, both on the body and on that part of the brain devoted to computation. First, I need to determine my maximum heart rate, which charts say is, for women, 208 minus 0.82 times your age (for men, it's 220 minus their age). I already know I have bradycardia, a slower than normal heart rate, so these general guidelines are going to be off for me. Then I have to determine what 80 percent of my maximum heart rate is. (I'll just lower this a few beats to make up for my slow pulse.) Now comes the not-inconsequential physical challenge: I have to exercise for 18 minutes at 80 percent of max, then 3 more minutes all-out. (I am doing this at a gym on a treadmill with a heart rate monitor, my stopwatch on my wrist.) Once I stop, I check my heart rate. Then I wait (panting and sweating) two minutes. Then I check again. My heartbeat should drop by 66 beats, the test experts say, but more is better. The faster the recovery, the fitter you are. The fitter you are, the younger you are, biologically. Mine drops 68 beats. That's good, but I am eager to see if serious aerobic exercise can make it even better.

Next comes strength. Some articles I read suggest you test this by doing arm curls or chest presses with free weights, but I like the simpler approach: How many pushups can I do before I can't do any more? For women, this test involves "modified" pushups with knees on the floor. This seems easy . . . for the first 10 or so. After that, not so much. Form has to be perfect. Hands placed at chest level, back straight, nose almost touching the floor each time. I am doing these on the floor of my writing room, much to the amusement of my daughter, who "just happened to be walking by." I am discerning a pattern here. I am able to do 27, which, according to one chart, puts me in the "excellent" category for a woman in her 50s. Again, not the decade I had in mind. Worse, another chart I consult expects a fit woman in her *60s* to do 25. I add strength training to my growing to-do list.

Finally comes the flexibility test. This is where all those years I haven't been practicing yoga would come in handy. The test can be done in several ways. I choose the easiest. I sit on the floor with my legs stretched out in front of me, slightly apart. Then I extend my arms, one hand on top of the other, and bend at the waist, reaching for the space between my feet. Oww. What are those tight bands down the backs of my thighs? Hamstrings. And they are, well, hamstringing my flexibility. The chart I am looking at says a woman under 45 should be able to reach two to four inches beyond her toes. That would not be me. "Older" women should be able to reach the soles of their feet. That I can do, but not without pain. Must work on this. I remember, way back, thinking of myself as "limber." Can I get back to that?

TWO WEEKS LATER, I AM HEADED TO THE BOWERMAN Sports Science Clinic at the University of Oregon. The "Bowerman" in the name is Bill Bowerman, the man who brought jogging to America, cofounded Nike, and invented the company's signature running shoe in his garage using his wife's waffle iron. The sports clinic is where elite athletes, NCAA stars, and future track-and-field Olympians go for athletic evaluations so they can maximize their training and be even faster, stronger, and more awesome than they already are. There, amid high-tech machines—x-ray absorptiometry scanners, high-power cycle ergometers, and computers loaded with the latest analytical software—overachievers with single-digit body fat percentages can undergo any one of 10 different tests. It's safe to say that the sports clinic has never seen the likes of me.

But the tests, I discover, are spendy. I know people at the university. I make inquiries. The price is firm. Unless I am willing to be a guinea pig for a small class of undergraduates who are learning how to operate the equipment and do the testing. Before they are let loose on elite athletes, they need to practice on . . . whoever will put up with them. This would make the tests free. I e-mail the grad student in charge the next day and hear back almost immediately. They are eager for a warm—albeit aging—body.

So here I am on a Monday morning for a VO$_2$ max test, which, I have been told, is the best single indicator of physical fitness. The test measures the body's maximum capacity for transporting and using oxygen during exercise. The more oxygen you are able to use, the better shape your heart, lungs, and arteries are in, the fitter you are, the younger you are. Actually, you have to be reasonably fit to do the test in the first place because it involves, as the graduate student explains to me, "a physical effort sufficient in duration and intensity to fully tax the aerobic energy system." In other words, you have to sweat buckets for a long time. And not have a heart attack. Or faint. You can take the test while cycling on a stationary bike or running on a treadmill. In either case, you wear a heart monitor synched with a computer, a pair of pinching nose clips, and uncomfortable headgear with a mask-and-hose contraption that captures and measures the air you expel. Your score is expressed as millimeters of oxygen per kilogram of body weight per minute, which is one too many metric conversions for me. The important thing to know is that the higher the number, the fitter the person. Athletes score higher than couch potatoes. The young score higher than the old. (And men, by virtue of having generally larger hearts and bigger-capacity lungs, score higher than women.)

Upstairs, the students are gathered around the machinery waiting for me—three guys with sinewy, distance-runner bodies; a compact, intense Chinese woman who, I learn, used to be a competitive gymnast; and the grad student, a young woman who runs the 800 for the university track team. There's nothing like hanging around super-fit young people to make you crabby.

On the first Monday, I do the test on the stationary bike. The next week I come in and do it all over again on the treadmill. Both tests start out pleasantly enough, if your idea of pleasant is having your nose pinched closed and your mouth covered by a plastic mask and exercising until you want to cry or puke or both. "Good job!" one or another of the students tells me as I soldier on, using that voice I used with my oldest son the year he played baseball on the losingest team in the history of Kidsports. The little gymnast woman, a look of deep concern permanently etched on her face, makes me point every 30 seconds to numbers on a poster, each number keyed to my "perceived rate of exertion." I hang on at "moderately hard" for as long as I can and then have to admit to "really hard" and then "really, really hard" before I signal that I can't go on. The test has lasted for 15 minutes.

The stationary bike is tough because of the unforgiving racing seat (enough said). The treadmill is hard because the headgear that supports the mask and air hose jostles and pulls at me when I run. Both of the tests are hard, period.

"Awesome," the cute male undergrad says as I get off the bike, dripping sweat. My score on the bike is 33. My score on the treadmill is 34.

Not so very awesome. According to the VO_2 max charts I find, my scores are just a tick above average for a 46- to 55-year-old woman. To give context here, world-class female endurance athletes can have VO_2 max scores that exceed 70. My friend the Internet tells me that a five-time Tour de France winner measured 88 at his peak, and a Norwegian cross-country skier who won a record eight gold medals at the Olympics measured 96. In case you're interested, thoroughbred horses have a VO_2 max of about 180, and Siberian dogs running in the Iditarod Trail Sled Dog Race have VO_2 values as high as 240.

VO_2 max decreases with age—for horses and dogs too. No news there. But everything I read about fitness says challenging aerobic and strength training can significantly improve the body's ability to use oxygen efficiently. Higher VO_2 max figures reflect a strong, efficient heart and unclogged, elastic arteries. It means muscles are getting what they need. It means a younger biological age.

I do another test at the clinic the following week, one that has little to do with biological age and a lot to do with sweating and bleeding and being a good-citizen guinea pig. I'll spare you the details of what I wasn't able to spare myself. After the test, as I'm getting ready to say goodbye to the students on that final day, the diminutive Chinese woman persuades me to do just one more test. It's the flexibility test I did at home. Dutifully, I obey. This time when I bend at the waist, I more easily, less painfully reach my toes. I figure that's either because I am warmed up from the previous test or because my finger is throbbing so much from the blood draws done during the previous test that I don't feel my hamstrings. She smiles politely and asks me to do it again. "You do better," she says. The sentence parses like a command, but I hear it as inspiration: "You *can* do better. Let me *see* you do better." I take a breath, exhale, and extend out. And out. My fingers are beyond my toes, two inches beyond my toes, two inches farther than when I performed this test at home. I don't think I've suddenly become young and limber. I think I just learned the value of someone pushing me. I'm going to want to work with a trainer.

THERE ARE SO MANY MORE TESTS I COULD TAKE: LUNG capacity tests and anaerobic power tests and DEXA scans, hydrostatic weigh-ins, and echocardiograms. In the interests of quantifying my health, I could wear a heart rate monitor all day. I could put wireless sensors in my sneakers and on my bike and have them deliver data to a little transceiver plugged into my smartphone. I could monitor my sleep. I could join MedHelp, one of the largest Internet forums for health information, where more than 30,000 new personal-tracking projects are started by users every month. I could join a user group called Quantified Self and share my obsession with others. Or I could, as they say in the land of Bill Bowerman: Just Do It.

I think I'll just do it.

five

Out on the Frontier

I KNOW I'VE CROSSED THE LINE WHEN I CALL MY HUSBAND, all excited, and practically yell into the phone, "I'm getting a muscle biopsy!" Yes, this is good news. Very good news. A physiologist I've been sweet-talking has just agreed to do the biopsy, which means I can discover the state of my mitochondria—the specialized energy centers in our cells. Almost as important, it means I have a potentially entertaining way of writing about one of the geekier subjects in this book (the aforementioned mitochondria)—because, after all, who *doesn't* want to hear about a muscle biopsy?

The line I've crossed is what I will do (to myself) to turn back the clock and, incidentally, to get a story. Having my face computer-aged to 75 and subjecting my fragile ego to viewing the result? Harrowing. But sure, okay. Intense pulsed light treatments? A little painful, but no problem. Breathing into a mouthpiece connected to a plastic hose connected to a computer while cycling at full speed as a good-natured but inexperienced grad student draws my blood every three minutes? That's *close* to the line. But a biopsy? A procedure defined as "the medical removal of tissue from a living subject"? I'm looking at that line in my rearview mirror.

I don't know what will be in store for me when I present myself at 8:30 sharp tomorrow morning at Dr. Hans Dreyer's lab just west of the University of Oregon campus. When Dreyer e-mailed me a "sure. 8:30. fasting" message a few days ago, I was so thrilled he would do the procedure that I didn't ask for details. All I know is that the muscle biopsy will yield a tissue sample that can be examined for mitochondria, both their number and their health. I've read that Canadian researchers who biopsied muscle from both sedentary and active adults between the ages of 53 and 75 found that couch potatoes' muscles had few healthy mitochondria, but active people's muscles had almost as many functioning mitochondria as you'd find in 20-somethings. I'm no couch potato, so my hopes are high.

I AM—AND I INTEND FOR YOU TO BE TOO—FASCINATED BY mitochondria. It is their health and well-being that, perhaps more than anything else within our control, is central to turning back the clock. At the Las Vegas conference, I read the abstracts of several papers about mitochondria and sat in on one session that simultaneously captivated and confused me. Now I've had time to educate myself, and here's what I've learned:

Mitochondria are specialized, self-contained subunits within most of our cells. Referred to variously as "the powerhouse of the cell," "the power plant of the cell," "the energy furnace of the cell," and, most charmingly, "the little fireplace of the cell," a mitochondrion is what keeps the cell—and, by extension, you and me—alive and lively. If you look up "mitochondria" in Wikipedia—which I did not do until this minute, I swear (my research methods are far more sophisticated)—you will find the following: "This article is about cell biology. For the Canadian death metal band, see Mitochondrion (band)." Just so we're on the same page here.

When we talk about—and/or rail against—our metabolisms, our bodies' ability to use fuel to create energy (or store it as fat), we are talking about what mitochondria do. In just about every cell in the body, from brain to bowel, mitochondria convert oxygen and food into an energy-releasing molecule called ATP that powers most of the cellular processes. The number of mitochondria in a cell depends on how much energy that cell requires (and how much you demand of it). Heart cells have thousands; skin cells have one. Lots of efficient mitochondria produce lots of energy—for the cell and for us. Meager, sluggish mitochondria, not so much.

The body is pretty smart. If a cell demands more energy—let's say you shut down the computer and go for a long walk, and your leg muscles must now perform—the little cellular furnaces stoke themselves hotter and make it happen for you. During cardio exercise like running, mitochondrial output can be as much as 400 times higher than when you're at rest. But here's the catch: As mitochondria generate energy, they also produce a nasty by-product, like a coal-burning power plant that feeds the grid while spewing pollution. The cellular "pollution" is what's commonly known as free radicals. These are unstable oxygen molecules that are missing electrons. They want to be complete—they are chemically compelled to be complete—so they go around stealing electrons from other molecules, thus making those molecules unstable. You've read about "free radical damage" and "oxidative damage"? This is it. You've read about taking antioxidant supplements and eating foods high in antioxidants? The oxidation they are "anti" is just this, the electron-hungry oxygen molecules out there (or rather, *in* us) creating havoc. But, as I said, the body—especially the healthy, well-cared-for body—is pretty smart. Efficiently functioning mitochondria try hard to clean up after themselves by producing their own antioxidants.

Now is the time to mention that mitochondria have their own personal intracellular DNA, the blueprint they carry of themselves. This is very unusual. And if it wasn't so much of a science-nerd digression, I'd tell you why. Just know that the reason this is important is that each mitochondrion's own DNA is an unfortunately convenient target for the rampaging free radicals. When that DNA is damaged, the mitochondrion's private repair and replicating apparatus is damaged. That's not good. If it can't effectively repair itself or replicate a good version of itself, the injury is progressive. Less able to perform internal repairs, it becomes increasingly inefficient, which means it produces more "pollution," which makes it even less capable of fixing itself. And so on.

A wealth of solid scientific evidence links mitochondria and aging. The connection was definitively established by a landmark Swedish study in which scientists developed a strain of mice with damaged mitochondria. The mice seemed normal until young adulthood, after which they quickly declined, becoming old, feeble, and ill. All of them were dead at 61 weeks. The normal life span for a lab mouse is 150 weeks. In humans, damaged mitochondria have been linked to type 2 diabetes, heart disease, obesity, and Alzheimer's—the classic diseases of aging. RealAge, the enormously popular Dr. Oz–related Web site, lists inefficient mitochondria as a "Major Ager."

The problem is this balance between energy output and internal pollution. We want more mitochondria producing more energy with less pollution. That's a real turn-back-the-clock strategy. Can it be done? Actually, that's two separate questions: Is it possible to increase the number of mitochondria in our cells? Is it possible to increase their efficiency— or to mitigate free radical damage? I am happy to tell you that the research says yes and yes. Basically, there's the hard way and the easy way.

Hard way first: sweat and more sweat.

Yeah, I know.

But the biochemical truth is, if you demand more, you will get more. If you make your heart work hard or your skeletal muscles work hard, the mitochondria within will meet the challenge by upping energy output and producing more of themselves. They also boost their internal mop-up process, producing more antioxidants to counteract free radical damage. Thus, making your mitochondria work harder doesn't have to mean increasing free radical damage.

Too many studies to ignore show that exercise increases both the number of mitochondria and their metabolic activity. In a Mayo Clinic study, healthy nonexercisers who biked three times a week significantly increased the action of their mitochondria. In another study, "consistent moderately intense" exercise for 12 weeks resulted in a 50 percent growth of mitochondria in the exercisers' thigh muscles. Hans Dreyer, who will be biopsying my thigh muscle tomorrow, is a believer in aerobic exercise to increase mitochondrial activity. A Canadian study touted the benefits of short bursts of high-intensity exercise. This is what's known as interval training, often referred to as HIIT (high-intensity interval training). Another study concluded that just plain *high intensity*—15 minutes of exercise performed at about 80 percent of maximum heart rate—led to an increase in the number and size of mitochondria.

Moderate exercise, high-intensity exercise, interval exercise, aerobic exercise—the message is pretty clear: *Exercise.* It's free (almost). It carries with it many benefits. It has no negative side effects. On the other hand, it requires a consistent, long-term commitment. It takes time. It's hard. And a lot of people—happily, I am not one of them— hate to do it.

So what's the easy way? As befits our 21st-century culture, it's taking a pill.

David Sinclair, PhD, an Australian-born Harvard Med School biologist, is at the forefront of research on how to keep mitochondria supercharged. In the early 2000s, he began focusing on an enzyme that, when activated, invigorated mitochondria. His happy—and much touted—discovery in 2003 was that this enzyme could be activated by a compound called resveratrol, which, although found in many foods— blueberries, cranberries, mulberries, and peanuts, for example—is present in significant amounts only in red wine. Pinot noir apparently is the best bet.

Headlines proclaimed, "Drink Wine: Live Longer," and the so-called French paradox all of a sudden seemed less paradoxical. *Mon dieu!* The reason the French can eat all that Camembert and chateaubriand in béarnaise sauce and still have significantly less heart disease than Americans is that they also drink a lot of wine. Talk about win-win.

In his Harvard lab, Sinclair transformed old mice into young mice with red-wine-derived resveratrol. He reversed heart disease. He reversed liver disease. He made them frisky. They lived an extra-long time. Good for them. I say it's about time lab mice catch a break. And, *potentially*, good for us. Other studies appeared to confirm resveratrol's salubrious effects on cholesterol, blood pressure, and the elasticity of arteries, among other things, and the race was on to create a turn-back-the-clock pill for us non-mice. The pharmaceutical giant GlaxoSmith-Kline bought Sinclair's little start-up company for $720 million and started clinical trials on this ostensibly amazing natural compound.

But 10 years after Sinclair's initial experiments, the literature on resveratrol remains contradictory and confusing. (At the Las Vegas conference, resveratrol was a popular topic, from a number of presentations to scores of booths dispensing a bewildering variety of samples.) Resveratrol may work—but there's considerable controversy over exactly how. The biochemical processes it affects are, as one research chemist put it, "wildly complex"; the other effects resveratrol seems to have are best described as "unclear"; and the therapeutic dosage is as yet unknown. Although Sinclair and others remain true believers and continue their research, GlaxoSmithKline halted clinical trials of resveratrol in 2011. As a naturally occurring substance, it was unpatentable, which meant the company might not be able to create a proprietary drug (and make boatloads of money). Also—and it's a big "also"—in a human trial on bone marrow cancer patients, megadoses of resveratrol induced kidney failure. The research continues in the lab, and it could be that something wonderful comes of it, but right now—hype notwithstanding—resveratrol is not the answer.

You may have noticed that there are many other mitochondria-enhancer contenders out there: herbal supplements; vitamin, mineral, and phytochemical combinations said to fortify, support, and otherwise invigorate mitochondria; special formulations sold as mitochondria "energizers." You can buy this stuff on the Internet. As with other anti-aging nostrums (remember the redox signaling supplement?), you can find compelling testimonials from happy, youthful, energized users. What's wrong with this scenario? Because, of course, you know there's something wrong.

Actually, there are a few things wrong: First, there's very little good data on these supplements, meaning long-term studies on us humans. Second, even if you wanted to risk it—after all, what could be the harm in taking herbs and vitamins and amino acids? It's not like taking a *drug*—the supplement industry is, as I'll get into in Chapter 10, largely unregulated. That means you can't be sure of what you're getting or how much of it you're getting or where it came from. And, should you need another reason: The cost can be prohibitive.

Sweaty, smelly exercise is looking better all the time.

THE NEXT MORNING, BRIGHT EYED AND EMPTY STOMACHED, I present myself at Hans Dreyer's lab. It's in a medical research building attached to a major hospital, and it looks, feels, and smells like a hospital: Band-Aid-colored walls, fluorescent panel ceiling lights, the whoosh of central air conditioning. I feel my blood pressure rise. I hate hospitals. As I wait for Dreyer to gather what he needs for "the procedure," I have time to think about just how *much* I hate hospitals, and just how much time older people spend in them. One of my goals in life—and certainly a long-term goal in this counterclockwise journey—is to spend as little time in them as possible as I get older. I'm all about that "compression of morbidity/rectangularization of life" thing: healthy, healthy, healthy, dead. That's the way to do it.

Dreyer comes out of his lab and walks me over to the procedure room. He is a short, compact, athletic-looking guy who might have been a high school gymnast. He's dressed in a doctor's smock over a T-shirt, cargo pants, and dorky sandals, a mixed message that I can't quite decipher but nonetheless find comfort in. I am directed to lie down on a hospital bed and roll up my sweatpants to expose my left thigh. I crane my neck to watch Dreyer prep the site, draping, swabbing, etc., as if— well, as if something major is going to happen. All the while I am asking mitochondria questions, scribbling notes in my reporter's notebook held overhead using one of those pens NASA developed that can write upside down. He's telling me how very hard it is to get good mitochondria data, how the sample has to be perfect, the storage and transport perfect, the prep in the lab perfect, the machine flawless. I didn't know this until now, but my samples will be FedExed to a Colorado State University lab this afternoon. The machine used to measure mitochondrial respiration (the taking in of oxygen and nutrients, the production of ATP/energy) is a $24,000 piece of equipment. It's in the budget for Dreyer's latest grant, but right now his lab is without it.

I'm doubly disappointed, first, because I had this Bill-Nye-the-Science-Guy image of Dreyer taking my sample across the hall to his lab, prepping a slide, and having me look through a microscope at living tissue, *my* living tissue; second, because the results won't be back until next week. But I soldier on. "This will feel like a bee sting," Dreyer says, holding aloft a lidocaine-filled syringe. He injects carefully. "Followed by a little burning," he adds. Unnecessarily. Finally, with two grad students looking on, Dreyer goes to work digging around in my thigh for two perfect muscle samples. "Little chunks," he says. Either he hears my sharp intake of breath or he realizes how the word "chunks" sounds because he quickly adds: "I'm just looking for two to five milligrams of pristine section."

A few minutes later, he places little pieces of muscle meat on a square of sterile gauze and proclaims himself pleased with the samples. One of the grad students whisks it away while Dreyer sutures me up. Yes, I need a suture to close the incision, and, because I am leaving town in three days and can't come back to the lab in time to get it removed, Dreyer gives me my very own suture kit. The fact that I get to remove my own suture is somehow unbelievably cool. I have perhaps crossed another line.

It takes a week and a half for the results to come. That means I have plenty of time to work up a full head of angst. Now that I know just how important high-functioning mitochondria are to turning back the biological clock, I want them. Bad. I want scientific proof that what I've been doing (more on that in a moment) works. My ego—yes, that—is crying out for gratification. Is it any worse to be ego-involved in the state of one's mitochondria than it is, for example, to be ego-involved in the number of books one sells, or whether one's child gets into AP Bio? I'm not sure. But ego-involved I am.

Finally, Dreyer e-mails me the results. "Your muscle had the highest rates of oxidative phosphorylation and electron transport capacity compared to other 'healthy' controls." Scarily, I actually know what this means. And it's good. Compared to the muscle tissue of other subjects in a group of volunteers he's testing, mine had the greatest capacity to consume oxygen and make energy using carbohydrates as fuel. Dreyer also compared my sample to those in another database of 20-something college women, a group he and another researcher are evaluating at high altitudes in Peru. "Compared to the mean values obtained from the young ~20yo females, your sample was very similar in terms of oxygen consumption, and showed a slightly greater level of oxphos efficiency [economy of energy production]." I'm liking it. I'm liking it. And then comes the best part: "As such, our preliminary analysis would suggest your muscles' mitochondrial capacity is similar to fit young women." I give myself a high five. (Followed too swiftly by regret that my thighs don't *look* like those of a 20-something woman.)

I need to add an explanation here. Although you won't read about how I sweat and grunt my way through every exercise and activity shown to have turn-back-the-clock potential (which is to say just about every exercise and activity on earth) until Chapter 11, I have been moderately active for my whole life, and I actually started my high-intensity physical regimen at the very beginning of my quest. I had hoped Dreyer would do a biopsy then, but I didn't meet the qualifications for the research study he was doing at the time (one in women over 65 who had knee surgery), and I discovered that you can't just order up a biopsy. But right after my high-tech Tanita scale revealed that my body was one-third fat and my VO$_2$ max test showed significant room for improvement, "get lean and fit" became number one on my long list of counterclockwise goals. Through the long months of sweating and grunting, as I continued to research other chapters, conduct interviews, and travel to North Carolina and Las Vegas, I kept in contact with Dreyer. Finally, because he needed healthy control subjects to compare to his college-age-females-at-high-altitude study, he called me in. All of this is to say that my amazingly wonderful, superactive, fully charged, practically teenaged mitochondria are undoubtedly the result of months and months of very hard work. But, *damn*. Way to turn back the clock.

CHAPTER
SIX

Size Matters

MITOCHONDRIA ARE MAIN CHARACTERS IN THAT HIDDEN drama of cellular aging, the narrative we know little about until it plays out on our public stage, and we see and feel ourselves age. But out on the frontiers of anti-aging, there is another character you've probably never heard of (and neither had I): telomeres. As with mitochondria, the research is impressive—Nobel laureate impressive, as a matter of fact—and the promise of long-term, high-level wellness seems tantalizingly close.

I first heard about telomeres at the anti-aging conference in Las Vegas, where I sat through parts of three completely incomprehensible PowerPoint sessions scribbling notes that, when I read them at home, were even more incomprehensible than the sessions themselves. Only now, after a combination of deep reading and getting people way smarter than me to answer my stupid questions (my MO for background research), I am able to make some sense out of this.

So, first: What are telomeres? They are protective caps at the ends of chromosomes that have been likened to the plastic tips at the ends of shoelaces. Just as those plastic tips keep your shoelaces from unraveling, telomeres keep your DNA from beginning to fray (or deteriorate, or fuse with neighboring chromosomes) during cell division. If cells divided without telomeres, the coded information at the ends of the strands would be lost, and the cell would die or, possibly worse, live on to malfunction.

Here's the rub: During cell division, the protective telomere "cap" is consumed, sacrificing itself to maintain the integrity of the cell. Happily, the cell makes an enzyme called telomerase that works hard to try to replace the cap after each division, but the more divisions a cell goes through, the shorter its telomere becomes. Telomere shortening means the cell's life span is shortening. That's why the length of a telomere is thought to be an important marker of cellular aging.

What do we know about telomeres and aging? Quite a lot. Studies show associations between shorter telomere length and just about everything that can—and frequently does—go wrong with an aging body. A University of Utah study I read found that people with shorter telomeres died 4 to 5 years earlier than people with longer caps on their chromosomes. They had three times the mortality rate from cardiovascular disease and eight times the death rate from infectious diseases. A number of other studies confirmed these and other unhealthy associations, implicating short telomeres in strokes, heart attacks, cancer, dementia, and diabetes. Add to that declines in lung, liver, and kidney function and in the immune response. Throw in osteoporosis and depression, and you've pretty much got the dirty-laundry list of aging.

But we age at different rates, right? While everyone's telomeres grow shorter, some people's grow shorter *faster*. Why would that be? Research shows that a sedentary lifestyle—you knew I was going to say that, didn't you?—is a major factor. So is chronic inflammation (a low-level but persistent response from a taxed immune system) and insulin resistance (aka metabolic syndrome, an all-too-common obesity-related, prediabetic condition). Here's something really interesting: Stress is also associated with shortened telomeres. "Our cells," says Elissa Epel, PhD, a pioneering telomere researcher, "are listening to our thoughts." In an important study that compared the telomeres of under-stress mothers of chronically ill children with those of mothers of healthy children, the difference in length was significant. Women with the highest stress levels had telomeres the equivalent length of those of women 10 years older. Stressed *sedentary* women were the biggest losers.

As I read about telomere length and its importance in aging—which means, of course, its importance in staying youthful—my first thought is: How long are *my* telomeres? All those stressed-out women got their telomeres measured. It can't be that complicated or laborious a process. Surely it doesn't involve someone making an incision in some part of my body and poking around for a "sample." After not much digging, I'm excited to discover that blood is all that is needed, and that a major telomere study is being conducted by Elizabeth Blackburn, PhD, at the University of California, San Francisco. Blackburn, a molecular biologist, one of *Time* magazine's 2007 "100 people who shape the world," and winner of the 2009 Nobel Prize in Physiology or Medicine, launched the field of telomere research 30 years ago. So anything she's involved with is golden. The study is called Know Your Telomeres, and researchers are looking for up to 240 nonsmoking midlife women. Participants get their blood drawn (and telomeres measured) once at the beginning of the study and once one year later. In between, there are phone interviews. And you even get paid! I'm ready to sign up. But when I enter all the required information at the study's site, I receive an automated rejection. Apparently, participants must live in or near San Francisco. That's where the initial study visit will take place as well as the blood draws. I write a note, saying that I will pay my way down to San Francisco for the study visit and the blood draws. I call and plead my case. No dice.

I do *not* want to throw myself on the mercy of the Internet. I see that there are "No doctor needed!" "Quick results!" ads for telomere-testing labs. But telomere testing is so very new, with its methods and technology just evolving. How do I know what's a scam and what's not? That's why I'm delighted to learn that Nobelist Blackburn has cofounded a company, Telome Health, which will be offering telomere tests to the public. "Will be" turns out to be the catch. The test is not yet available, and there's no good indication when it might be. But I do find a lead to a Spanish company called Life Length that has an information-rich Web site and what looks to be an impressively credentialed advisory board. I'm not pleased to learn that they've just introduced telomere testing in the United States—which makes me wonder if they've gotten the kinks out and how large their database is for comparison purposes—but they appear to be my best bet. As they deal only with medical professionals, I ask my friend and naturopath, Andrew Elliott, to make the connection and see about getting me tested. When the word comes that the test will cost $900, Elliott—on his own initiative—writes back to the company rep saying that I am doing research for a book, and can we possibly negotiate a lower price. The sales manager e-mails Elliott that the company will cut me a deal if I mention its name in the book. Which I believe I just did.

The test kit arrives at my naturopath's office a few days later, with vials for blood nested in Styrofoam nested in a reinforced box, a next-day return mail pouch, and separate instruction sheets for me, the phlebotomist, and the person in charge of mailing the sample. Also a secret log-in code I must use to fill out a lengthy online health questionnaire, without which they refuse to do the analysis. As my daughter would say: *"Whatever."* The next morning, I'm at a local lab to get my blood drawn. When I hand the phlebotomist the instruction sheet, she doesn't glance at it. "We do hundreds of blood draws a week," she says curtly. I try to explain that this is a new and unique test with specific instructions that might also be unique. She's not interested. Before I leave the lab, I ask the receptionist if I can speak to whoever will be mailing the sample. It needs to be refrigerated, and it needs to be in the mail, overnight, by this afternoon, I tell her. "Don't worry," she says, in that same dismissive tone I got from the phlebotomist. "We do this all the time." *No you don't!* I want to yell. *I bet this is the first telomere test you've ever drawn blood for!* But I am nice and polite and just ask her to please make sure the mailing person looks at the instruction sheet. The test itself will be done quickly, but the company claims a backlog—is this obscure $900 analysis really that popular?—so the report may take up to four weeks to arrive at my naturopath's office.

THIS GIVES ME PLENTY OF TIME TO RESEARCH MY TELOMERE-augmentation options, should I need them. Most genetic markers are not modifiable, but it turns out that this one is. I discover that the most promising—and scariest—way is genetic manipulation. It works miracles. It dramatically reverses many signs of aging. It makes the old young again. Old *mice*, that is. The research, which really does show extraordinary turn-back-the-clock results, is all rodent based. And the aging mechanisms in mice are not necessarily those found in humans. And manipulation in the lab does not necessarily correlate with how real bodies work. And then there's this other little problem. Switching on the telomerase gene, which is what the researchers did in these mice, makes it possible for a cell to replicate forever. It makes the cell immortal. We have a name for immortal cells, cells that won't die of their own accord, cells that keep making more of themselves: cancer. Although none of the genetically tweaked mice developed cancer, telomerase therapy remains quite controversial because of this possibility.

How about a kinder, gentler approach? There's some—not much, but some—research on vitamins and supplements. A study published in the very credible *American Journal of Clinical Nutrition* found that telomere length was longer in midlife or older women who regularly took multivitamins (yay! I do that!), and that higher intakes of vitamins C and E from food were also associated with longer length. The supplement industry is, you remember, unregulated. That means, among other things, that a company can make whatever (veiled) claims it wants about what a supplement does. There are claims that omega-3 fatty acids, vitamin D, folate, and vitamin B_{12} may provide telomere support. (If not, they do many other good things in the body.)

Some anti-aging docs are promoting Chinese gingerroot, *Ginkgo biloba*, and astragalus root extract for telomere health. In a 2011 study conducted on a commercial age-management product made of astragalus root extract, researchers found that the product "moderately activated" telomerase in cultured human immune cells. In the body, the product (TA-65) decreased the percentage of short telomeres in several kinds of immune cells. It's worth noting that five of the seven researchers involved in this study disclosed competing financial interests, meaning they stand to make a profit from the sale of TA-65.

Finally, there's intriguing research on something called carnosine, an antioxidant-rich combination of two amino acids found in the brain and muscles. A 2004 study found that, in the lab, the telomeres of cultured lung cells grown in carnosine "exhibited a slower shortening rate" and an "extended lifespan." But it's a long distance between cells in a petri dish and cells in the body.

I would be remiss if I didn't tell you about the $5,495 Rejuva Matrix, a (according to the product brochure) "solar homeopathic mat developed to provide non-ultraviolet frequencies similar to those from the sun." The mat provides an electromagnetic field of 54 to 78 giga-hertz at 50 to 78 decibels, whatever the heck that means. The promoter of said mat (a presenter and exhibitor at the Las Vegas anti-aging confer-ence, in fact) told me that lying on the mat for 30 minutes a day five days a week for three months increased the average telomere length 1 percent for six people in his pilot study. After 10 months, he recorded a 2.9 percent increase. Stranger things have been true.

Probably the biggest news in the telomere-lengthening world is also the most prosaic: Changes in lifestyle are showing real promise, with a critical mass of studies showing associations between telomere length and nutrition, exercise, and stress reduction. Once again, the sexy and/or quick fixes lose out to the almost clichéd advice to eat a low-fat, high-antioxidant diet; avoid sugar, alcohol, and tobacco; exercise regularly; and find balance in your life. Some of the most intriguing studies involve state of mind, which makes sense given the link between telomere length and stress. In a three-month study of people who learned how to medi-ate, telomere shortening slowed compared to that of nonmeditators. In one of many suggestive studies from Elissa Epel—the "our cells are lis-tening to our thoughts" researcher—the telomeres of those who live in the present measured longer than those preoccupied with past or future.

At last, Life Length sends the telomere results to my naturopath. I'm initially excited to see that I'm getting a 15-page report. But it turns out that only three of those pages are specifically about my telomeres. And the information is confusing. The average length of the telomeres in my blood sample is about twice the length of what Life Length deems "short"—which sounds good but is actually close to meaningless because telomere length is very individual. My "short" telomere may be someone else's medium-length telomere, or vice versa. Based on a simple graph provided on page four of the report, it seems that more than 75 percent of midlife women have a higher percentage of short telomeres than I do—which sounds good. But how many women have they tested? Are they healthy women? Stressed women? Do they exercise? To whom am I being compared? And how accurate is this test anyway? How skilled was the analyst? And how pristine was my sample? (I am thinking about all the potential problems Hans Dreyer talked about with the muscle sample.) Was my sample refrigerated after the blood draw? Did it get to the testing facility on time? There are just too many unanswered questions to put much stock in the results. As my naturopath says in an e-mail after we've discussed and debated the results: "I think you have done a leading-edge test and it will take years to understand what the numbers mean and how to use them in a useful way." In a later e-mail, and in a lighter mood, he writes, referring to the cost of the test: "perhaps the money spent on the test could have been better spent buying lottery tickets. A winning one probably has the potential of quickly lengthening telomeres!"

I am very glad to have discovered the budding science of telomeres, excited to have read the research that puts such stock in healthy lifestyle changes as a prime telomere-lengthening strategy—and disappointed that the test was such an anticlimax. Perhaps it's time to stop playing around on the edges, out on the frontiers, of anti-aging and get down to the nitty-gritty.

seven

Shortcuts and Quick Fixes

WHAT'S THE SCARIEST NUMBER YOU CAN IMAGINE? THE national debt? The number of e-mail messages in your in-box after a week's vacation?

No. It's your percentage of body fat at midlife. Okay, it's *my* percentage of body fat at midlife.

Of all the biomarkers of age, of all the stats that determine how old you really are biologically, percentage fat and its slender sibling, percentage lean, are among the most significant. You will remember—or, forgive me, I will remind you—of these disturbing facts: The average American loses 6.6 pounds of lean body mass during every decade from young adulthood into middle age. At age 45, the rate accelerates. And, as lean decreases, fat increases. The body of the average 25-year-old woman is 25 percent fat. The body of a (sedentary) 65-year-old woman is 43 percent fat (for a man, 40 percent). With the decrease in muscle comes a decrease in strength and general vitality (fitness, aerobic capacity). This condition even has a name—and it's *not* "getting older." It's sarcopenia, Greek for "reduction of flesh." I think it's a game changer to consider that something we are accustomed to blaming on chronological age might be a "condition" caused not so much by the number of years we have lived, but rather by how we have lived those years.

The fat-to-lean ratio is not just about appearance, although it goes without saying that, chunky-thighed, pudgy-cheeked babies notwithstanding, less fat and more muscle can make a body look decades younger than its calendar years. So appearance matters, yes. But there's far more going on here. The high-fat–low-muscle thing—sarcopenia—causes, triggers, or is closely linked with other markers of aging. Metabolism, for example. Young people, with their lower percentages of fat, have higher metabolisms. That's because one pound of fat burns two calories a day, and one pound of muscle can burn 35. While some metabolic slowdown might be attributable to just the passage of time, it's far more likely that we're slowing down not just because we're older, but also because we've become increasingly fatter. And by "we," I mean *me*. As I've been researching biomarkers, talking to researchers, hanging out at labs and clinics and conventions, standing on bioimpedance machines, and submerging myself in tanks of water (I spared you the description of that experience), I've become increasingly focused on fat-to-lean. I need much less of the former and much more of the latter in light of the unhappy news my Tanita scale delivered that almost one-third of my body is fat.

In addition to slowing down my metabolism—making it, need I add, easier to gain even more fat—high body fat is related to increased glucose intolerance, which leads to insulin resistance, the first step on the path to type 2 diabetes. Not a road one wants to travel. A high body fat ratio is also implicated in elevated bad cholesterol (which I have), and my all-about-arteries friend Professor Doug Seals cites studies showing that a high percentage of abdominal body fat is related to "old" (inelastic) arteries.

So, how to reverse this trend? To burn fat I need a stoked-up metabolism, but to achieve this fat-burning metabolism I need . . . less fat. I'm feeling stuck. I go back through all my notes, my stacks of books, the scores of articles I've torn from magazines. Here, apparently, is all I have to do:

- Lift weights
- Engage in aerobic exercise
- No: Do interval exercise
- Wait: Do high-intensity interval exercise
- Practice yoga
- Eat six small meals a day
- Eat spicy foods
- Omit sugar
- Increase fiber
- Drink coffee
- No, don't
- Consume gallons of water
- Avoid stress (yeah, right)
- Sleep a lot

Really?

This is way too much. And it will take way too long. Isn't this the 21st century? Isn't this the US of A, land of instant gratification and quick fixes? Doesn't the booming anti-aging industry provide some options here? Surely there is a quick fix for this.

My first thought: thyroid. My mother often complained of a "sluggish thyroid" that, she insisted, made it easy for her to gain weight and hard to lose it. My aunt said she had thyroid issues. My sisters-in-law all talk thyroid. Thyroid hormones are well known for their role in helping to regulate metabolism. Low thyroid means a lethargic metabolism. I know it's awful to wish for something to be out of whack, but I can't help thinking how great it would be if all I had to do was take a pill every morning. Like magic (well, like complex biochemistry), my metabolism would be supercharged, and fat would just disappear.

I call my doctor and ask for a thyroid test. I remind him that I have a very slow heart rate, and that my hands and feet are often cold—two signs of hypothyroidism. It's just a simple blood test that looks for the level of TSH (thyroid-stimulating hormone) being secreted by the pituitary gland. While I'm waiting for the lab results, I read up on what I kind of hope is my condition. It is most common in women, and the incidence increases with age. It might be linked to bad cholesterol. I'm as excited as one can be when anticipating a disease. Alas, the doctor calls with the bad news: My TSH level is perfectly normal.

My next thought, I am somewhat embarrassed to admit, is liposuction. Or, as the surgeons involved in this practice sometimes prefer to call it, "circumference reduction." I heard all about this, including new and wonderful noninvasive ultrasound fat-liquefying techniques, during my time with the preeminent plastic surgeon Dr. Jewell. In terms of quick fixes, this ranks pretty high. An hour or so on a table, and I could reduce my body fat percentage by maybe two or three points. I force myself to watch a liposuction surgery video on YouTube (joining the 74,866 others who did so before me), and it is simultaneously revolting and mesmerizing to see liquefied fat splashing into a glass jar. I peruse close to 100 before-and-after photos of various parts of various people's bodies and imagine my own sculpted, contoured, reduced-fat silhouette.

Here's what stops me: Money. (Thousands.) Ego. (Would I respect myself in the morning?) Math. It dawns on me that although reducing my fat percentage would automatically increase my lean percentage, I would not, in fact, be actually increasing muscle mass at all. I would have the same number of pounds of muscle, consuming the same perhaps 35 calories per pound that I had before the, as the YouTube surgeon put it, "evacuation." What I need is more calorie-burning, metabolism-boosting muscle. Now.

It turns out that the marketplace—the supplement/nutraceutical/pharmaceutical/anti-aging commercial marketplace—is chock-full of products that promise just this. Ads in men's and women's health and fitness magazines and all over the Web tout "extreme energy and muscle builders" that "mobilize fat" to give "the best body ever." More muscle and less fat? It's hard not to take a closer look. The ads for these "professional strength," "clinically proven," "scientifically backed" pills and powders feature men and women with strong, sculpted bodies. The men sport the obligatory six-pack (I've never understood the aesthetic appeal); the women have sleek, toned thighs for which I would sell my soul. Or my firstborn.

But not so fast. As I try to follow up the claims, I discover that the top-selling fat-busting, energy-boosting supplement, Hydroxycut, has encountered some major problems. The FDA received almost two dozen reports of serious health issues suffered by users, from jaundice, seizures, and cardiovascular problems to liver damage so severe that the person required a transplant—to one documented death. The FDA ordered a recall back in 2009. Whatever happened with all that, the product line is very much alive today—and available everywhere.

I check into some other products that promise to, as the ad for one boldly announces, "immediately trigger gains in lean muscle." Yes, I want that. The ads for these powders and drinks keep referencing "the key ingredients known to build muscle," but never say what these key ingredients are. Deep reading of labels augmented by quick tutorials from Wikipedia and enhanced by detailed explanations from my science journalist husband help unravel the mystery. Besides caffeine, three or four different iterations of sugar, some vitamins, and various food dyes, there seem to be two "key" ingredients. One is something called creatine, produced by the liver and kidneys and transported to muscles for their use. The body also gets creatine from the diet. Meat has a lot of it. Bodybuilders, powerlifters, wrestlers, sprinters, and others who want to gain muscle mass swear by it. Although I'd never heard of creatine before, when I mention it to my high school daughter, she nods knowingly. "Oh yeah," she says, "all the football players chug that stuff." By "stuff" she means creatine-rich power shakes. The other key ingredient is arginine, an amino acid that helps activate a blood-flow enhancer that presumably increases energy, aids in burning body fat, and, according to a brochure I picked up at the Las Vegas anti-aging convention, enhances sexual performance. (I wonder if the football players know *that?*)

I discover that both of these compounds, while they have supporters in the world of sport and fitness, are not without their problems. The Mayo Clinic lists 22 known side effects for arginine, from the innocuous (bloating, restless legs) to the portentous (high blood pressure, increased risk of bleeding). But, on the other hand, in clinical trials arginine was used safely "with minor side effects" for up to three months. Creatine, which appears to do what it purports to do—increase both strength and muscle mass—also gets mixed medical reviews. Some research suggests that a certain level of supplementation is "largely devoid of adverse side effects." But there have also been reports of kidney damage, heart problems, and altered liver function. The past president of the American Academy of Family Physicians, Jim King, MD, told a *Men's Health* journalist, "I feel it would be better for no one to use creatine."

I'm vacillating. Nothing is without risk, right? Maybe I could begin my day with a creatine shake for a week or two to see what happens. But wait a minute. Buried in that *Men's Health* article I read is this important piece of information that, not so surprisingly, none of the ads or brochures chose to mention: The "magic" of these supplements is not that they, themselves, build muscle. It's that they give you increased energy to work harder in the gym, lift heavier weights for more reps, and build the muscle yourself. Oh. I have to *work* for this? Not exactly the quick fix I'm looking for.

Far more promising—and, perhaps, more perilous—is hormone replacement therapy. DHEA (a hormone precursor) and HGH (human growth hormone) are both darlings of the more-lean-and-I-mean-*now* crowd. I learned quite a bit about hormone replacement, especially the bioidentical variety, at the Las Vegas conference, but the focus of the presentations I attended was not muscle building. Still, the theory is the same: Hormone levels decrease as we age. Replacing those depleted hormones, upping the levels to match our peak years, can transform aging bodies into more youthful bodies. And so it is, some research shows and true believers most fervently believe, with DHEA, a substance that helps regulate the way cells consume fats and sugars and that modulates the balance between using energy and storing energy. "Storing energy," by the way, is a nice way of saying larding on fat. DHEA levels peak in our mid-20s. By age 65, we have maybe 10 to 20 percent of what we did in our young adulthood.

DHEA enthusiasts believe that the substance exerts a powerful influence on body composition, and at least two small but credible studies published in the mid-2000s support that idea. In one, sponsored in part by the National Institutes of Health, four months of DHEA supplementation (plus a program of resistance training) helped a group of older women and men gain significantly more muscle and strength than did a group who trained with no DHEA. In another study, this one published in the prestigious *JAMA: The Journal of the American Medical Association*, nonexercising older women who took DHEA supplements lost an average of more than 10 percent of their visceral fat (the bad stuff around the organs) and 6 percent of subcutaneous fat. The placebo group showed "miniscule" changes. A rat study a few years later demonstrated that old rats fed a high-fat diet with DHEA supplementation increased muscle and decreased body fat—both the amount of fat and the number of fat cells.

The problem—yes, there's always a problem—is that the body converts DHEA into testosterone and estrogen. Upping the testosterone level can cause unwanted side effects like acne, hirsutism, and high cholesterol. Upping the estrogen level can act as a stimulant to hormone-dependent cancers such as breast cancer. I might consider DHEA if pimples and chin whiskers were the only potential side effects. These side effects are not common, and they're not all that serious. If you see one coming, you stop taking the DHEA. But trading more muscle for the possibility, even the smallest possibility, of an increase in the chance of breast cancer? I don't have to think about that for a nanosecond. There are other ways to get lean.

Like, for example, the king of the muscle-building, fat-busting hormone replacement world: HGH. Human growth hormone, as it is naturally produced in the body, is an amazing substance: It builds muscle and bone, promotes the breakdown of fat, boosts the immune system, regulates blood sugar. All of these are biomarkers of youthfulness. But the party ends at puberty. Every decade thereafter, the body produces less and less HGH until, at midlife, you've got perhaps 25 percent of the growth hormone you had at 20. (Fifty percent of elderly folks have no detectable HGH at all.) It makes sense, then, to supplement, right? If you had a lot at age 20, and you were doing great at age 20, then why not artificially supplement to get back to your 20-year-old self?

The buzz about HGH began in 1990 with a study published in the *New England Journal of Medicine*. When 125 men (ages 61 to 81) were given HGH injections three times a week for six months, their muscle mass increased substantially, their fat decreased even more substantially, and their bone density increased. It was a very small study; the cost of HGH supplementation then was $1,000 a month, and some disagreeable side effects were noted. Regardless, the study caused a sensation. The age of age management began in earnest. Growth hormone use and abuse by professional and amateur athletes followed. Internet hawking of what was purported to be HGH skyrocketed.

Although the *New England Journal of Medicine* later took the unprecedented step of denouncing the misuse of the study the journal had chosen to publish, the commercial marketplace paid little attention, and serious researchers continued looking into the promise and peril of the hormone. And studies through the 2000s confirmed much of what that original study had found. In two systematic reviews of the scientific literature that looked at "gold standard" research (controlled, randomized, double-blind), one analyzing 31 articles, the other 44 articles, the findings were clear: HGH injections increased lean body mass, decreased fat, and improved total cholesterol numbers.

But outside the research setting, bodybuilders were using HGH for prolonged periods, and the news there was not good. They began exhibiting the symptoms of a syndrome called acromegaly that's caused when the pituitary gland produces too much growth hormone: Their hands, feet, noses, lips, and ears enlarged. The bones of the jaw, fingers, and toes thickened, causing noticeable, sometimes severe disfigurement. They had heart and kidney problems. They developed diabetes, liver disease. They suffered joint pain and fatigue. This was serious business.

When I mention HGH to an athletic trainer I know, a guy who used to compete as a "natural" (that is, no hormones, no steroids) bodybuilder, he grabs me by the shoulder. "You're not thinking of doing that, are you?" he asks, very concerned. "We could tell who was using in the gym," he says. "Using," he'd said. The language of drugs. "These guys looked like apes," he tells me. "Please. Promise me you won't do this."

I didn't really have to promise because, as I soon discovered, it would be illegal for me to be treated with HGH. Prescribing the hormone to treat "aging or aging-related conditions"—that is, the natural decrease in HGH production that comes with age—is punishable by a five-year prison sentence. But what about all the stuff for sale on the Internet? It's pretty much fakery. What about the anti-aging clinics and spas that offer hormone replacement therapy that includes HGH?

It turns out that you can circumvent the law. Or, as a renowned endocrinologist I interviewed told me, "Anyone with symptoms of middle age and a positive bank account can find a clinic that will administer the hormone or a substance that will stimulate the body to produce the hormone." George Merriam, a Harvard-trained MD who has conducted some promising HGH studies on older people, explained it to me this way: HGH can be legally prescribed to remedy hormone-deficiency disease, so you create an "adult-onset growth hormone-deficiency disease"—which, basically, any midlife person could have by virtue of having a naturally declining level of HGH. The symptoms of this disease read like the minor complaints of any run-of-the-mill adult: "general muscle loss," "fatigue," "poor-quality sleep." The prescription? HGH injections. The cost is extraordinary. The long-term risks—at least those we know of from the bodybuilders' experiences—are downright scary. But those short-term results, proven results, significant muscle-building results, are seductive. Just not seductive enough for me.

OKAY, SO NOW YOU'RE THINKING: WHAT FUN IS THIS? SHE'S too much of a chicken to try much of anything. Wrong! I can, in fact, be seduced by get-lean-quick schemes. I can, like most of the American public, be a sucker. I blame Candace for this one. She's a locker-room friend I see every so often at the gym. I had been noticing for a while that Candace was not looking good. She was putting on weight. Her complexion was pasty. Her hair was limp. Then, after not running in to her for maybe six weeks, I saw her in the locker room one morning, and she looked amazing. It looked as if she'd dropped a good 20 pounds and gone back in time a good 10 years. Her skin was glowing. She was almost sizzling with energy. I had to know what accounted for this extraordinary—and very rapid—change.

"It's hCG," she tells me, smiling broadly. "It changed my life."

I had heard about hCG at the Las Vegas conference. In fact, it seemed as if every other booth in the exhibit hall had brochures describing hCG protocols and products. One hard-sell, maximize-your-profits booth in particular made such a poor impression on me that I remember vowing to pay no attention to whatever this hCG thing was. Now I was paying attention. I pumped Candace for information and heard about her amazing 22-pounds-in-32-days weight loss, most of which, she said, was fat, about the emergence of muscles she didn't know she had, and, most important, about the doctor (a local naturopath) from whom she received a homeopathic hCG tincture and a detailed protocol. Then I did my own research.

What hCG stands for is human chorionic gonadotropin, a hormone secreted during pregnancy. (It's actually what those pee-on-a-strip pregnancy tests are measuring.) A gifted British endocrinologist named Albert Simeons first proposed using hCG injections to stimulate rapid fat loss with little muscle loss while doing research in India in the 1950s. He noticed calorie-deprived women giving birth to big, healthy babies and came to believe that the hCG their bodies were naturally secreting was protecting their fetuses by quickly mobilizing and using any fat deposits they had and any fat they consumed in their diets. In the face of the severe calorie restriction that was their daily life, the hormone had reprogrammed their brains, he thought, to make their system hyperefficient at burning fat. From this theory he developed a very specific hCG protocol that involved hormone injections and a 500-calorie-a-day diet with a very short list of allowable foods: no grains, legumes, dairy, or fat; an oddly small selection of fruits and vegetables; a daily allotment of three ounces of very lean protein. A kinder and gentler—not to mention less expensive—approach that did not involve injections was homeopathic hCG, a super-diluted concentration of the hormone delivered under the tongue by eyedropper.

My friend Candace had gone on this homeopathic hCG protocol for four weeks. She said she was never hungry, not once, and the weight just disappeared. She felt lean and clean. When you read about such things on the Internet, your "too good to be true" detector goes off immediately. But there was Candy, right in front of me, looking amazing. I called her naturopath the next day.

And for the next three weeks, I ate 500 or fewer calories a day and took homeopathic hCG supplements. Breakfast was an apple, sliced so thin as to be transparent (because that made lots of pieces, and I could pretend I was eating a big breakfast). Lunch was a two- or three-item salad (celery, lettuce, cuke, or cabbage—the choices were limited). Dinner was three ounces of white-meat chicken (seared—no oil allowed!—in a nonstick pan) and a salad made from the short list. I was allowed one snack, another apple, which I savored with such intensity that I scared my daughter. When I asked the naturopath why the choices were so very limited, why a person couldn't just eat, say a 70-calorie pear instead of a 70-calorie apple, she didn't have a convincing answer. "That's the Simeons protocol," she said. "It works. Don't mess with it."

So I didn't. The first week, I lost nine pounds. Yes, nine. The second week I lost another four pounds. By the end of three weeks—that's 21 days—I had lost 17 pounds. After the first two days, I was not hungry. Really. I was also not very energetic.

You will not find any reputable studies that say the hormone itself helps with muscle-sparing weight loss. (And the notion that a *homeopathic* version of hCG like I took—containing an almost immeasurably small concentration of the hormone—would work is considered just plain silly by mainstream researchers.) Go to any reputable Web site—MayoClinic.com, for example—and you will read that the hCG protocol doesn't work. What works is consuming so few calories. What works is starving yourself. So why didn't I feel starving? In retrospect, I think it was classic mind-over-matter. Or an example of the placebo effect. I wanted not to feel hungry. I expected, because of Candace's firsthand report, not to feel hungry. I didn't feel hungry. And, of course, on 500 calories a day, I lost a lot of weight.

You are now expecting the other shoe to fall, and I will not disappoint.

The body composition scale said that 5 of the 17 pounds I lost were water, and another 5 were muscle. *I had lost muscle.* Even though I had continued to exercise during the three weeks, my energy level was low—not surprising given the severe calorie restriction. I just wasn't able to exercise for as long or as vigorously as I had been. I just wasn't able to protect my muscles from being used as fuel. I had lost muscle, and I knew it was going to be hard to find it again.

Three weeks after I stopped the protocol, I had regained all but 2 of the 17 pounds—and, according to my Tanita scale, none of the weight gain was muscle. I was now fatter than when I started. Was I depressed? You bet. But I also figured it served me right. I had fallen for a too-good-to-be-true quick fix, and it had backfired. I was more disgusted with my lack of good sense than I was depressed about my worsened fat-to-lean ratio.

On the upside, this little experiment hadn't resulted in my growing a massive jaw and protruding brow, sprouting hair on my face, elevating my blood pressure, or giving myself liver disease. So I think I got off easy. The lesson I take with me on this leg of the counterclockwise journey: Hormone hawkers to the contrary, there is no quick fix. I am actually going to have to work at this. Overtime. And work means more than putting in some gym time. But just what does it mean? Where do I go from here?

In one of the magazine articles I read about taking steps to maximize health and vitality, I come across this aha-worthy sentence: "Don't paint over a dirty house." I scrawl it on a sticky note and tack it to the side of my computer screen so I can savor the revelation—and act on it. I have to clean "house" (my body) before I can "paint" (transform myself into something fresher, newer). It's time to scrub and scour.

eight

A Clean Slate

WHAT WOULD YOU DO IF YOU KNEW YOU WERE ABOUT TO start an increasingly restrictive 14-day detox regimen, a semi-draconian plan that promised to be rejuvenating, energizing, and result in the pristine gut of a 20-year-old but denied you, well, just about everything? Wait a second. Didn't I just put myself through a more-than-draconian 500-calorie-a-day plan? Yes, I did. Here's the difference: That was a quick-fix impulse, the kind of decidedly unscientific foray into too-good-to-be-true land that fuels much of the anti-aging market. I fell for it. I wanted to fall for it. But I've really thought about this *new* draconian plan. The promise is not a quick fix. The promise, buried in the hype that unfortunately accompanies almost everything that has to do with our health, is more subtle. The detox plan itself, as you'll see, is also more subtle. Or at least progressive, not the zero-to-60 jolt of the 500-calorie hCG fiasco.

Still, there was nothing subtle about my personal preparation for detox: I made a beeline from the nutritionist's office, where I received my marching orders, to the Supreme Bean, where I sat with a double-shot cappuccino and a bag of Trader Joe's pretzel rods to contemplate my dietary future. Then, after a dinner that would soon be a big no-no (chicken Parmesan, pasta), I inhaled not one, not two, but four of the amazing dark-chocolate-chip-and-almond cookies my daughter had whipped up to take to school the following day.

And now it is the following day, the first day of detox. I awake with a fuzzy mouth and a dull headache and a guilty conscience. I read somewhere that the day before a person vows to start any kind of diet is often a vigorous exercise in overindulgence. There's nothing like the promise of deprivation to make one go calorie crazy. Which I did, and for which I will now pay.

If you believe that our 21st-century bodies are in need of detoxification—which I do, for reasons I will tell you in a minute—and if you believe that detox and turning back the biological clock go together—which I do (more on this soon)—then doing something is mandatory. The question is: What? Long term, the answer is clear: Educate yourself about the proven and potentially harmful chemicals that are a part of everyday life (food, cookware, cleaning products, cosmetics, for starters); read labels on everything; avoid as much of the nasty stuff as you can; replace with the cleanest alternatives you can find.

All good and sensible. But you could choose to jump-start this whole process by giving your body a kick in its toxic butt. (Fat is one of the places the body sequesters and holds on to toxins, so I mean this literally.) This butt-kicking jump-start is what I've chosen to do. And I've chosen this particular detox program over the zillions of others out there for several reasons. First, it is not silly (or potentially harmful), like the mystifyingly popular regimen of hot water laced with lemon juice, cayenne, and maple syrup, which is devoid of so much the body needs to function well, including protein, fiber, and most vitamins and minerals. My plan is not a quick-weight-loss scheme masquerading as detox. Second, it was recommended by a credentialed nutritionist and given the nod by a naturopath I trust. And third, it is supposedly targeted at overall detoxification and not aimed at one specific area of the body—because, folks, I'm doing this only once: no liver detox followed by colon irrigation followed by a fill-in-the-blank cleansing. This is it.

A metabolic detox, my brimming-with-health nutritionist carefully explains to me, is a systemwide cleanse meant to scour liver, colon, gastrointestinal tract, lymphatic system, skin, and lungs. "Scour" is my word, not hers. I have this image of Roto-Rooter or a bottle brush. She uses far gentler terms like "purify." This regimen, she says, eliminates foods that are hard to digest, focuses on "colon-friendly plant-based foods" (not exactly restaurant-menu language), supplements the diet with vitamin- and mineral-charged rice protein powder shakes, stabilizes the blood sugar level, and gives the body a rest so it can devote energy to detoxing itself. The aim is to reduce inflammation and cellular "rust" (oxidation) throughout my body. You will remember that chronic inflammation and free radical "rust" have both been implicated, big-time, in cellular aging and in most of the diseases that shorten both our life spans and our health spans.

The first four days of this metabolic detoxification program are, she informs me, "pretty easy." If your definition of "pretty easy" includes giving up caffeine, alcohol, anything with refined sugar (just about all processed foods, from bread to ketchup), and all "flesh foods"—the least appetizing way of referring to "meat" I've ever heard (but maybe that's the point)—then this introductory phase qualifies. This morning, I at least get to have yogurt, which, along with all dairy, will soon be verboten. I mix it with an organic apple and a few "heart healthy" almonds as I sip, somewhat smugly, on herbal tea.

Well, actually, it's green tea. With caffeine. But only a little. It's just one hour into the first day, and I'm already cheating. But only a little. And only to protect my family. Lunch is a black beans, brown rice, and tofu combo, which, to Eugene, Oregon, is like a Philly cheesesteak is to Philly. It's Upper Left Coast soul food. So far, except for not being able to eat anything my family is eating and getting into a flesh-food fight with my husband, things are going well.

Why am I doing this? Why detox? "You're not all *that* toxic," my husband says helpfully as he washes down his thick-slab, peppered bacon with a nice hot cup of coffee laced with half-and-half. I glare at him.

Why, indeed.

THERE ARE THOSE WHO BELIEVE THAT WE EAT, BREATHE, and live toxins, that modern life itself is toxic. Some of these folks are kooks and alarmists; some are scammers looking to make a buck on fear-mongering. But others are reasonable, thoughtful, educated people: scientists and researchers, health professionals, environmental watchdogs. The EPA recognizes 4 million toxins. Some 80,000 chemicals are in use commercially, but only 15,000 of them have been screened for potential health effects. A Centers for Disease Control and Prevention (CDC) study of 2,000 people nationwide found traces of more than 60 toxic compounds (including some very nasty stuff like fire-retardant chemicals, arsenic, mercury) in their blood and urine. Another CDC study of even more people found that almost all had traces of the chemical used to make the coating of most nonstick cookware, and 90 percent had traces of the chemical used to create plastic bottles. How harmful are these chemicals to our health? The jury is still out, but most people—me included—are not interested in waiting until there is a decisive verdict.

It's hard (and foolhardy) *not* to be concerned. Preservatives, artificial colors, artificial flavors, pesticides, insecticides, fertilizers, herbicides, fungicides, hormones, antibiotics, mercury, lead, chlorine, PCBs, aspartame, MSG, saturated fats, trans fats, and the new Big (bad) Kahuna, high-fructose corn syrup (HFCS), are known to have harmful effects on the body—which is the definition of a toxin. Sugar (and not just the HFCS variety) alters the body's hormonal balance and creates, in the words of University of California, San Francisco endocrinologist Robert Lustig, MD, a "toxic environment." (And we in the United States are eating about three and a half times the amount of sugar we did a generation ago.) A smart and engaging lecture Lustig gave, Sugar: The Bitter Truth (look for it on YouTube), was one of the prompts that got me serious about this detox thing.

So were scary comments like these, from books I am reading about detoxification: "You are saturated daily in a bath of metal toxins." (Ouch.) "All our bodies are receptacles for a multitude of industrial chemicals." (Call in the hazmat team.) "We all carry the residue of modern living deep within our bodies." (Poetic but scary.) A kinder, gentler, but nonetheless powerful way of looking at this is the rain barrel analogy. The toxins we take in are like drops of rain falling in a barrel. (The barrel is the body.) Each exposure is tiny, like a single raindrop. Nothing to concern ourselves about. But over time, the drops accumulate until the rain barrel is full, then overflowing. Detoxing is doing something to empty the rain barrel, or at least to lower the water level. Whatever the metaphor—toxic bath, industrial chemical receptacle, rain barrel—the idea is that all of us carry a "body burden," the load on our system caused by the accumulation of tiny amounts of hundreds, perhaps thousands, of known toxins and questionable chemicals.

Obviously, the longer we spend eating, drinking, and breathing—that is, the older we are (chronologically, that is)—the bigger the potential buildup, the heavier the body burden. What this means exactly is still unclear, but the idea is that toxins gunk up the works inside, causing irritation, inflammation, and malabsorption and poor use of nutrients. There are long lists of conditions thought to be linked to our toxic intake: fatigue, constipation, weight gain, poor concentration, poor memory, poor digestion, impaired immunity—and more. This sounds suspiciously like the dark side of aging to me. A list in another source includes Alzheimer's, diabetes, hypertension, arthritis, cancer. A company that hawks a particular detox product online lists 77 distinct symptoms of toxic overload, from dark circles under the eyes to stuttering. But just because Internet hucksters have gotten ahold of the detox idea and are claiming that anything and everything that could possibly go wrong with you is caused by toxins—and can be cured by their detox product—doesn't mean the concept (and reality) of body burden is wrongheaded.

But why would a detox program or product be necessary? Isn't the body a self-cleaning machine? Aren't we built, with our protective layers of skin, our air-filtering lungs, and, most of all, our magnificent blood-purifying livers, to take care of all that? Doesn't all the blood in the body pass through the liver, where toxins, impurities, and assorted debris are cleared from it? Yes. But apparently, we are overloading the system. We're creating more work than our livers can handle, which is stressing and aging this premier cleansing organ and in the process aging the entire body.

And the cycle is self-perpetuating. An overtaxed, compromised liver does not detoxify substances as rapidly or as completely as a healthy liver, and so the body burden builds, which further compromises the liver, which further gunks up—and ages—the rest of the system. And so on. No wonder the French are so focused on the liver. (For us Americans, it's the heart.)

The "overwhelm the system" concept makes sense. This is certainly what happens when an alcoholic overwhelms the system with drink (a toxin) and in doing so manages to damage and scar the liver and generally compromise his or her health and well-being. Alcoholics fast-forward the biological clock, advancing it beyond—sometimes way beyond—their chronological years. How many robust, lively, clear-eyed, pink-cheeked alcoholics do you know? So it's definitely worth considering the reverse: Purifying, cleansing, and strengthening the body's natural detoxification systems could slow the biological clock, maybe even undo damage we didn't know we had done.

So how do we know what our "body burden" is? Can we accurately measure the level (or even the existence) of our toxicity? If you cruise the Web—I did, so you don't have to—you'll find scores of sites promoting "easy-to-use home specimen collection kits" with accompanying testing services. Just send in a strand of hair, a gob of spit, a cup (no, not actually a full eight fluid ounces) of pee, a smear of—well, you know—and for $49 or $499 or $4,999 (yes, you can spend $5,000 on this), some lab somewhere will send you back an impressive-looking report listing all the toxins they find. And generally the list is long. Maybe that means you have a heavy body burden. Maybe it means the company has sloppy (or untested) testing procedures. Maybe it means the company wants to sell you its detox product. There's no meaningful regulation or oversight.

Obviously, when the CDC tests the blood and urine of thousands of people, the agency uses the services of a fully vetted and respected lab. But for the rest of us, it's buyer beware. That's why I decided not to possibly piss away (so to speak) my money on a test. I would just do the detox. It couldn't hurt, and the more I read and the more health practitioners I talked to, the more I thought it would help me in my counterclockwise journey. I did take a free online "What's in You" body burden test that gave me an overall "medium" score on the site's version of a toxicity scale. I also answered 15 questions on a toxicity questionnaire the nutritionist gave me. Happily, I could answer "no" to eating fast foods, drinking soda, and consuming sugar-free foods (except for the sugar-free gum I sometimes chain-chew when I write). I had to answer "yes" to eating refined carbs (remember that bag of pretzel rods?), eating nonorganic produce, and a few other questions. It was not surprising to see where the creators of this assessment felt the foodborne toxic load would be coming from: processed and packaged foods, drive-thru foods, white foods (sugar, flour), and pesticide-doused produce.

I AM NOW FOUR DAYS INTO MY REGIMEN. IN ADDITION TO giving up alcohol, caffeine, meat, and sugar, I have eliminated dairy and eggs from my diet. Do I feel less toxic? I'm not sure. But I do feel lighter. I don't mean weight, although it's possible that I have lost a pound or two. I mean attitude. Also, I am definitely sleeping better. And, most miraculously, I have lost my craving for pretzels and handfuls of those breakfast cereals that have no business calling themselves cereals or being eaten for breakfast. I am not hungry, as in growling-stomach hungry, but I find that I am reminded of food countless times a day.

And it's not tempeh in hemp sauce I am being reminded of. As I walk from the parking structure to the gym, I smell doughnuts (there's a bakery a block away), the air redolent with fried dough and sugar, and although I eat maybe a doughnut a decade and have never craved doughnuts the way I've craved Peanut Butter Cap'n Crunch, I want one, or two, or three, right then. It's not about hunger. It's about living in a world of food cues. I drive past my favorite Thai restaurant, and I can almost taste the Spicy Eggplant with Shrimp. A friend drops by the house and, oblivious to my situation, starts rhapsodizing about garlic-studded roast pork. I haven't eaten pork since Jimmy Carter was president, but my mouth starts watering. I didn't know a body could produce this much saliva this quickly. I'm just lusting after the forbidden. I must stay the course, I tell myself, pouring my eighth cup of herbal tea for the day.

As I keep my eyes on the prize—a rejuvenated, revitalized, detoxi-fied me—I am keenly aware that I am one of millions of self-detoxers. Detox is very big business. How big? In 0.2 second, Google finds more than 15 million listings for the word "detox." (Okay, I admit this also is the title of a Dr. Dre album. And alcohol and drug detox add plenty to the stats. But *15 million?*) Amazon lists 1,500 detox books and almost 3,000 detox products, from cleansing kits to tea bags, foot pads to flu-ids, powders to pills, micronized alkaline water to forest sap made from Chinese herbs, potions concocted from aged garlic extract, psyllium seed husks, algae, and bentonite clay liquid.

Every product label is adjective laden: super, secret, supreme, max-imum, ultimate, miraculous, surefire. There's Power Cleanse, Vital Cleanse, Squeaky Clean, ReNew Life Cleanse, Garden of Life Perfect Cleanse. Although the adjective winner might be Nature's Secret Ulti-mate Cleanse, I like the audacious imperative of Flush & Be Fit. Every product is a "breakthrough." Every product promises to reduce what-ever needs reducing (bloating, cravings, a laundry list of symptoms) and boost whatever needs boosting (metabolism, energy, sex life). Some products, like the costly Clean Program ($425 for shakes and supple-ments), are bolstered by bestsellers, hyped by media attention, and fueled by celebrity endorsements. Gwyneth Paltrow is a big fan of Clean. Demi Moore and Mariska Hargitay are satisfied cleansers. Who wouldn't want to be as luminous as those women?

In addition to supplements, drinks, and dietary regimens, there are infrared sauna treatments, colon therapy, chelation therapy, lymphatic massage, and apparently so many other detox choices that there exists an International School of Detoxification, established to educate and assist us in all our detoxification needs. I have to say, enrollment is tempting, if only for the suitable-for-framing Certification in Detoxification to hang on the wall, a real conversation starter when company comes over.

The number of products, services, and therapies all proclaiming extraordinary success is overwhelming. I spend several days, and I mean full working days, checking out offerings and claims. More interesting than the rampant hucksterism I find (please don't fall for the foot detox pads!) is the quick lesson I get in medical history. It turns out that body cleansing is not a New Age invention, but rather a practice, devised by the ancient Egyptians and later amended by the Greeks, based on the idea of "autointoxication." That's the notion that foods (or, later, the body's own "humors") could putrefy, rot, and create toxins within the digestive system, and that these toxins would then make their way into the circulatory system, causing illness or even death. The concept was later broadened to a more general belief that the body was not capable of fully disposing of its own waste products. As late as the 19th century, studies in biochemistry and microbiology seemed to support this notion, and mainstream physicians endorsed it. In fact, the father of immunology, a renowned Russian biologist (and winner of the Nobel Prize), was a particularly strong supporter. He believed these self-made toxins could shorten the life span. Then, in the post–World War I era, the tide turned, new studies appeared, and mainstream medicine rejected both the autointoxication hypothesis and the curative treatments as unscientific and anachronistic.

Which is where we are right now. Mainstream medicine and medical practitioners, supported by what we know about how the body works, hold firm to the self-cleaning paradigm. Alternative and holistic practitioners don't argue that the body isn't designed to mop up after itself. They argue that the mess to mop has become bigger and messier than our bodies were built to handle. Mainstreamers retort that it is difficult to accurately measure the presence of toxins, that we don't really know what a "toxic level" is for any given person, and that direct links between most individual toxins and specific conditions have not been established—all good points. Alternative folks reply with the powerful stories of parades of people they have treated who came in sick and weary and left healthy and rejuvenated. This, sniff the main-streamers, is merely "anecdotal evidence." They will not be persuaded (and perhaps you will not be persuaded) until large-scale, double-blind, placebo-controlled studies are conducted and appear in peer-reviewed journals, with the results thereafter reproduced by additional large-scale, double-blind, placebo-controlled studies. Would gold-standard studies be a good thing? You bet. But I am not holding my breath, and neither should you. As I've said before, such studies are extraordinarily expensive and are almost always undertaken when there is the promise of big money to be made from pharmaceutical sales. That's not a likely scenario here. But if you are careful about it, if you don't fall for nutri-tionally compromising schemes or unregulated invasive treatments, there doesn't seem to be any harm in detoxing, and there is at least the potential for good.

Detoxing can be as simple as replacing the infamous "Dirty Dozen" (the twelve common fruits and vegetables that carry the greatest amounts of pesticide residue) with organic produce; watching your mer-cury intake by being judicious about your consumption of the big fish with the highest levels, like swordfish; and staying away from processed, packaged, and junk foods. You can add high-fiber foods, drink lots of water, take saunas, exercise—all good things to do whether or not you labor under a body burden. You could add what some nutritionists and holistic practitioners consider purifying foods: garlic, apple cider vine-gar, lemon juice, cayenne, ginger, yogurt—and, if you are really serious, seaweed and algae (spirulina, chlorella).

Or you could follow a plan. The Web is stuffed to indigestion with detox diet plans, including my favorite, Reverend George Malkmus's Hallelujah Diet, which is based on what he thinks God wanted us to eat in the Garden of Eden. No apples, I guess, but otherwise lots of raw produce, including daily barley grass drinks. I hadn't imagined grain fields abutting the Garden of Eden. A number of the regimens look a lot like the one I have chosen, a progressive elimination plan designed to give the insides a little R&R while possibly determining food sensitivities.

I AM NOW SEVEN DAYS IN. I AM NO LONGER EATING ANY grains, nuts, or seeds, in addition to my previous list of no-nos: dairy, eggs, meat, sugar, alcohol, caffeine. What *am* I eating? Vegetables, fruits, and legumes plus the rice protein shake. My family of omnivores is grumbling, but my stomach is not. I have ceased fantasizing about coconut prawns and potstickers. I am feeling particularly optimistic and full of energy. Maybe it's the detox; maybe it's how simple life becomes when you don't have to think about food. Now that I am not planning and shopping for meals (thus the grumbling from home), now that my own choices are few, and dwindling, I have more time for everything else. I am emptier but life is fuller. Today two people told me that my skin looked lovely.

This from the staff of the Mayo Clinic: "Some people report feeling more focused and energetic during and after detox diets. However, this may be due to a belief that they're doing something good for their bodies."

I get it: the placebo effect. It matters to researchers whether it's the treatment that is working or the belief that the treatment is going to work. But does it matter to you and me? If I feel better, I am better, regardless of what got me there.

But I do understand why Mayo—and mainstream medicine in general—is anti-detox. It's not just that the hard science isn't there. It's that people can actually do themselves harm by following some of the harsher regimens. The Master Cleanse, for example. That's the one where you live on "lemonade" made from water, lemon juice, cayenne, and maple syrup, supplemented with cups of very salty water. Short-term effects can be unpleasant: fatigue, nausea, dizziness, dehydration.

Long-term effects, assuming someone could actually stay on this regimen long term, translate into loss of muscle mass (thanks to the absence of muscle-building protein), which is exactly what you don't want if you are trying to lower your biological age. All-liquid regimens, as a rule, are a mistake—and sometimes a big one. In the 1970s, between 2 million and 4 million people were reputed to have tried what was known (with unintended irony) as the Last Chance Diet. There were reports that 58 people died from heart attacks while following this starvation diet that allowed only liquid protein derived from slaughterhouse by-products. Cleanses with harsh laxatives are unkind to the colon, stripping it of helpful bacteria and teaching it to be lazy, teaching it to act old.

And speaking of the colon, no discussion of detox can avoid talking about colon cleanses, aka colon irrigation, aka colonic hydrotherapy. But let's just call a spade a spade: We're talking enema here. When I tell friends that I am writing about and participating in detox, the first thing they ask is whether I've gone in for a colonic.

No. And I don't intend to. Colon cleansing is based on that ancient "autointoxication" theory that nasty stuff is putrefying in our guts and we need outside intervention to get rid of it. But the best evidence says that the bowel itself is not dirty, and barring drugs, disease, or mechanical blockage, it cleans itself. Could it be overburdened, as some believe the liver is? That is certainly the belief of people who schedule regular colonics. Certain colon-cleaning preparations have been associated with electrolyte imbalances that can cause muscle spasms, irregular heartbeat, blood pressure changes, convulsions—even heart attacks. Incompletely sterilized equipment or equipment used improperly (as in perforating your bowel wall) can cause infection and worse. Frequent colon cleansing—an activity I find difficult to imagine—can lead to dependence on enemas and the loss of the ability to take care of one's own business.

So, no thanks. Also, I sat through a "live" colonic irrigation on YouTube, which involved 10 minutes of a mildly freaked-out British guy lying on a table with a tube inserted where such tubes are inserted. He was not having fun.

Another much-touted detox regimen is chelation therapy, a treatment to rid the body of heavy metals like lead, arsenic, or mercury. It was first developed as an antidote for World War I soldiers exposed to arsenic-based poison gas attacks. The idea was that there were certain chemicals that, when injected, could bond with the heavy metal to create a water-soluble compound that would enter the bloodstream and make its way to the liver and kidneys and out of the body. After World War II, chelation was used to detoxify workers suffering from lead poisoning as a result of their jobs repainting the hulls of ships. In the mid-1970s, the therapy was used to save the life of a nuclear worker badly contaminated by the radioactive metal americium.

Which is to say: Chelation therapy works—if you are actually exposed to high doses of heavy metals, and if the chelating agent is specific to the metal, and if the treatment is carefully overseen by someone who knows what he or she is doing. Which is to say: Ignore all chelation treatments advertised on the Web.

It's not that heavy-metal toxicity is a hoax. It's real. Heavy metals can and do accumulate in various tissues in the body, and that is not good. But, short of exposure to poison gas or radioactive metals or lead paint, what constitutes potentially dangerous exposure is debatable. Is my mouthful of amalgam fillings that include mercury a hazmat zone? Does my once- or twice-a-month exposure to mercury via high-on-the-food-chain fish like tuna demand chelation? Testing for levels of toxicity, as I mentioned before, is often less than accurate—and sometimes downright deceptive—as are claims of successful detoxification through chelation.

It's difficult to be a savvy consumer in this unregulated world of alternative health products. When I followed up on one much-advertised chelation product, I was initially delighted to find references on the product's Web site to published scientific studies presumably providing evidence of the product's efficacy. Most people—including me if I were not researching this for a book—would stop there. "Ah," they (I) would say, looking at the citations. "Here's proof." One of the citations was for *JAMA*! That's the *Journal of the American Medical Association*, one of the most prestigious mainstream medical journals in the world. Or was it *JAMA*? I looked again and saw that, no, it was *JANA*, an easy mistake to make when reading quickly. *JANA* is the *Journal of the American* Nutriceutical *Association*, an organization founded to promote the health and medical benefits of food-derived supplements. I found the paper online and read it. Who would go that far? Hardly anyone. The research in question turned out not to be about the product's ability to remove heavy metals from the body. It was, instead, about the reported success of the delivery system used to get the product into the body. And the study was done on rats. (The "delivery system," by the way, was a suppository. I'm not sure if I feel sorrier for the rats or the lab techs.)

Regardless of shams and scams, hyped products with little research behind them, and problems defining toxicity, let alone pre- and post-detox testing, I am attracted to the basic idea of body cleansing. I trust that my body was designed to keep itself clean, but I know how dirty our world has become. That's why I am willing to engage in active self-cleansing. But all detox is not as invasive, unpleasant, or just plain difficult as it may appear to be.

Internal—colon- and liver-centric—detox is one thing. But sweat is presumably another way the body rids itself of toxins, and helping it do so can be oh-so-much-more appealing than drinking cayenne-spiced lemonade or getting an enema. Saunas, steam rooms, and sweat lodges have long been touted as detoxifiers. In the interest of research, I devote one week to serious sweating. On Monday, Wednesday, and Friday, I sit in a eucalyptus-infused steam room. On Tuesday, Thursday, and Saturday, I head for the infrared sauna. It's a tough life. My conclusions: I break a sweat faster in the sauna, but I feel better after leaving the steam room. Both experiences are relaxing and enjoyable. Both experiences, after I replenish with water and take an invigorating shower, make my skin glow and elevate my mood.

But have I detoxed? Sadly, no. In researching the benefits of sweating, I discover that it's largely a myth—but a nice myth!—that we sweat out toxins, and that the more we sweat the more we cleanse ourselves. Experts who study sweating, like Dee Anna Glaser, MD, a founding member of the International Hyperhidrosis Society (a medical group dedicated to the study and treatment of heavy sweating), say that perspiration contains only trace amounts of toxins (and virtually no heavy metals), and that sweating heavily does nothing to increase those levels. "Baloney" is what one university scientist called claims that heavy sweating washes away pesticides and industrial chemicals. Others warn against excessive sweating, which can actually impair the body's natural detox systems. Dehydration, they say, can stress the kidneys and keep them from doing their job. Severe dehydration is serious business. In 2009, during a New Age retreat in Sedona, Arizona, 3 people died and 21 more became ill while sitting in an overcrowded and improperly set up sweat lodge.

Okay, so sweat in moderation. Ridding the body of "trace amounts" is better than no amounts at all, isn't it? And time spent in a sauna or steam room is quiet time, time away from electronic devices and worldly imperatives. Chronic stress can be as "toxic" as a diet of deep-fried Snickers in the sense that both can sicken us from within, wear us down, age us. Anything we can do to lighten that load, especially as we grow (chronologically) older and our lives become increasingly complicated, is a good thing. That it feels good too is a bonus.

IT IS DAY 14 OF MY 14-DAY DETOX REGIMEN, AND SOMETHING has definitely happened. You know how sometimes you lose track of, lose touch with, your own body? It takes you places; it does things for you; you dress it, put food in it, but you don't fully, deeply inhabit it? This happens to me when I feel stressed or gain weight or don't get enough sleep—which is to say: more often than not.

I wake up this morning, my final day on the program, and the best way I can explain this—and I know it might sound flaky—is that I have come back to my body. I'd been feeling increasingly energetic as the detox progressed, so part of inhabiting my body is that sense of renewed energy. I'd also felt increasingly focused, but not in that edgy way caffeine focuses you. There's more clarity, more precision—and more calm—to this focus. And, although I'd been going without so many of the foods I enjoy, I didn't feel deprived or resentful, as I do when I'm on a diet. I'd started to feel, and feel now on day 14, unburdened, empowered, upbeat. And, yes, youthful.

Did giving my insides a two-week staycation rejuvenate me? Yes. Is it possible to quantify this? No. Neither can I tell you exactly why I feel rejuvenated. Is it because this particular detox regimen flushed nasty chemicals from my body? Is it because my rested liver kicked into high gear? Is it because I thought detox would do me good so it did? I wish I knew.

And I wish there was hard science to back up my overwhelming sense of wellness. There isn't. There are only anecdotes. Like this one. But the experience has been so positive that, whatever else I do on this journey, whatever else works or doesn't, I believe I will come back to this. Lack of persuasive scientific verification aside, I am ready to commit to a twice- or even thrice-yearly detox regimen. For now, my house is clean, and I am ready to paint.

CHAPTER

nine

Eating Young

WE EAT TO NOURISH OURSELVES, TO ENERGIZE OUR BODIES and our minds, to fuel the lives we live.

Ah, if only it were that simple.

In fact, our relationship with food is anything but. We eat out of joy, and we eat out of sadness. We eat out of boredom, guilt, love, and addiction. We eat to reward and to punish, to celebrate and to mourn, to remember and to forget. Food is not just food. It is culture and religion, art and science, politics and commerce. And it is also, as Hippocrates famously said, medicine.

I think about food a lot. I like to eat. I like to cook. I have a garden. I have four chickens who lay eggs. I pay attention to what I eat. And then I don't. I, as they say, "honor the temple of my body" with healthy, wholesome food. And then I eat Cap'n Crunch out of the box. If "we are what we eat," which seems a biological truism as well as a well-worn adage, and if what I want to be is younger from the inside out, then Cap'n Crunch is probably not an option. What is?

I wonder: Can I eat myself younger? Yes, say the health magazines and fitness Web sites. Yes, say the testimonials from people who claim they've turned their clocks backward, revitalized their bodies, cured everything from arthritis to adult acne with one food or another, one dietary regimen or another. Yes, say the Internet hawkers of berries and powders, green foods and bee foods, fermented drinks, and the seeds of exotic plants. Are there really foods that can slow, halt, or reverse aging? Are there "superfoods"? What do we know about the power of food to keep us, or get us, healthy?

There's one school of thought that says that food is important, but perhaps not as important as we think or would like to believe. Because the food we eat is one factor we can directly control—unlike, say, a genetic glitch or hidden environmental toxins or, for that matter, the simple passage of time—we attribute to it a degree of importance inconsistent with reality (or science). We think: *Nothing bad can happen if I just eat organic, if I just get enough fiber, if I never say yes to an Oreo again. I can protect myself from discomfort, disease, from aging, if I eat [fill in the blank].*

But food is not everything. It is, however, something, and it is something I need to be smarter about, especially now that I am as clean and pristine inside as I probably ever have been. There's pretty good science out there to help me. Although to my knowledge no one has ever conducted a large-scale, controlled, randomized, double-blind study of

Cap'n Crunch, there is some solid research that links certain foods with disease. Aging is not, itself, a disease, but eating in an attempt to lower the chance of disease is certainly an anti-aging strategy. So what do we know? We know—sorry, beef lovers—that red meat is implicated in colon cancer. This isn't PR from the poultry farmers or propaganda from the international vegan conspiracy. It is the finding of a 20-year study funded by the American Cancer Society that involved 150,000 women and men. We know—old news now, although it hasn't appreciably changed eating habits—that diets high in sodium are associated with increased blood pressure and decreased arterial health, both of which are important biomarkers. My quadruple-bypass father, the only person on earth observed salting an anchovy pizza, is a poster boy for this.

And it's hard to miss the more recent flood of bad news about high-fructose corn syrup—an ingredient in everything from baked goods to cereals, soft drinks to salad dressings—and its connection to obesity, increased risk of type 2 diabetes, high blood pressure, elevated bad cholesterol, and even long-term liver damage. There's been active debate over whether HFCS is really any worse than plain old table sugar, although it doesn't seem as if winning such a debate would be much of a victory for either side. Regardless, the fact remains that high-fructose corn syrup is most often found in junk foods and low-quality foods that also contain other things you don't want a lot of, like fats, salt, and additives. (In my defense, let me say that Cap'n Crunch does not contain HFCS, although two of the first four ingredients are sugars.)

What about the good news? What do we know about food and youthful biomarkers, food and disease prevention? A Harvard Medical School study set out the basics when it found that the so-called Mediterranean diet—rich in colorful fruits and vegetables, low in meat and dairy, and high in omega-3 foods (fatty fish, walnuts, flax seed, and canola oil)—was associated with a 30 percent lower mortality rate in the population being studied. We know, from other credible studies, that foods rich in omega-3 fatty acids can boost the immune system and protect against—and maybe even reverse—heart disease. New studies are identifying potential benefits for a wide range of conditions, including cancer, inflammatory bowel disease, and other autoimmune diseases such as lupus and rheumatoid arthritis. We know that foods rich in fiber (bran, beans, and berries are top sources) help lower cholesterol, boost the immune system, and protect against heart disease, diabetes, and some cancers. We know that foods rich in antioxidants (like brightly colored vegetables and fruits) may do the same. Particular antioxidants like vitamins C and E have not fared well in large clinical trials—that is, researchers have found little evidence that taking individual supplements prevents disease. But observational studies keep finding that people who eat the most-antioxidant-rich diets are the healthiest.

In fact, people who eat mostly plant-based diets are the healthiest *and* "youngest." In a landmark study in the 1980s—it was called the "Grand Prix of epidemiology"—researchers compiled one of the most comprehensive databases on multiple causes of disease and found that diets rich in animal products correlated with high cholesterol and increased heart disease and cancer, while the opposite was true of diets consisting mostly of plant foods. Extensive research into the "secrets" of the world's healthiest and longest-lived cultures (in the Caucasus, the Andes, northern Pakistan, and Okinawa, Japan) shows startlingly similar dietary habits: More than 90 percent of their diets comes from plant foods; fat and salt consumption is low, and—it goes without saying—they don't eat processed foods. These are folks who not only live into their 90s, they live healthy, active, vital lives into their 90s. It's not just the absence of disease that is startling. It's the presence of high-level health.

TRUE, FOOD ISN'T EVERYTHING. BUT MUCH OF THE HOPE (AND hype) surrounding the anti-aging movement is focused on food (or dietary supplements), and in particular on what are being called "superfoods." This is not a scientific term. It is not a term used by dietitians or nutritional scientists. I was a little surprised, given how widespread the term is, to discover that it has no agreed-upon definition or parameters. But that hasn't stopped the claims and promises. In fact, it has encouraged them. So what is a superfood? And might superfoods be the hedge against aging that many claim them to be?

The best definition I could piece together for "superfood" is that it is a food particularly rich in vitamins, minerals, antioxidants, amino acids, enzymes, and other essential nutrients with proven health benefits. It has more of the good stuff per calorie than other foods and fewer (or none) of the properties considered to be negative. A persistent argument in favor of superfoods is that our rapid pace of life, the poor quality of the typical American diet—we are both overfed and undernourished—and the pervasiveness of environmental toxins make superfoods a dietary must. Superfoods are said to "work wonders" and bring "amazing health results." They are credited with preventing (sometimes curing) diseases, increasing energy (including the sexual variety), "flushing out toxins," and "leaving you with a healthy glow." I am quoting from various Web sites here. And there are legions of them.

Where to start?

This is what I decided to do. I conceived of my immersion into the world of superfoods as a monthlong journey, with each week a personal exploration of a different list of superfoods. I would eat those foods and those foods only and keep a journal detailing any changes in health or attitude. In week one, I wanted to begin with the 10 superfoods mentioned most frequently in the lists of "top superfoods" compiled by the most credible sources I could find. I checked the Mayo Clinic, the Center for Science in the Public Interest, the USDA, *Prevention* magazine, AARP, several university-based nutrition centers—and yes, Dr. Oz. There was amazing agreement.

Here are the top 10. The first 6 appeared on all the top 10 lists I consulted.

Broccoli—the "eat it, it's good for you" food that George Bush (the elder) proclaimed his distaste for—is one of the most nutrient-dense foods on earth. It's a superstar of the top 10 list. It has protein; bone-building calcium; fiber; vitamins A, C, and K; a phytoestrogen shown to benefit cognitive skills; and a chemical that, at least in animal studies, reversed age-related damage to body tissues and organs. Done.

Blueberries are one of the USDA's top ORAC foods. That stands for "oxygen radical absorbence capacity," which means these foods are antioxidant powerhouses that, as the USDA says, "attack aging at its roots" and can "help slow down the effects of aging in humans" by protecting the body against cellular damage. (Remember the pollution caused by those cellular engines, mitochondria?) Or that's what the USDA used to say. Recently, the agency has recanted, removing the ORAC list from its Web site because "metabolic pathways are not completely understood and non-antioxidant mechanisms [are] still undefined." In other words: More research is needed. But studies at Tufts support the "powerhouse food" approach, finding that several compounds in blueberries help to mitigate inflammation. (Inflammation has been linked to just about every disease of aging.) It's worth mentioning that blueberries are sweet, delicious, and grow in my garden if the chickens don't get them first.

Salmon is possibly my favorite food on earth, so I was delighted to find wild salmon on everyone's top superfoods list. It's one of the richest sources of omega-3 fatty acids, which help to lower cholesterol, prevent blood platelets from sticking to artery walls, decrease inflammation, decrease the risk of strokes, and prevent heart attacks. Salmon has lots of protein, is a good source of iron, and is low in mercury—a concern for fish lovers. In 2009, Madonna went on a well-publicized salmon binge to "knock 12 years off her appearance," as the *Boston Globe* reported.

Hard to separate the effects of salmon, a 24-7 personal trainer, and possible skilled plastic surgery, but the woman looks amazing.

Almonds (walnuts too, and pistachios) are proven reducers of bad cholesterol. Like broccoli, they are rich in a type of antioxidant thought to be instrumental in battling free radical damage. They're high in fiber, in phytochemicals that may protect against cancer, and in arginine, a precursor to human growth hormone. They are also high in calories, which is a reason I've avoided them. But not this week.

Spinach won't make your biceps bulge like Popeye's, but it's an extraordinary source of immune-boosting, cancer-fighting compounds with a high (albeit recently rescinded) ORAC score.

Beans also make the short list because they are very high in soluble fiber, which has been linked to lower risks of heart disease, diabetes, and certain cancers; reduced cholesterol and blood glucose levels; lower blood pressure; and less inflammation. I was surprised to learn that black beans have more than three times the fiber of oatmeal, which is hawked relentlessly as a health food.

The last four items on my superfoods list appeared on most but not all (six or seven out of eight) of the master lists I consulted.

Sweet potatoes, with their prodigious vitamin A content (good for the skin and eyes), their host of powerful antioxidants, and their potassium, which helps blunt the effects of sodium on blood pressure and bone loss, are nutritional powerhouses. I grew up thinking sweet potatoes appeared on the dinner table only once a year, topped with brown sugar and mini marshmallows. Apparently, that's no way to treat a top 10 superfood.

I was thrilled to see yogurt make the list. I hate hearing about how dairy is bad for you. I consider my personal discovery of Greek-style yogurt one of the high points of my life. The Greek-style kind (thicker and creamier) has triple or more the protein of regular yogurt. Yogurt is calcium rich, like milk (and can be tolerated by many of the lactose intolerant), and is full of what is euphemistically called "active cultures"—better than saying it's good for you because it's loaded with bacteria. But it's the good kind, the gut-enhancing kind.

Quinoa (KEEN-wah) is the only grain on the list. It's high in protein, fiber, and iron. Besides, the NASA scientists tasked with feeding astronauts in space chose it because it supplied the most "essential life-sustaining nutrients" of any single food. What they meant was that it contained all the essential amino acids and was thus a complete protein—not that it contained every nutrient needed to sustain life.

Rounding out the list is the keeps-the-doctor-away apple, with its heart-healthy, cholesterol-lowering fiber (eat the skin—buy organic) and free radical–fighting antioxidants. (I must admit the following: Avocados and apples were tied, but I hate avocados, so they didn't make my list.)

Given the variety here—vegetables, fruits, grain, dairy, fish—I figured week one would not be much of a challenge. I was wrong.

DAY ONE OF WEEK ONE. I IMMEDIATELY SCREW UP BY automatically going through the Quick Fixx drive-thru for my morning latte. I realize this as the nice lady hands me my drink, and I wish I could report that I don't drink it. I can't. I do. But I do toss the chocolate-covered espresso bean. Breakfast of yogurt, blueberries, and chopped almonds is wonderful, which is a good thing as it turns out that this will be my breakfast every day throughout the entire superfoods experiment. Lunch of spinach leaves with quinoa, apples, and almonds is dry (olive oil will not appear on the horizon until week two), and by midafternoon I am jonesing for Rold Gold honey wheat pretzels, which contain not a single superfood among their 12 ingredients. (Yes, I look. Yes, there is a bag in the cupboard.) It's interesting that I'm already craving what I cannot have. Or am I? I should be used to the drill, having weathered both the super-restrictive 500-calorie hCG diet and the progressive elimination detox regimen. Maybe I'm not *really* craving those pretzels, I am just anticipating that I *may* crave those pretzels. I'm practicing craving. I need to take this one meal at a time. I hold on, knowing that dinner will be wild Chinook salmon, a sweet potato, and broccoli. That evening, in a post-salmon state of contentedness, I am drinking herbal tea and doing really well until my daughter takes over the kitchen to make coconut oatmeal cookies for a school potluck. The house smells like heaven on a sunny day. Alas, I am in superfood hell.

Day two is a repeat except I *purposely* get the latte, I add broccoli florets to the lunch salad, and my daughter makes Rice Krispies Treats after dinner. On day three I have to make a formal presentation at a lunch meeting, a semifancy catered lunch meeting. I bring a plastic container with a cold piece of salmon sitting atop a thick layer of spinach. I think it's going to be awkward. It isn't. Everyone at my table wants to know about superfoods. They express sincere interest as they munch on items selected from a gourmet cookie tray. I push through the week, "cheating" one day by eating a tin of sardines for lunch (another high-omega-3 fish), which tastes a lot less like cat food than I thought it would. I Facebook about this and get the sympathy I need to make it through two more days. For my final dinner, I am, for the fifth time this week, eating salmon, sweet potatoes, and broccoli. My daughter is at a friend's house. My husband has made himself "bisghetti," leftover spaghetti mixed with crumbled bacon and a fried egg and topped with Parmesan cheese. If this guy outlives me, I'm going to be royally pissed. But right now, I'm just smug. I feel focused and energized, healthy, glowing, alert but calm—all those good adjectives. It occurs to me, though, that this may be the result of what I didn't eat this week—pretzels, Cap'n Crunch, my usual five or six sticks a day of Sweet Mint Orbit gum, my daughter's cookies—as much as what I did eat.

For week two, I go back to my top superfoods lists and add the next

10 most touted foods to my menu: olive oil, eggs, tofu, garlic, onion, brown rice, green tea, colored peppers, kiwifruit, and—my raison d'être for compiling this runner-up list—dark chocolate.

Olive oil—a "good" fat and a good source of vitamin E—makes the list for its potent antioxidant properties and its proven connection to lowering blood pressure and improving cardiovascular health. Eggs, once maligned as a high-cholesterol bad guy, are enjoying a new (scientifically warranted) reputation as a low-calorie, nutrient-dense food with a rich mix of essential amino acids and a high level of antioxidants. I've read that eggs from free-range chickens like my marauding backyard brood are even healthier. Tofu—or, more generally, soy—is full of vitamins, minerals, plant proteins, fiber, and omega-3s, all heart healthy and inflammation reducing. It's the richest known source of phytoestrogens, which have been linked to lower risks of hormone-related cancers. As for garlic and onion, aside from being just what you want sautéing in your Official Oil of Choice (the aroma of which, for me, trumps that of oatmeal coconut cookies), they have powerful antioxidant and anti-inflammatory properties. Brown rice, like other fiber-rich whole grains, may lower the risks of heart disease, diabetes, and some cancers. I'm just happy it made the list because there is only so much quinoa a person can eat.

That brings us to antioxidant-rich green tea, about which there is exciting news. A Hong Kong study that looked at 2,000 older women and men showed a significant link between drinking green tea and the length of telomeres, those caps that protect the ends of chromosomes from damage. Colored peppers (red, orange, yellow) and kiwifruits come under the umbrella of "brightly colored fruits and vegetables" that have abundant vitamins and antioxidants.

And now, the star of the list as far as I'm concerned: dark chocolate. The news is *all* good. The women's magazines and popular health sites have been all over this, but you will be happy to know that there is real—and impressive—science behind the hype. Dark (70 percent cacao or darker) chocolate is good for you. How good? Let me count the ways: It improves the health of arteries and the cholesterol profile, lowers high blood pressure, reduces inflammation, boosts the immune response, protects skin from UV damage (chocolate as internal sunscreen!), improves cognitive functioning, and elevates mood. It's not often one envies those who participate in medical studies, but when I read about the volunteers who got to eat a Dove dark chocolate bar every day for a week, I thought, *Now* that's *the kind of guinea pig I want to be*. The only bad news: You can't eat all you want. An ounce or two is all you get. Which, given my past week's menu of spinach leaves and canned sardines—okay, I'm exaggerating for effect—sounds heavenly. Oh, and here is where I mention that I also added red wine for week two because of the exciting—yes, and controversial—research on the anti-aging effects of resveratrol, a compound found in the skin of red grapes. Pinot noir and merlot are cited as wines with the highest levels of resveratrol, so I'm afraid I will be forced to indulge.

The week goes by quickly. I can dress my salad—which now includes colored peppers and purple (also called red) onions—in garlic-infused extra-virgin olive oil. I can eat a hearty bowl of vegan soul food (brown rice, black beans, tofu, veggies). One night, my husband, who is not a big fan of what my superfoods experiment is doing to dinnertime, relents and makes me a savory spinach omelet. I brew a cup of green tea in the morning, sip a glass of wine with dinner, and, every evening, nibble at a square of 77 percent dark chocolate. Life is good.

I ask my daughter if she notices any changes. She looks at me with the merciless gaze a teenage girl saves just for her mother. I want her to say (because this is what I see): "Your eyes are brighter. Your skin is glowing. And say, have you lost a little weight?" Of course, she says none of this. But later, unbidden, she remarks that I "seem happier." She squints, appraising me. "I mean, your mood is better," she says.

She's right. I've noticed this too. Maybe it's the dark chocolate. Or the glass of wine. Or it could be that this superfoods menu is regulating my blood sugar: no ping-ponging between cranky hunger and post–Cap'n Crunch highs. I think it's all of this and something more. I think it's the mindfulness of eating this way, the discipline that takes away the opportunity to make choices I will regret. The lightness I feel in the absence of that regret.

I am feeling so good that I don't want this week to end, so I amend my plans for week three. I decide not to change my basic 20 superfoods (plus wine) regimen. But, as enhancements to that diet, I will seek out and try the exotic and trendy superfoods I've been hearing so much about. You know, the ones with big price tags from faraway places. I go to my local health food store to track down what I can.

In the bulk section of the store, I locate: dried goji berries from the protected valleys of Inner Mongolia; açai berries from the Amazon; maca powder from Peru; spirulina, originally from the lakes of the Valley of Mexico but now cultivated throughout the United States; chia seeds from a plant grown in Guatemala; bee pollen from the legs of bees who visit a species of eucalyptus found only in Australia; and hemp seeds from (who knows why?) Manitoba, Canada. I've gone almost around the world, and I haven't moved an inch from my spot in front of the bulk bins. A few aisles away I find a very small bottle of wheatgrass juice and a big bottle of kombucha. I'm set.

At home, I lay everything out on the kitchen counter to sample and snack on throughout the week. I start with goji berries because they look the friendliest, kind of like slightly oversize, past-their-prime red-orange raisins. They are tough and chewy, but not in an unpleasant way, and taste like a cross between dried strawberries and dried figs. The word on gojis (aka wolfberries, desert-thorn berries) is that they are a very rich source of antioxidants and, ounce for ounce, have 500 times more vitamin C than oranges. Web sites tout them as all-purpose anti-agers that increase immunity, protect arteries from plaque buildup, improve eyesight, and protect against Alzheimer's. The little berry is, indeed, a nutritional powerhouse, but whether its wealth of vitamins, minerals, and proteins translates into such wide-ranging health benefits is yet to be proven. They are tasty, though.

Açai berries are next. I remember all the hoopla about these small, purple, grapelike fruits, the extraordinary claims, the connections to Amazonian legend and lore. Back in the mid-2000s, a multilevel marketing company made açai almost a household word. The tonic it sold ($40 a bottle), via a pyramid scheme, was said to, among other things, cure arthritis, reverse diabetes, protect against cancer, lower cholesterol, and, last but not least, increase penis size. In the almost 10 years since açai debuted in the commercial marketplace, there's been no credible scientific evidence that the berry performs any of these miracles— although sales appear to be brisk. Açai is similar to goji in its antioxidant profile, so that's good. What's not good is how it tastes—bitter, sour, tart, not like any berry you'd want to eat. Açai marketers finesse the unpleasant taste by either referring to it as "having undertones of dark chocolate" (and by "dark chocolate" I think they mean that inedible baking chocolate, not a 70 percent cacao Dove bar) or urging you to buy açai drinks that are a mixture of fruits and berries so you don't actually taste the açai. To test that theory, I sneak some açai berries into my daughter's apple juice, banana, and frozen strawberry smoothie one morning. Let's just say that the hypothesis is not borne out, and I am forbidden from ever again making a smoothie for her.

Before moving on to more pleasant topics, let me say a word about the spirulina powder I bought at the store: blech. That's the word. Spirulina is a microalgae, which is a nice way of saying pond scum. It smells like the green slime that grows just below the waterline on the pilings of old wharves. In its defense, spirulina apparently is among the highest-protein foods on earth, and a few studies out there suggest it might help lower cholesterol and boost the immune system. Regardless, I can't stand the smell, and I throw the bag in the garbage. Later that week I pick up a spirulina protein bar that tastes like what I imagine licking the side of an abandoned pool would taste like, only crunchy. The crunchy bits stick between my teeth, so I get little surprise tastes for hours.

I do brave the unknown by drinking a mixture of maca—a silty, wheat-colored powder—and water because I've read that maca was consumed by Inca warriors to increase strength and endurance. The drink is, well, interesting, simultaneously creamy and bitter. After I drink it I don't storm the city of Cuzco chanting victory slogans, but I do feel alert and slightly on edge, like I've had a double shot of espresso. Chia seeds (yes, the same seeds that sprout to become Chia Pets and "Chia Professor" Albert Einstein's hair) are ever-so-slightly peppery and pleasant until they turn gluey in your mouth. That's probably because of their fat content, the good kind (omega-3). They are also high in antioxidants and fiber. Andrew Weil, MD, likes them sprinkled on cereal, yogurt, and salads, and endorses adding them to chicken feed to enhance the omega-3 content of eggs. I follow all this advice. The chickens seem happy, but they are hardly picky eaters. It turns out that I much prefer hemp seeds, which are a good vegan source of protein, an excellent source of omega fatty acids (with a great ratio of omega-6s to omega-3s), and replete with all those phytonutrients that plants provide. Does munching on these tiny seeds—they taste just like sunflower seeds— lead to youthful arteries and cardiovascular health? Possibly. Omega-3s' heart-health evidence seems strong. Will hemp seeds get you high? You'll either be happy or disappointed to know: nope.

The final baggie on my kitchen counter contains bee pollen, which, along with far too many other exotic offerings I'm reading about, is touted as "nature's perfect superfood." Health benefits, none proven, are said to include heightened energy, improved metabolism, enhanced immunity, and decreased inflammation. There are even some anticancer claims. It's hard not to love this sweet-tasting golden dust, which is excellent sprinkled on Greek yogurt, and I salute the industrious bees for their great work, but I'm not banking on this stuff—or any of the other touted but untested items I gathered this week—to turn back my biological clock. Still, throughout week three, I find myself sprinkling bee pollen, snacking on goji berries and hemp seeds, and washing down gluey mouthfuls of chia seeds with swigs from the kombucha bottle.

Kombucha, a not distasteful carbonated, fermented drink rich in antioxidants, is interesting. It has both celebrity—Madonna, Halle Berry, and Gwyneth Paltrow swear by it—and science behind it. A Swiss study found antimicrobial, antibacterial, and antifungal effects. Two other studies—these are test-tube studies, not humans-drinking-kombucha studies—supported the drink's capacity to combat free radicals, which cause much of the damage we call aging. So things are looking good for kombucha. It's also palatable and not horribly expensive. It's a keeper. I can't say the same about wheatgrass, touted as a powerful detox tonic and general cure-all. It tastes like liquid lawn, and there's no credible science behind it. I won't be downing wheatgrass shots again anytime soon.

On the sixth morning of week three, I wake up with a sore throat and an itchy nose. What? Okay, I didn't expect superfoods to instantly elevate me to an exalted level of youthful vigor and wellness, but getting sick? I haven't had a cold in three years. I go to the kitchen, drink the rest of the bottle of kombucha, and munch on goji berries and hemp seeds while brewing a cup of açai green tea. I tell myself that sequence doesn't equal consequence. Two hours later, my throat is better, and my nose is fine. Was it the superfoods? I can neither blame them for my momentary lapse of good health nor praise them for my quick recovery.

BUT AT LEAST I AM HEALTHY—AND RARING TO GO—FOR MY fourth and final superfoods week. This week I am going raw, the most extreme of the eat-your-way-young approaches, a diet believed by some to be the ultimate in counterclockwise eating. There's an almost cultlike aspect to eating raw, with true believers telling stories of miraculous recoveries from serious or seemingly intractable illnesses. Raw foodists claim improved energy and vitality, an elevated sense of well-being—and more. Here's what a recently raw Chicago restaurateur, quoted in O magazine, had to say: "When I transitioned to an all-raw lifestyle, I felt like I could walk on water. I didn't just stop aging; I began to feel as if I were actually growing younger."

"Raw" means eating basically unheated, uncooked, unprocessed foods, and, because most raw foodists are also vegans, no sushi, steak tartare, or even raw (that is, unheated, unpasteurized) milk products. The diet consists of vegetables, fruits, seeds, nuts, and sprouted grains, nothing heated above some magic temperature, which might be 104°F or 106°F or maybe 112°F. There is disagreement on the exact number, but unanimity on the scientifically bogus reason not to heat or cook food. Raw foodists assert that foods heated above some specific temperature lose much of their nutritional value and are not only less healthful, but also even harmful to the body. Raw foods, they say, have natural enzymes critical to the well-being of the body. Heat destroys those enzymes and leaves toxins behind. They call cooked food "dead food" or sometimes even "poison food." The problem with this reasoning is that the body itself, in order to digest food, breaks down all these enzymes regardless. So eating raw to preserve enzymes doesn't work. And, while some foods do lose nutritional value when cooked—especially vegetables boiled forever in water—others don't. Cooked tomatoes, for example, deliver more nutrition than raw because, as Cornell University food scientists discovered, cooking increases the bioavailability of beneficial compounds called phytochemicals. But, as I discover, the research does support other reasons to eat raw.

Some medical trials link raw vegan diets with low levels of "bad" cholesterol and triglycerides. One study mentions the diet's benefits for lowering obesity and hypertension, and another shows reduced symptoms of fibromyalgia and rheumatoid arthritis. Of course, it goes without saying that a diet packed with vegetables and fruits (raw or otherwise) and absent processed foods is going to have health benefits. But there are also studies that link raw vegan diets with low "good" cholesterol, vitamin B_{12} deficiency, lower bone density, amenorrhea, and dental erosion.

The raw foodists, though, are true believers. They tell themselves and each other powerful stories of healing and regeneration. I want to meet a true believer, and so I begin my raw week by lunching with a 17-year veteran of raw foods at a trendy raw restaurant in Portland. We've communicated via e-mail, so I know she works at a health food store, informally schools others in the joys and rigors of raw, regularly arranges or attends raw foods potlucks, and is 65. I expect to see a vibrant, energetic woman who does not look her age. This woman looks her age, and maybe more. Over a lunch of raw soup (a gingery, cilantro-y gazpacho), a green salad, a hummuslike dip spread on oddly textured raw crackers (pressed dehydrated nuts and seeds), I listen to her personal story. Like many of the raw foodists whose blogs I've looked at in preparation for this week, she has long been health conscious. She started many years ago as an organic whole foods eater, then became a vegetarian, then a vegan, then a vegan who experimented with a partial raw foods diet, and now a 100 percent raw foodist.

Our lunch conversation is friendly and spirited—but odd. On the one hand, she tells me that the raw foods diet makes her feel "clean" and "fresh." On the other hand, she thinks it has destroyed her teeth. She has arthritis that the diet has not helped and another worsening medical condition for which she is not receiving treatment because she thinks the diet will take care of it. She has had this condition since her children were little. Her children are now grown with children of their own. She talks about loving food—growing her own herbs and vegetables, making her own almond milk and cashew cheese—but sighs and looks down-right weary when she talks about spending five to six hours a day, every day, in food preparation. A raw food diet, I am learning, is not just about throwing together a salad or making a fruit and vegetable smoothie; it is about using allowable foods in allowable ways to make what I think most of us would consider semirecognizable foods. The raw crackers I eat at the restaurant, for example, involve grinding various seeds and nuts, pressing this mixture into a thin, flat sheet, and dehydrating it twice, once for 12 hours in a dehydrator, and then again, for another 12 hours, in the open air on the kitchen counter. This is also, my companion tells me, how one makes "crust" for a raw pizza.

I ask her what her favorite raw foods entrée is, and she details a dish she recently ate at a raw potluck. She calls it "ravioli." The pasta is very thin slices of raw red beets cut into rounds with a cookie cutter. Between two rounds is a cheese made from raw cashews. The sauce is uncooked salsa with basil substituting for cilantro. She says she has a great recipe for raw lasagna and will e-mail it to me.

Back home, I try to make a go of it. After three weeks of grilled salmon and two weeks of dark chocolate and red wine, it is not easy. For a few days I do okay with fruit smoothies and green salads topped with nuts and seeds. I buy several packages of the same raw crackers the restaurant served. I discover raw cacao nibs, which are what chocolate starts off as, but the crunchy little bits taste bitter and dirtlike. I buy a raw meal replacement formula, which is so vile that words fail me. I buy Kale Krunch, a raw snack food that comes in many flavors and, well, words fail me.

Finally, I bite the (raw, unprocessed) bullet and decide to go "gourmet raw" by attempting the lasagna recipe my lunch companion e-mails me. When you read a recipe that begins "three days before," you know you're in trouble. It does, in fact, take parts of three days to make this entrée. The cheese is made from raw, organic cashews soaked overnight in spring-water, blended with a mixer, placed in a cloth bag to "weep," allowed to ferment, combined with a few other raw ingredients (tahini, miso, nutritional yeast), and then refrigerated. The pasta is very thin ribbons of raw zucchini marinated for two days in garlic-infused olive oil. The filling is raw spinach and raw mushrooms, marinated overnight in olive oil. The sauce, at least, is easy, made on the spot, a combination of raw and sundried tomatoes with the requisite Italian herbs. When assembled, the dish is very pretty. When eaten, it tastes like slightly too oily salad, not bad until you encounter a little ball of cashew cheese, which is sour and simultaneously mushy and grainy. I know cheese, and this is no cheese. My loyal and long-suffering family sits at the table. They admire the dish. They take several polite bites, except my daughter, who takes one not-so-polite bite that is quickly and showily deposited in her napkin. Then we do what any red-blooded American family would do: We order pizza. Real baked-in-an-oven, grease-spots-on-the-box pizza. If this is "dead food," then I've died and gone to heaven. Later that night, I cook the raw lasagna, hoping to make it more edible. I do not succeed.

Superfoods month is over. I am not, as I'm betting is clear, a convert to raw. I will not be chugging spirulina smoothies or snacking on Kale Krunch again anytime soon. But the health-and-wellness (and anti-aging) perks of a mostly plant-based diet are not lost on me. The evidence is there, and I've felt it myself in everything from increased energy to elevated mood. My skin feels softer. The whites of my eyes are whiter. Is my hair actually thicker? It seems to be. Yesterday my longtime hairdresser remarked on how "ridiculously fast" it's growing. I am sleeping soundly, and awakening refreshed. Food is not everything. It's not *the* answer. But it is *an* answer. Another answer that's shouted from the anti-aging rooftops is supplements. That's next.

ten

Better Living Through Chemistry

WE AMERICANS SPEND $28.1 BILLION A YEAR ON DIETARY supplements. That includes everything from the prosaic one-a-day vitamin pill to exotic herbal concoctions, from mineral blends to multisyllabic probiotics with names you'd need a Latin scholar to translate, from fish oils to pulverized mushrooms, plus all manner of ancient elixirs and an extraordinary variety of "essential" thises and "crucial" thats that we had no idea were either essential or crucial. Dietary supplements promise to cure what ails you: arthritis, cardiovascular disease, fibromyalgia, migraine, adrenal fatigue, failing eyesight, high cholesterol, low libido. They promise health and high-level wellness, boosted energy, enhanced concentration, and, of course, a litany of anti-aging benefits.

When I begin this part of my investigation, I am already popping six pills a day and spending close to $100 a month on supplements. I don't take anything too exotic, just E, B complex, calcium (two a day), a multi, and CoQ_{10}. Do I need them? Do any of us? I don't really know. I take them because somewhere, sometime, someone (a friend, my naturopath, a *New York Times* health story, a column in a women's magazine) told me I should. I am concerned enough to do something but clueless about what I'm actually doing. Like many of the people spending that $28.1 billion, I react to the latest news story, adding and deleting supplements as they are touted and then later demonized. Take vitamin E for heart health! No, don't. Mega-C is insurance against cancer. Not really. *Ginkgo biloba* is a memory booster. Or not. Just in the past year, even before I went on this focused turn-back-the-clock quest, I experimented—without a great deal of thought—with black cohosh, red yeast rice extract, grape seed extract, tart cherry capsules, full-spectrum pomegranate, resveratrol, and holy basil, in addition to my usual alphabet lineup of vitamins.

I shouldn't need the excuse of this counterclockwise quest to get wiser and more informed about supplements, but apparently I do. I know that this supplements-and-nutraceuticals terrain is rocky, littered with extravagant claims and exaggerated youth-in-a-pill promises. But are supplements really necessary to maintain youth and vigor? Are they key to optimum health? I know that good health—or, to raise the bar higher, high-level wellness—is based in part on superior nutrition. Dietitians speak with one voice when they say that we should get our nutrition from foods, not pills, that a "good" diet will take care of all our needs. But then they tell us (with one voice) that the typical American diet is sadly deficient in fresh fruits and vegetables and lacking in fish, that the typical American diet is 40 percent fat, that we each eat 130 pounds of white sugar a year and consume three to five times the amount of sodium our bodies need. While the nutritionists and dietitians continue to wage a battle for the hearts, minds, and stomachs of the American public, it seems that those of us who don't hew to a virtuous and carefully considered superfoods diet every day—that would be me—ought to consider taking supplements as, well, a supplement to our daily regimen. I don't eat poorly. Fruits and vegetables are my friends. Fried foods, fast foods, and junk (with the exception of certain addictive and utterly worthless but delicious cereals) are my enemies. But I neglect whole grains. I am not a protein lover, unless I discover some high-fat cheese that I wish I hadn't. I like my daughter's cookies way too much and have been known to go on frozen yogurt binges. I am inconsistent.

The basic question seems simple: Which supplements have real impact—or at least hold strong promise—in the anti-aging arena? But as I begin to do the research, I immediately uncover four obstacles to finding good answers: First, even for those substances generally agreed upon as being good and necessary (the traditional vitamin and mineral lineup, for example), no one has determined optimum levels. The RDI (reference dietary intake)—which is what the percent daily value you see on food and vitamin supplement labels refers to—is the level needed to prevent particular illness-related deficiencies, not to (if possible) supercharge health. And then there's this significant complication: Let's call it body ecology. The body is a system, an intricate, interwoven, redundant, double- and triple-feedback system. Extracting one element from food—calcium, for example—and taking it in an isolated, concentrated dose may do far less good than we imagine, or far less than calcium does when we get it from food. Our smart, sophisticated bodies may be benefiting from the synergistic effects of calcium plus everything else in the food, which is why nutritionists want us to eat real foods and not depend on pills.

The other two even more serious issues related to supplements are both impediments to our being smart about their use. The first is that, protestations to the contrary, supplements and nutraceuticals are a largely unregulated industry. Supplement manufacturers won a major victory back in 1994 with the passage of an act that restricted the ability of the FDA to exert authority over supplements as long as the manufacturers made no claims about their products treating, preventing, or curing diseases. The FDA "regulates" dietary supplements as a category of food, not drugs. Pharmaceutical companies that manufacture and sell drugs are required to obtain FDA approval before bringing the drug to market, which involves assessing risks and benefits—generally through extensive wide-scale testing, first in the lab, then in lab animals, and then in humans. Manufacturers of dietary supplements, on the other hand, do not need the approval of the FDA to market their wares. If there's a new ingredient in the supplement, the manufacturer notifies the FDA beforehand, giving the agency 75 days to do a little homework. Basically, it's the FDA's responsibility to prove that the supplement is unsafe, not the manufacturer's responsibility to prove it's safe.

This may be more government policy than you thought you wanted to know—it sure is more than I wanted to know—but it does scream "Caveat emptor!" And we are the emptors. A quick search for "anti-aging supplements" (which nets an extraordinary but somehow not surprising 12.4 million hits) brings up a snazzy Web site promoting a "new," "revolutionary," "rejuvenating" product that—in FDA-compliant prose—does not *promise* to treat or cure or rejuvenate, but instead cleverly states that the supplement will "help" our bodies "come back to life" against an extraordinary range of conditions including (in alphabetical order): Alzheimer's, cellulite, diabetes, fatigue, hypertension, impotence, osteoarthritis, and osteoporosis. Really?

The fourth complication, which probably underlies all three previous complications, is that good, solid science about supplements is hard (not impossible, but hard) to find. As I've mentioned before—but this is an important point, so I'm going to say it again—it is extraordinarily expensive to mount years of clinical trials to see if a substance is both effective and safe. The folks who can afford to do this—generally but hardly lovingly referred to as Big Pharma—undertake such efforts because they stand to make billions of dollars on successful drugs—drugs that alleviate symptoms or cure illnesses. Drugs they can patent and sell exclusively. But vitamins, minerals, amino acids, and herbs are not patentable. Why spend hundreds of millions of dollars in R&D when you won't have a proprietary product? Why, indeed. What good science there is comes mostly from university researchers (who often support their labs through government grants, which creates its own set of challenges).

So, noting that the deck is stacked against me (all of us), let me see what I can find out about supplements that can help maintain energy and wellness—and, just maybe, in the long term, tweak the biological clock. With so much marketing masquerading as information, it's vital to get the facts from sources that are not simultaneously trying to pimp products. I survey my far-flung field of experts, an open-minded MD, a conservative naturopath, a registered dietitian who teaches college courses, a personal trainer, two nutritionists, three university research scientists, and my science writer husband. One source rises to the top: the Linus Pauling Institute (LPI) Micronutrient Information Center. It's a not-intimidatingly-extensive no-nonsense compendium of the latest scientific research on the roles of vitamins, minerals, other nutrients, and dietary phytochemicals (plant chemicals that may affect health) in promoting wellness. There are citations—references to published scientific studies—for every statement. Linus Pauling, after whom the institute was named, is now remembered as the guy who thought vitamin C would cure colds (and maybe cancer). But he was also and more importantly a groundbreaking biochemist, arguably one of the most brilliant scientists of the 20th century, and the only person in history to win two unshared Nobel Prizes. He pioneered the field of orthomolecular medicine (a term he coined), which seeks to maintain health and prevent disease by optimizing nutritional intake and prescribing supplements. I trust, and my sources trust, the LPI's micronutrient site.

Here's what I find after a deep and thorough reading of the material: Most of us are not getting enough micronutrients from the food we eat. Micronutrients (vitamins and minerals) are nutrients the body requires in small quantities to help orchestrate a whole range of functions. We're unable to produce them ourselves, so we have to get them from food. "Marginal" or "subclinical" deficiencies in micronutrients—that is, not huge deficits—have been linked to general fatigue, impaired immunity, poor cognition, and increased risks of heart disease, osteoporosis, and cancer. In other words, the opposite of staying youthful and vital, let alone turning back the clock. Based on a significant body of research, the LPI's conclusion is that we should all be taking at least a daily multivitamin-and-mineral supplement. There are no "you'll live to be 120 and doing the tango" promises—the LPI's tone is far more sober—but the fact that the recommendation is evidence based and comes from a source not selling vitamins makes it especially compelling. Following a trail of links, I find a study on the effects of multivitamins on a group of healthy midlife women and men, and the results clinch my resolve to never forget to swallow my daily capsule. The vitamin takers had stronger immune systems, better problem-solving abilities, and longer attention spans than the nontakers.

The LPI site singles out certain common nutrients for special attention: vitamins A, C, and D; calcium; and magnesium. Elsewhere, vitamins C, E, B_6, folate, and B_{12} are highlighted as important parts of any supplementation plan. I've taken my daily multivitamin pill for years without much thought about its individual components. I grab my bottle from the medicine cabinet for some serious label reading. Happily, all the necessary elements are there. Unhappily, the multi does not contain the LPI's recommended doses of C, D, or calcium. I already take extra calcium in a separate cal-mag-zinc supplement. I'll add separate C and D to the mix.

Omega-3 fish oil is recommended most strongly, with "a large body of research" suggesting that higher intakes are associated with lower heart disease risk. Okay, I can do that. I eat fish maybe once a week—except during that wild salmon binge in my superfoods month—so this would be a good idea for me. I am disappointed to learn that a supplement I started taking years ago, coenzyme Q_{10}, although an important antioxidant and essential to the production of energy within cells (and apparently helpful to people with certain hereditary disorders), does not have the science behind it. There's one potentially promising rat study, but the LPI concludes that "there is no scientific evidence that coenzyme Q_{10} supplementation . . . prevents age-related functional declines in humans." It seems the body produces CoQ_{10} naturally; deficiencies are quite rare, and most people don't benefit from supplementation.

About the recently touted curcumin (turmeric), the news is a little better. Preliminary trials suggest that it may have an antiinflammatory effect in humans, and with so many diseases being linked to chronic inflammation, this is good news. There are promising findings in animal models of Alzheimer's disease—but the evidence is far from conclusive. What looks great in the lab and works for our rodent friends quite often doesn't pan out for us. So, as far as the LPI is concerned, the jury is out on curcumin, despite the hype. On the other hand, Doug Seals, the University of Colorado professor who is one of the country's foremost experts on vascular aging, likes curcumin a lot. He thinks its antiinflammatory and antioxidant potential is strong. I look back at my notes from the long conversation I had with him several months ago and see that he calls the evidence (in mice) "convincing." Considering the cautious LPI non-endorsement and this enthusiastic semi-endorsement, both from high-cred sources, I think it's worth a try.

I remember that Seals is also enthusiastic about nitrites and nitrates, about which the LPI site is silent. Nitrites—yes, the allegedly evil stuff used in curing meats—and nitrates—yes, the compound used in fertilizers and explosives—are apparently both potent antioxidants. Oxidative stress is one big reason arteries age, and Seals firmly believes that we are as old as our arteries. Young, elastic, supple, clog-free arteries translate into biological youthfulness. People who have low levels of nitrites and nitrates in their blood have significantly higher incidences of heart disease and diabetes, Seals told me. Aging decreases the levels in the body, so supplementation makes a lot of sense to Seals. Actually, he would much rather have people eat their way to higher levels, but because one of the best food sources is beet root juice, he knows he's not going to win that battle. He recommends a sodium nitrite pill, which I discover is in the midst of a clinical trial for the treatment of peripheral artery disease. It's difficult to consider taking something you've been told for so many years to avoid—both the sodium and the nitrite—but Seals is a careful, conservative, just-the-facts-ma'am kind of guy. I think I'll follow his lead.

I find some potentially excellent anti-aging news about two substances I haven't heard much about before, something called L-carnitine (an amino acid derivative) and alpha-lipoic acid (ALA). The research—and there is a lot of it—on L-carnitine is exciting, albeit rodent based. Aged rats fed L-carnitine were rejuvenated, showing significant reversals in age-related declines in liver and heart function, energy metabolism, and memory. Their mitochondria were happy campers. L-carnitine also blunted the effects of oxidative stress. All good news. Apparently such good news that, even though research with humans is still in its infancy, and even though there is some concern over how much of an oral supplement the human body actually absorbs (it may be as low as 14 percent), the LPI recommends taking 500 to 1,000 milligrams of L-carnitine daily. I'm on it.

Research on alpha-lipoic acid is also mostly test-tube and lab-animal based, but again the results are so encouraging that the LPI gives it a thumbs-up. ALA is a potent antioxidant that (in the test tube) directly scavenges and neutralizes free radicals, possibly one of the best ways to prevent age-related declines. I call up Tory Hagen, PhD, a biochemist, principal investigator, and holder of an endowed chair in health-span research at LPI, and listen as he enthuses about ALA. He tells me he went into this line of research looking to disprove its benefits, but what he found left him "intrigued." In animals, he saw that ALA improves cholesterol levels and helps them produce their own antioxidants. He mentions another study that combined ALA with other antioxidants or L-carnitine. The molecular cocktail turned back the clock on declines in memory (so far just in our friends the rats). But in one very small study Hagen conducted with elderly subjects, he found—to his delight— a reversal of measurable, age-related stress factors.

He's warmed to his subject now, and I am an eager listener. Imagine someone waxing poetic about something called glutathione. I know, it strains credulity, but Tory Hagen has been interested in glutathione—the most important antioxidant in every cell in the human body, he says—for nearly 25 years. He wrote his dissertation on it. Glutathione may be unparalleled in its disease-fighting, toxin-neutralizing, immune-boosting, artery-unclogging, anti-aging functions. In other words, it's very, very good stuff. On the Web you'll find link after link to supplement vendors selling the stuff. But, according to Hagen, direct supplementation doesn't work. It's far better to supply the body with the building blocks it needs to make its own glutathione. Which is where L-carnitine and ALA come in. They are, he says, "especially effective" in raising glutathione levels. And that's good because our cells need a lot, the more the better. Several glutathione supplement makers claim to have created a delivery system that protects the substance from being destroyed by stomach acid, but their statements, as they are legally obligated to say, "have not been evaluated by the Food and Drug Administration" or, as far as I'm able to determine, subjected to rigorous testing. So I'm going to go with the word of the man who's been studying the substance for a quarter of a century and isn't trying to make a buck from it.

"What I'm seeing is not a panacea," he tells me, "not a magic bullet, but it certainly looks like certain compounds can benefit or improve different organ functions." His words are measured, but there is real excitement in his voice. He can't wait to mount additional studies. Meanwhile, the LPI—and Hagen himself—recommends taking L-carnitine daily. The LPI's final statement on these two substances is more than enough to get me scurrying to my local health food store: Supplementing with these two "may help counteract age-related declines in metabolic efficiency, physical activity, and cognitive performance." That's what I like to hear.

WHAT ABOUT THE HERBAL TONICS USED FOR CENTURIES BY various Asian and Indian cultures? To ignore what advanced, health-conscious cultures have been using for centuries would be impossibly closed-minded. That's why I go to a three-hour lecture entitled Discovering the Fountain of Youth: Ancient Herbal Tonics for Longevity and Rejuvenation, given by a soft-spoken but nonetheless voluble Argentinean herbalist who's traveled the world studying the wellness-enhancing therapies of cultures that have been around a *whole* lot longer than ours. She brings many props to the lecture—pretty hand-made bowls filled with powders, pieces of roots, tough little berries, sprigs of plants. As she talks, the small, closely attentive audience passes them around.

The first—and the only one I'm already familiar with—is Asian ginseng, which she calls "the king of herbal tonics" because, she says, it is a "Jing tonic" that "promotes chi or qi." Met with blank stares, mine included, she explains that ginseng tea has been used for centuries to increase physical strength, stamina, and endurance, and to improve mental acuity. Western science, recently awakened to the herb's possibilities, appears to bear out ginseng's promise, with some studies showing mild cardiovascular benefits like shortened recovery time after exercise and a lowering of cholesterol. There's some indication that ginseng helps the brain produce endorphins (which make you feel good), so it's not surprising that ginseng seems to help relieve stress and anxiety and improve mental clarity. On top of that, there's some evidence that it might help boost the immune system. All that without side effects and with very little risk. I think I'll give the tea a chance.

Next on the herbalist's list is something called *fo-ti*, a plant native to China and Taiwan that she says, somewhat mysteriously, "replenishes vital essence." I find out later, when I deepen my research on these herbs, that fo-ti has a local nickname, *he shou wu*, which translates as "black-haired Mr. He" and refers to a Chinese village legend wherein an elderly Mr. He drank fo-ti tea and had his youthful appearance (and dark hair) restored. Used in China as a blood elixir and liver restorer, it appears (from several animal studies) that fo-ti may lower cholesterol, boost the immune system, and perhaps rejuvenate aging arteries. I'm not sure where to get this stuff, and I don't trust online sources. Luckily—well, I think luckily—I live in one of those places that has more herbalists, energy workers, and naturopaths than investment bankers, so I'm betting I can get my hands on this. If it works for me as it did for Mr. He, perhaps I can save some money on those every-eight-week "rejuvenating" hair salon treatments.

Now she passes around a little ceramic bowl that holds some wizened, dirt-colored lumps. These are dried reishi mushrooms, in use as a traditional Chinese medicine for more than 2,000 years. It's hard not to pay attention to something that people have been using for two millennia. The herbalist thinks reishi mushrooms are one of the most powerful immune-system boosters on earth and also puts great stock in their antioxidant and antitumor actions. The Canadian master herbalist Terry Willard, PhD, a noted expert on the subject, calls reishi a "medical wonder" capable of ameliorating an astonishingly long list of conditions and diseases. Reishi, he says, is a potent adaptogen, a substance that helps the body deal with a wide range of physical, biological, and environmental stresses. I discover that some Western research supports the antitumor idea—in fact, some cancer docs seem excited—and that other studies have found evidence for lowered blood pressure, cholesterol, and blood sugar. Although you can apparently buy this stuff (powdered) in capsules, the herbalist much prefers drinking it as tea. This is unfortunate. If the tea tastes anything like the dried mushrooms smell, this will be a challenge. Perhaps I can think of it as medicine rather than tea. It goes on my list.

She has two more herbs to tell us about. At this point in the lecture—we're more than two hours in—I am hoping the next plant boosts mental energy and improves focus and concentration (and that she gives away free samples). Oh wait a second, I already know a plant that does this: *Coffea arabica*. I wish I had a cup about now. But it could be that gotu kola comes close. A member of the parsley family that's native to India, Japan, China, and Indonesia, it's popular with yogis, the herbalist says, because it "opens up the crown chakra." Mine definitely needs opening up. The plant is known as "the fountain of life" because of a legend that an ancient Chinese herbalist used it and lived for 200 years. I wonder if he, like Mr. He, had a full head of black hair when he finally succumbed. As an herbal remedy, it's used to improve cognitive function and memory. One small study shows it seems to improve circulation. Another suggests it may reduce anxiety. In animals, it appears to have a sedative effect. I've seen gotu kola tea on the shelf at my local health food store. It looks like I'm going to be drinking *a lot* of tea.

The final herb of the evening is suma, the root of a rambling vine that grows in Brazil. It's apparently another one of these "good for everything that ails you" plants. In fact, it's nicknamed *para tudo* ("for all") because of its reputed wide-ranging effects. However: no charming legend of an über-healthy long-lived, raven-haired Brazilian. And very little research. I will cross this one off my list.

MOST PEOPLE, WHEN DECIDING ON WHAT SUPPLEMENTS TO take, don't sit through three-hour lectures by herbalists or decode research papers in peer-reviewed journals or interview scientists. They hear about the newest, best, most powerful *something*, and they Google it. They enter that world I referred to at the beginning of this chapter, the overhyped, underregulated land of marketers who have positioned themselves to cash in on our aging angst. With "synergistic vitality products" and "novel formations of anti-aging essentials" that include a dazzling array of vitamins, minerals, amino acids, seeds, berries, flowers, fruits, herbs, mushrooms—not to mention Spanish moss and an extract from "fresh, clean Scotch pinecones harvested from Wisconsin forests"— the products all promise vitality and robust health. They promise to turn back the clock. (But not in language so specific that it would put the FDA on alert.) Some of the ingredients in the products have good science behind them. Some have made cages full of rats very happy. Some have proven their worth in petri dishes. Some are wishful thinking. You would not know the difference based on the claims.

I'm not going to name names here—really, there are just too many—but I feel it is my duty to point out a particular subset of supplement hawkers. I am not talking about the online or brick-and-mortar supplement sellers, the retailers with big inventories to move. We expect stores, whether they sell computers or clothing or CoQ_{10}, to *sell*, to present (bombard?) us with insistently persuasive messages. *You need this. You want this. Buy this.* We do not expect doctors to sell to us. Yet that's what some are doing, or learning to do. They are attending roundtables entitled Making Money with Supplements—Five Easy Steps, or tuning in to Webinars entitled (I am not making this up) Turning Your Patients into Customers, in which the doctor learns "how to efficiently build rapport with patients to allow you to sell to them easier." No nuance there.

I am not suggesting that all doctors or health care providers who offer supplements for sale are more interested in new revenue streams than in their patients' health and well-being. My wonderful, caring, treasure-trove-of-information naturopath sells supplements from his office. He does so because then he can control the quality of what his patients take. (He fully researches and vets the companies he deals with.) And his price generally just covers his cost plus shipping, and is almost always less expensive than buying the same product at a health food store.

But I am, after this immersion into the world of supplements, saying again and emphatically: Caveat emptor. And I'm saying it to myself too, reminding myself, because sometimes the information is just so persuasive, it sounds so good, that you forget it is advertising. Just last week I read a forcefully worded, enthusiastically pro-supplement chapter in a best-selling anti-aging book. The author, an MD, suggested a program of nutritional supplementation that totaled—I kept count—27 capsules a day. I wondered how much that would cost. Turns out all I had to do was go to the guy's Web site, where it all was conveniently (and expensively) for sale.

BASED ON ALL I'M READING AND HEARING, AND ON THE advice of experts ranging from a senior scientist at one of the leading orthomolecular research institutes to a swirly-skirted, chakra-savvy herbalist, I am persuaded that supplementation is a good idea and (at the very least) a promising turn-back-the-clock strategy, regardless of what I eat. Here is a list of what I've decided to take or, in a few cases, continue to take. Let me offer this hint—you're going to thank me for this—about the purchasing of supplements. Check out (and join, for $2.75 a month) ConsumerLab.com, a noncommercial site that identifies the highest-quality health and nutritional products through independent testing. Tests establish the purity (degree of contamination) of the product and whether the amount of the nutrient as stated on the bottle is really in the bottle. Then a wonderfully helpful chart provides the cost per unit so you can comparison shop. Combining informed reading at the LPI Micronutrient Information Center site (http://lpi.oregonstate.edu/infocenter) with a stop at ConsumerLab really demystified this confusing world for me. It is also going to save me money. Although I now plan to take more supplements than I did before, in addition to three exotic herbal teas, I figure my monthly cost to be a few dollars *less* than what I had been spending. Here's my new list:

- A top-quality one-a-day multivitamin
- Additional calcium (with magnesium and zinc in proper proportions)
- Additional vitamin C
- Additional vitamin D
- Omega-3 fish oil
- Alpha-lipoic acid
- L-carnitine
- Curcumin
- Sodium nitrite (not happily, but I trust Doug Seals)
- Ginseng tea
- Reishi mushroom tea
- Gotu kola tea

I do not expect, as Tory Hagen put it, a panacea. I do not expect dramatic—or immediate—results. But slowly, over time, I am hoping (if the research is right) that I will become increasingly disease resistant and increasingly energetic, that my metabolism will fire up, that my arteries will become more supple, my heart stronger, my bad cholesterol lower, and that the seconds, maybe even the minutes, on my biological clock will begin to tick backward. Ask me in a year. Or five. But in the meantime, I'm not sitting back (or down) waiting for results. I am (and have been since I first began this quest) out and about—panting, sweating, grunting, and learning all I can about the anti-aging virtues of physical movement.

eleven

The Sweaty Truth

WHEN I FIRST SET FORTH ON THIS COUNTERCLOCKWISE journey, even before I headed to Vegas or the research labs or the plastic surgeon's lair, I headed to the gym. I knew that physical activity was going to be a key element in this journey. I mean, who *doesn't* know— even if they don't do it—that being active is the cornerstone of a healthy life. And I knew that one or two months of turn-back-the-clock exercise wasn't likely to make significant changes, if significant changes were to be made. Besides, I knew it would take me many months to personally sweat and grunt my way through all the possible activities linked to health, well-being, and youthful vitality. So, as I have been researching and testing myself, as I've been hCG-ing, detoxing, superfooding, and deciding on supplements, I have been sweating. A lot. I have walked, hiked, jogged, raced, biked, climbed, swum, spun, rowed, drummed, boxed, and hooped. I've Zumba-ed and Nia-ed, yoga-ed and Pilate-ed. I've curled, crunched, lifted, pressed, snatched, twisted, pulled, pushed, pumped, jumped, squatted—and jump-squatted. I've used ropes and bands; dumbbells, barbells, and kettlebells; stability balls, BOSU balls, and medicine balls; not to mention sledgehammers, concrete blocks, and enormous sacks filled with sand. I've sweated through classes, group training, personal training, and boot camps. I transformed a spare room into a workout space. I transformed my daily schedule to include—in fact, to begin with—exercise. Note the *daily*. Note that there are seven days in the week. I made a whole new set of exercise-enthusiast friends. (We call ourselves the Sweat Chicas.)

Why?

Because—although you may not want to hear this, although you may *still* be waiting for me to tell you that there's some easy, hitherto-unknown secret to staying youthful—it looks as if the hard, sweaty truth is: Exercise is It.

Say the folks at the National Institutes of Health: "People who exercise regularly not only live longer, they live better."

The report on the MacArthur Foundation Study of Successful Aging, a groundbreaking, myth-exploding 10-year project that revolutionized the study of gerontology, concludes by touting the "powerful effects" of exercise and calling it "the only anti-aging regimen that actually works."

The renowned scientists who head the USDA Human Nutrition Research Center on Aging at Tufts University believe that, besides quitting smoking, "there is no single thing that will increase vitality at any age other than exercise."

One of the major conclusions of the Harvard Nurses' Health Study, among the largest (more than a quarter of a million women) and longest-running (almost 40 years) investigations of factors affecting women's health? "Higher levels of midlife physical activity are associated with *exceptional* health status." (emphasis mine)

Says vascular-aging guru Doug Seals of the University of Colorado: "Based on all available evidence, exercise has *the* most powerful anti-aging effect, head to toe."

Yes, I know what you are thinking: "Exercise is good for me, blah, blah, blah, what else is new?" But this *is* new. Scientists are a cautious bunch. On the whole, they need several dozen peer-reviewed, double-blind, placebo-controlled studies to comfortably say the sky is blue, and even then, they would qualify the statement by saying it *appears* to be blue. This consensus on exercise, these kinds of unequivocal statements—they are exceedingly rare. Still, if you, like me, have thought of exercise as something you (grudgingly) do only to keep your weight in check, or if you have convinced yourself that this whole exercise thing is way overblown, you likely need more persuasion. You need to know just *how* good, just how *extraordinarily* wide ranging the effects can be, just how *dramatic* the results can be, just how *central* to the turn-back-the-clock quest exercise really is. Listen up:

- A four-decade, 50,000-person-strong study of activity, health, and longevity (the College Alumni Health Study) found that the more active you are, the more vitality you have, the clearer your thinking, and the better your sleep. People who exercise "live better . . . look better . . . feel better . . . and live longer." A study from the Cooper Institute for Aerobics Research neatly quantified this: "For each minute increase [over a five-year span in how long subjects could go on a treadmill], there was a corresponding 7.9% . . . decrease in the risk of mortality." A large study comparing exercisers and nonexercisers that was published in the *New England Journal of Medicine* found the active, lively, disease-free health spans of exercisers (who didn't smoke and weren't overweight) were five years longer.

- An eight-decade-long investigation of 1,500 Californians found that being active in midlife was the single most important predictor of good health.

- In a review of more than 40 studies on the benefits of exercise, researchers writing in the *International Journal of Clinical Practice* reported consistent evidence that regular exercise can help prevent more than 25 diseases and health conditions later in life. Among these are the diseases that rob us of vitality and youth—not to mention years: heart disease, diabetes, high blood pressure.

- Three decades of intensive medical and anthropological research focused on the world's healthiest and longest-lived cultures found that—from Japan to Pakistan, Russia to Ecuador—these healthy, vital outliers had two things in common, one of which was that challenging physical activity was a part of their daily lives. (The other, you may remember from the superfoods chapter, is that they eat mostly plants.)

Hundreds of studies credit exercise and regular physical activity with boosting the immune system, lowering blood pressure, reducing blood sugar, reducing bad cholesterol, reducing systemic inflammation, strengthening the heart muscle, improving circulation, and increasing the ability to resist stress. Scores of other studies detail the positive effects of exercise on the brain: enhanced memory, improved learning ability, longer attention span.

And what about this? Research shows that chronologically older exercisers have arteries as supple as adults half their age and the heat tolerance of much younger adults. And what I consider the very best news of all: Exercise imparts major turn-back-the-clock benefits regardless of how old you are when you start. In several startling—at least I was startled—studies published in the *New England Journal of Medicine*, people ages 75 and older benefited extraordinarily from starting an exercise program. It increased their muscle strength and mobility and reversed the progressive effects of what's called "functional decline" (the ability to perform the daily tasks of living).

Yet, as I discover when I read the stats on our national habits, fewer than 2 in 10 Americans get the recommended amount of exercise—a very modest 30 minutes five days a week—according to the latest figures compiled by the Centers for Disease Control and Prevention. More than 25 percent of our countrymen and countrywomen get *no* exercise at all. What happens when you don't challenge your body on a regular basis—or ever? Well, there's this little problem we have with obesity, and by "little problem" I mean "national epidemic." But that's merely the visible outcome of our couch potato status. Here's what I discovered is going on inside.

Some researchers call it "disuse atrophy." Essentially, our bodies are far too efficient to waste energy on the care and feeding of parts that aren't very often called into use or taxed in some way. For example: muscles. It's the clichéd but scientifically proven Use It or Lose It theory. The research on this is beyond convincing. There's a well-established "decay curve" that accompanies even a short period of bed rest (that is, doing absolutely no exercise) at any age, and this is what it looks like: Muscle mass decreases, fat percentage increases, heart output decreases, bad cholesterol increases, lung function decreases, red blood cell production slows, calcium loss from bones accelerates. And that's after two *weeks*. Imagine the cumulative effect of a lifetime of inactivity: Everything you want to have more of to be healthy and youthful decreases; everything you don't want, all those conditions that rob you of vitality, they increase.

What's interesting to me about all this is how inactivity has so long been conflated with aging that, until recently, all of these unhealthy, vitality-robbing increases and decreases were considered "natural" consequences of getting older. In fact, many, to some degree or another, are "natural" consequences of *inactivity*. This is not to say that there are no age-related changes in the body. Of course there are. But many—decrease in muscle mass, decrease in metabolism, decrease in aerobic fitness, decrease in bone density, just to name a few—are, if not caused by a lack of physical activity, then exacerbated and accelerated by it. That 1 percent loss of muscle every year that "happens" after the age of 40? That 5 percent decrease in metabolic rate "expected" each decade after the age of 40? That bone loss that begins to outstrip bone mineral replacement after age 35? Real data from real people. But, as I've said before, we're just discovering how much of this is the result of the passage of time, and how much is the consequence of time passed on the couch.

A number of studies I am reading help to answer that question, if indirectly, and you're going to like the answers. (Well, not if you are a confirmed couch potato. But if you want to take as much control as possible over the aging process, this is all good news.) Let's take the "inevitable" age-related wasting of muscle (remember the "disease" of aging known as sarcopenia?) and the resulting frailty. In an eight-week study that had very elderly (ages 87 to 96) women lifting weights, the women tripled their muscle strength and increased the size of their muscles by 10 percent. In *eight weeks*. In another weight-training study with nonagenarians, muscle strength increased by 174 percent, and walking speed increased by 50 percent. After three months of weight training, a group of older men doubled the size of their quads and tripled the size of their hamstrings. A slew of randomized, controlled trials confirm that muscles remain responsive to training into old, old age with, say some researchers, improvements in strength equal to 15 to 20 years' "rejuvenation." Not only that, but Tufts University researchers looking at the broader effects of weight training on people in their 60s also found decreases in blood pressure and a reversal of metabolic decline. Weight training turned back the clock that age (and previous inactivity) had fast-forwarded.

And the news about aerobic activity is just as good. When Doug Seals tested the stiffness of midlife men's arteries (stiff arteries, remember, are one of the biomarkers of aging), he found that the arteries of the men who exercised were basically in the same shape as those of men 30 years younger. A few years later, he and his colleagues found the same results in women exercisers. Physically active middle-aged women had "young" arteries.

Having young arteries means lower blood pressure, a sign of a youthful, efficient body. In a Japanese study that compared the blood levels of an artery-constricting, blood-pressure-elevating protein in young, middle-aged, and older women, the older women (in their 60s) had almost three times the concentration—until they started doing aerobic exercise. After three months of cycling on a stationary bicycle for 30 minutes five days a week, the women reduced their amount of the "aging" protein by more than 40 percent. In the Harvard Alumni Health Study, arguably the gold standard for epidemiological investigations (studies that look at patterns of health across large populations), "vigorous exercise" was associated with a greatly reduced risk of hypertension. In a meta-analysis of studies on women's exercise and cholesterol levels that was truly "meta"—compiling the results of all the randomized, controlled trials published over a 50-year span—the results were dramatic and clear-cut: Exercise was deemed "efficacious" for reducing bad cholesterol (by up to 5 percent) and increasing good cholesterol (by up to 3 percent) without any other intervention.

From Stanford came a 12-year study of joint and muscle pain that followed 900 adults initially in their 50s. If you guessed that those who exercised regularly had much less pain, you'd be right. From Tufts came a study of weight-bearing exercise and bone loss reporting that eight months or more of such exercise "effectively reduced the rate of bone loss" in these women. Other researchers found that endurance training (exercising at a lesser intensity for a longer time) upped aerobic fitness by "the equivalent of 10 to 20 years rejuvenation." Elizabeth Blackburn's group at the University of California, San Francisco, touted the "significant moderating effect of exercise" on the length of telomeres, which normally shorten with age (and chronic stress).

Specific findings about the brain and exercise are so encouraging that even in the absence of any other research, they would be enough to keep me going to the gym. My mother had Alzheimer's—a huge shock, given the extraordinary genetic heritage she had been blessed with—so I am perhaps even more keen than the everyday petrified-of-Alzheimer's person to do whatever I can to die of something else. Like maybe, at age 98, my parachute failing to open. I was thrilled to find a Finnish study in which middle-aged men and women who exercised two times a week (and ate healthily) had a 50 percent reduction in the risk of Alzheimer's. Japanese researchers found evidence of "exercise-enhanced cognitive function." Not only did a single bout of exercise fuel the brain—that is, increase the amount of food energy going to the brain—but exercise over a period of several weeks also appeared to change brain chemistry, allowing the brain to store "fuel" as reserves. A superfueled brain may be able to compensate for and mitigate other losses. These were rats, alas, whose brains were being superfueled, but the findings were dramatic enough—and suggestive enough—that the study made national headlines. In a University of Illinois study on humans ages 55 years and older, researchers found, as expected, age-related "robust declines" in brain tissue density. Bad news. But "losses in these areas were *substantially reduced* as a function of cardiovascular fitness." (emphasis mine)

I've saved the best brain news for last. It comes from work done by Brown University neuroscientist Peter Snyder, PhD. It's long been known that the hippocampus (along with other parts of the brain) shrinks with age. The hippocampus is this tiny structure deep in the center of the brain that encodes new information so we can access and recall it later. Without it, we could not form new memories. Just in the past decade, scientists have discovered that certain areas of the brain are capable of making new cells and new connections between cells throughout our lives. And guess what? Aerobic exercise—"a moderate amount on a regular basis," according to Snyder—promotes the growth of new neurons in the hippocampus. Who wouldn't want that?

I think I hear you saying: *Okay, already. I'll exercise. I'll exercise. Just tell me what to do!*

SO...WHAT *IS* THE BEST STAY-YOUNG FORM OF PHYSICAL activity? This is just what I was asking myself when I began the exercise part of this quest. As I looked into the many and varied forms of physical activity I could engage in, I quickly became overwhelmed. I was overwhelmed by the research (I've highlighted only a small fraction of it). I was overwhelmed by the opinions (just about every trainer and exercise physiologist I spoke to had a "best"). And I was overwhelmed by the time commitment. I wasn't as concerned about finding an hour a day to devote to exercise—I had been sort of, kind of, almost, sometimes doing that over the years—I was concerned about the time it would take to plan for, seek out, learn, and experiment with different exercises. It had been a no-brainer to drive to the gym and jump on an elliptical machine or a bike. Now I was going to have to think and plan. And be awkward. Truthfully, this is where researching for the book trumped living my life. Had I been on a purely personal, private quest, I don't think I would have pushed myself as I did (as you'll see). I don't think I would have tried so many things. I'm not sure I would have moved out of my exercise comfort zone. Just pulling together the class schedules from various studios and gyms would have done me in. Contemplating boot camps would have ended with contemplation. I knew I owed it to myself, to my health and vitality, to try what there was to try. But what kept me planning and scheduling and rescheduling and day-in-and-day-out *doing* was, at certain key moments, my commitment to chronicling this quest. I was out there, sweating and grunting, as your representative. I owed it to you. (So thanks. Really.)

I thought I could narrow my choices by asking, What's the best anti-aging exercise? Here's what I discover:

"Gentle jogging," say Danish researchers who have been tracking the health and well-being of more than 20,000 Copenhageners since 1976. No, it's resistance training. That's the true fountain-of-youth exercise regimen, according to research in (not surprisingly) the *Journal of Strength and Conditioning Research*. It builds youthful muscle and increases good growth factor hormones in the blood. But what about all this talk of HIIT—high-intensity interval training? It's tough; it's quick; it supercharges the body; it amps up the mitochondria. And 10 one-minute sprints (each followed by a 75-second recovery) three times a week appear to do as much good as 10 straight hours of that "gentle jogging" thing.

When a *New York Times* health reporter asked top exercise experts which exercise is best, she got as many answers as there were experts. One guy—and by "guy" I mean the chairman of a noted university's department of physiology—likes the burpee, which is possibly my least favorite thing in the world to do with my body. If you don't know what a burpee is, consider yourself lucky. If you want to preserve your innocence (which I would recommend), just skip this next sentence. A burpee is a Marine Corps/football player–type calisthenics move in which you drop to the ground in a squat, kick your feet behind you to the plank position, then pull your feet back into a kind of squat, then leap up as high as you can. You can throw in a pushup while you're down in plank, if you so choose. It is not a choice I would suggest. And you do that over and over again, as fast as you can, for one minute. Another university physiologist waxes rhapsodic about the squat. It activates the body's biggest muscles. It's simple and easy to do. A "very potent exercise," he says. A leading researcher in the field of endurance exercise at the Mayo Clinic endorses "brisk walking"—which is kind of like "gentle jogging," isn't it? Swimming (a whole-body exercise) and water aerobics (easy on the joints) have their advocates, as does yoga. And then there's a growing chorus of experts who sing the praises of high-intensity intervals. CrossFit, a kind of HIIT, is currently all the rage.

So what's a person to do?

I did everything . . . so you don't have to. And I'm here to report back. I know: There's nothing quite as boring as listening to the details of someone else's workouts (unless it's listening to the accomplishments of someone else's children), so I promise not to drag you through every experience. But I am going to tell you *something* about *some* of my mighty—and sweaty—efforts to turn back the clock if only because, in the throes of one or another exertion, the only thing that got me through was the thought *Well, at least this will make a good story for the book.*

That's what I was thinking, for example, when I slipped on my own sweat and did a face-plant on my yoga mat during my second—and last—attempt at hot yoga. The room was a toasty 102°F. And, because people who love yoga are not always people who love to use deodorant, the air was thick, I'd go so far as to say *solid*, with the exertions of two-dozen hardworking human animals. Yoga is good for so many things we associate with youth and vitality: posture and alignment, strength, balance, flexibility, dexterity, range of motion. Among the physiological benefits of yoga, many of which are backed by research, are decreases in heart rate and blood pressure, improvements in cholesterol numbers (increased good, decreased bad, decreased triglycerides), and increase in cardiovascular efficiency. Yoga enthusiasts claim their practice results in better sleep; more energy; a bolstered immune system; enhanced concentration, attention, and memory; and a generalized sense of well-being. This all sounds perfect, like a terrific long-term turn-back-the-clock strategy. The few serious yoga folks I've encountered, the amazing Katya Hayes of Queen's Bay, British Columbia, being at the top of the list, have extraordinary grace and a kind of luminescent energy that makes you want to stay within their orbit.

I had taken yoga classes in the past and liked the discipline. I tried to keep it up at home by starting at least a few mornings a week with three sun salutations. But I didn't do enough, and I wasn't serious enough to feel dramatic benefits. It did increase my flexibility, and I liked what yoga did for my everyday posture. Sometimes I think that just posture alone may be the dividing line between young and old. But hot yoga, or "Bikram yoga" as it is sometimes known, was something else entirely. The extreme moist heat (presumably to mimic the conditions in India—although seriously, *why*?) supposedly makes it "easier" to achieve more challenging poses because your muscles are nice and warm. The extraordinary flexibility you can achieve can, hot yogis believe, turn back the clock for tendons and joints. But I defy you to get the sole of your foot to stay on the inside of your thigh (tree pose) when your legs are slick with sweat. When I achieved the face-plant during an intense downward dog sequence, I didn't realize that I had given myself a bloody nose because it was just more rivulets working their way down another surface of my body.

Before I leave the topic of extreme perspiration behind, I'd like to tell you about Tabata, a form of high-intensity interval exercise you've probably never heard of. Unlike the CrossFit craze (which I participated in later), with its more than 4,000 certified affiliated gyms, a growing system of instructor credentialing, and stone-cold-serious regional, national, and international competitions, Tabata is obscure. When I explained what it was to a veteran trainer at a big New York gym recently, it was the first he had heard of it. I would never have known about it myself but for the overnight appearance (in a long-vacant store-front in a local strip mall I frequent) of a business that called itself, mysteriously, The Box. I looked in the big front window and saw a small, almost bare room. A few mats stacked against one wall, a collection of kettlebell weights—the epitome of "no frills." Some kind of serious fitness work was apparently going on right here under my nose, at my own neighborhood strip mall. What was it? The sign on the door gave no clue, only the hours the classes met, beginning at 5:00 a.m., which was, at least, a clue to the seriousness of the enterprise.

I showed up the very next morning. No, not at 5:00 a.m. I made it to the 7:00 class. I did not know what was in store for me, and I'm glad I didn't. The Tabata protocol—you know you're in for serious business when the instructor uses the word "protocol"—consists of 20 seconds of all-out effort followed by 10 seconds of rest, repeated eight or more times. When that set is finished, another one begins. And another. And another. The all-out effort is old-school calisthenics—burpees (yep, my least favorite exercise), squats, pushups, situps, and the up-and-back sprints not so affectionately known as suicides. The 20-second high-intensity intervals are endless. The 10-second rests are over before they begin. It is, in a word, brutal. In fact, as I saw that first morning, The Box is "decorated" with various hand-lettered signs proclaiming just that. "Understand . . . it is supposed to be BRUTAL!!" reads one sign. Others offer these encouraging messages: "You're not gonna DIE!!!" And "Pain is weakness leaving the body." In other words, you kind of have to drink the Kool-Aid.

Tabata, I learned from a photocopied information sheet I found on the battered desk at the rear of The Box, was developed by Japanese physiologist Izumi Tabata to apply maximum stress to the cardiovascular systems of Japanese Olympic speed skaters. It's a HIIT method so intense and so physically challenging that it was common during the sessions at The Box to see one or another seemingly fit young man make a beeline to the wastebasket by the door—this was where one went to throw up. The instructor looked like a marathoner or a Tour de France champion. The instructor looked like an Olympian. The instructor, in the unlikely event that he ever fell ill, would qualify for Medicare. If this is what one could look like—and move like—at 66 with Tabata, then what else, really, did I need to know?

Of course, I did the research, discovering along the way that brief spurts of very high-intensity interval training like Tabata had extraordinary anti-aging effects, including an astonishing 14 percent improvement in the best measure of overall aerobic fitness, VO_2 max, in only six weeks. (And these were already highly fit, highly trained subjects.)

I did several weeks of Tabata training beginning about three months after I started the exercise part of my quest. Just last week, I stopped by The Box to buy a new 20-session punch card. I hated it so much that I loved it. The high I got from finishing a session, the overwhelming *relief*, the full-body joy that overtook me when the session was over and I knew I did not have to do one more burpee or one more flying squat, was like nothing else I've ever felt. If you've ever suffered through intense pain and then had that pain almost magically dissipate, you know what I mean. You feel lighter. The world is suddenly clearer and brighter. Anything seems possible. This—all by itself—is like taking an anti-aging pill.

But the thing about Tabata is that you have to be in decent shape to try it in the first place. You have to be reasonably fit to make it through the protocol (with or without the sprint to the wastebasket). So how did I get in good enough shape to benefit from the backward-aging, aerobic-fitness effects of Tabata? It wasn't from my prequest sit-on-a-recumbent-bike-and-read-a-magazine exercise routine. I started running (if a 10½-minute mile can be considered running) and worked myself up to five miles two or three times a week. I even ran a few races, including, along with a team of a dozen mostly midlife women, the 36-hour adventure in bonding and sleep deprivation known as the Hood to Coast Relay. I awoke at 5:30 two mornings a week to go to a water aerobics class. I bought my son's girlfriend's touring bike and went on long country rides up and down significant hills. I worked out on weight machines and in the weight room, all of this in search of challenging exercise routines that I loved, would stay with, and, most important, had proven turn-back-the-clock effects.

At first, I hired a trainer to show me what to do and how to do it. Then I joined four other incipient gym rats—the aforementioned Sweat Chicas—for group training three times a week. The camaraderie was almost instantaneous. The shared sense of purpose, the humor (the more than occasional profanity!) made the workouts fun. Our shared commitment to our 7:00 a.m. slot got me out of bed on many a dark and rainy morning. We were lucky to find a demanding, inventive—and funny— trainer, a hunk of a guy in his mid-20s who, to our joy and amazement, never treated any of us like we could be his mother. (Actually, his mother was one of his clients, and he didn't even treat her like she was his mother.) We did circuit training. We did CrossFit, a tough, as-many-reps-as-possible (or "AMRAPs," in CrossFit lingo) strength and conditioning program used by police academies and tactical operations teams and military special operations units. CrossFit is high-intensity interval training, but it's quite different from Tabata. CrossFit is about weight lifting and rope climbing and pullups. Tabata is old-school calisthenics. I wouldn't dare tell this to a super-competitive, muscle-bulging fanatic, but CrossFit is not as brutal as Tabata. We did the Spartan 600 Warrior workout. (Don't ask.) We got visibly stronger. One morning, as I was grunting through some lateral lifts, I saw the outline of my deltoid muscle in the mirror. There was definition to my shoulders, a rounded contour, what trainers call a "cut line" defining the muscle. I let out a yelp.

Randy, the trainer, walked over to see if I was hurt. I lifted the weights so my delts popped. "Uh-oh," he said, a big grin on his face.

"We're gonna have to start charging admission"—he waited a beat—"to the gun show!" "Guns" is weight-lifting slang for cut, or "shredded," upper-arm muscles. I was, I must admit, inordinately proud of myself. A few weeks later I was working my way through a set of barbell rows when Randy stopped to note, and compliment, my latissimus dorsi (the large muscles on either side of the back). More muscle. More strength. I'm on my way to a higher metabolism. I could *feel* the clock ticking backward. Under Randy's tutelage, striving to meet his ever-higher expectations, we saw how many bench presses we could do, and then we did more the next week. We saw how much we could lift. We perfected our form. We lifted more. We did whatever Randy told us to do, and we liked it. When Randy left the gym to start his own business, we went with him. When he expanded and moved, we moved with him.

I also, along the way, signed up for various boot camps, from a Saturday-in-the-park experience that involved beating truck tires with sledge-hammers (try it, you'll like it) and pushing a half-ton pickup a mile down the street (not solo) to what is perhaps *the* iconic boot camp, the Biggest Loser. No, I was not a contestant. I was a paying guest at one of the BL's "resorts" (note ironic use of quotation marks), where for two weeks I engaged in seven hours of diverse and über-intense physical activity every day.

I did it not because I had seen the TV show (I hadn't) or because I had lots of weight to lose. I did it because it was the most challenging, immersive experience I could find. I needed to do whatever I could to continue improving my strength and stamina. I did it because I wanted to learn new exercises and fitness tips from trainers at the tops of their games. Which I did. I learned that core exercises rule. I learned that kickboxing is so much fun it ought to be illegal. I learned that HIIT can be done in the water. I learned—and this was the biggest and most important aging-backward lesson of all—that fitness is a lifestyle, not an add-on.

And, along with all the other hard and sweaty work I've done during these long months since my quest began, I just may have succeeded. Soon I will remeasure my biomarkers and retake various fitness tests. That has been my plan from the beginning, to retest (the muscle biopsy would be the exception), to calculate my "before" and "after," to—I hope—see progress, if going back (in time) can be considered going forward (in health and vitality). In the meantime, as I continue to buff my body, it occurs to me that I may need to pay attention to my attitude. Aging, it seems, is also in your head, not just in your muscles and bones. I've read that what—and how—you think about aging can have a real impact on how you actually age. I want to explore that next.

twelve

Thinking Young

OLD OLDIE WAS WHAT EVERYONE CALLED HER. SHE WAS MY mother's great-grandmother. Her bedroom was up in the attic of the big house, and every morning for as long as anyone could remember, she would wake before dawn, braid her long white hair, coil the braids around her head, and walk down three flights of stairs to the kitchen, where she would bake biscuits or rolls or quick bread for breakfast. That's how the rest of the family awakened, to that sweet, yeasty smell. Then one morning, there was no sweet, yeasty smell. Someone climbed the three flights of stairs to her room to see what was going on. She was there, in bed, hair fanned out on the pillow, eyes closed. She had died in her sleep. She was 97. Or 102. It depended on who was telling the story.

This afternoon I am telling the story, sprawled on an oversize, pillowy recliner in Rosemarie Eisenberg's cozy office. Rosemarie is a certified hypnotist and guided interactive imagery practitioner who uses deep relaxation, creative visualization, and hypnosis to get people to stop smoking or prepare to do battle with an illness or conquer a fear. I am here to have Rosemarie hypnotize me to "think young." When I told my husband what I was up to, he amused himself with the thought that when I got home from the session he would be able to snap his fingers or say a code word and I would all of a sudden start skipping across the lawn or giggling or playing hopscotch. That's not exactly what I had in mind.

I'd been doing a lot of reading in the "you are what you think you are" literature, and I wanted to explore the idea that mind-set—that is, what you think you are—might exert a discernible influence on who you are, or who you become, biologically. What, if anything, would happen if Rosemarie planted the suggestion—which is what she says hypnotism really is—of having a youthful mind-set? Would I feel younger? Would I *be* younger? This isn't as far-fetched as it may sound.

The idea that we can think ourselves young, that our minds can instigate changes in our bodies, is what Ellen Langer calls "the psychology of the possible" and others have called the "biology of hope" or the "biology of belief." Langer is my new hero, a brilliant Harvard psychologist who, for the past 35 years, has been designing ingenious social experiments to test the general hypothesis that our beliefs might be one of the most important determinants of health and longevity. Over the long course of that research, she has come to believe what yogis have known for centuries, what holistic and mind–body practitioners have been saying for decades (but without her good data): "If one's mind-set is altered, one's body will change accordingly."

It turns out that we already know this from what researchers have learned about placebos, those medically ineffectual treatments that nonetheless sometimes result in people getting better. In numerous carefully designed studies, one group of sufferers of some illness is treated with the "real" drug, the one a pharmaceutical company is testing; one group gets nothing; and one group gets a placebo. In study after study, regardless of disease, regardless of drug, some people in the placebo group get better. They respond as if they are being treated with the real drug. It's called the placebo effect, and it is not inconsequential. If you look at these studies, you'll see 15 or 20 or even 30 percent of the people in the placebo group improving. What's going on?

Although there's much controversy about what might be behind the placebo effect, it's clear that for some people a belief that something will work makes it work. Or, to put it another way: Expectation of improvement can lead to improvement. This is what Ellen Langer and others in her field are talking about: physiological responses to ideas, to mind-sets, to expectations. What you think is what you become.

Now suppose what you think is *old is bad.* Suppose, after years of hearing jokes about being over-the-hill at 40 or 50 or 60, after seeing thousands of commercials for Depends and Ensure and cell phone keypads with three-inch-high numerals, after watching hundreds of movies and television shows with cranky, crabby, asexual older people, suppose you begin to conflate "old" with sick, debilitated, and diminished? With forgetful, slow, weak, timid, and stodgy? Those last five adjectives are the most common "unthinkingly accepted" negative stereotypes of "old" in Western cultures, according to one group of researchers.

Things will keep getting worse as I get older. As I get older I will be less useful. As I get older I will be less happy. Those are three items from a morale scale developed by the Philadelphia Geriatric Center that speak to our dire expectations of growing older. In a blatant act of unscientific research, I ask my high school–age daughter to write down the first five things that come to mind when she thinks "old person." It takes her maybe 10 seconds. That's what's so powerful about stereotypes. They are instantly, thoughtlessly accessible. She hands me the sticky note with her scribbles on it: "Wrinkles. Bent over. Slow. Boring. Gross." I feel myself getting angry. I am about to launch into a lecture about vibrant, vital, energetic, interesting old people. But you know what? Part of me believes what she believes. Part of me, not a part of me I am proud of, buys into the stereotype. That's why I'm so quick to lie about my age these days. I don't want to be associated with the stereotype. And that's why I am going to try this hypnosis. I'd like to work on replacing, or overwriting, *old is sick* and *old is bad*. If I keep telling myself this, if I keep believing it, even a little—and if Ellen Langer is right—I may *make* myself old.

What's interesting about stereotypes and older people is that, as researchers at Brandeis and the University of Virginia have found, older people internalize and accept society's view of them. They view their own group every bit as negatively as they are viewed by others. And so older people think of themselves—and we, the not-yet-old, think of our future selves—as unhappier, less likable, less useful, more dependent. This is, researchers like Langer believe, a self-fulfilling prophesy of decline. You get what you expect.

But it works both ways. Mind–body guru Deepak Chopra, among many others, has written about the Abkhazians, a group I've noted before as being one of the healthiest, most vibrant, longest-lived communities on the planet. Yes, they eat a plant-rich diet, and yes, physical activity is a part of their everyday lives. But researchers think there may be something more to their vitality. They have no word in their language for "old people." They refer to the eldest among them as "long-living people." Note how "long-living" expresses an action, something they are in the midst of doing, while "old" is a static state, a pronouncement. Are Abkhazians healthy and vital in old age because their language allows—*expects*—them to be?

Langer looked at two other populations that apparently do not hold many of our common negative stereotypes about aging: mainland Chinese and the American deaf community. Although "memory loss" is repeatedly mentioned as a condition of old age by other populations, neither of these communities listed it very often. It is not part of their perception of old age. Interestingly, when Langer tested the memories of old people in these two communities, they were significantly better than in the general population. Dismiss that. Embrace that. Make of it what you will, but there are an awful lot of very smart people who think (and a mounting body of evidence supporting the idea) that, as Chopra has said, "Expectation rules outcome."

The evidence that perceptions of aging (another way of looking at expectations about growing older) affect what does in fact happen is pretty startling. A Yale study concluded that perceptions a person held about aging had more impact on how long he or she lived than did their blood pressure, cholesterol level, or whether they were smokers. Regardless of age, gender, socioeconomic status, loneliness, or—*get this*—the actual state of their health, the men and women with positive views on aging lived seven and a half years longer than those who bought into the negative stereotypes. Conversely, another study found that older adults who perceived their health as poor were six times more likely to die (within the time frame studied, that is) than those who thought they were in good health—*regardless of their actual health status.* One explanation is that if you think of illness and decrepitude as inevitable parts of aging, you are less likely to do anything to prevent, counteract, or treat them.

Here's another component to this "stereotype leads to perception leads to expectation leads to outcome" sequence that I find just fascinating. It's called "cueing" or "priming." The idea is that you get cues from your physical environment that prime your feelings, your expectations, and often your behaviors. Once primed, the body responds accordingly.

So if you are cued "old," your body acts older. It *becomes* older. If you are cued "young," the opposite might happen. I like this! It adds a dimension to my gym time and group workout routines. I am surrounding myself with healthy, energetic people. Our conversations are about strength and stamina, about future races and bike rides. I am being "cued" young.

Langer created a number of very interesting experiments testing this notion. In one, she took the blood pressures of women before and after they had their gray hair colored. After their hair was colored, the women told Langer that they not only thought they looked younger, they also felt younger. Interestingly, the women's post-salon blood pressure—a biomarker of aging—was lower than their *I-am-old* gray-hair blood pressure. Were they cued to age backward? It's an intriguing idea, an idea I now remember hearing, in a somewhat different iteration, from the plastic surgeon, Mark Jewell. He—and most cosmetic surgeons, I am betting—feels strongly that looking younger improves women's self-esteem. The physical state affects the mental attitude. Langer is exploring the other side of the coin: Mental attitude affects physical state. It makes perfect sense that both would be true.

In two other studies, she asked the question: If the life we live resembles that of a different age group, will we age more like that group than our own? In other words, will environmental and contextual cues affect our biology? She found that women who waited until their mid-30s to have their first child tended to live longer than women who gave birth in their early 20s. A possible explanation—Langer is all about possibility, not probability—is that the "old" mothers inhabited the social world of women 10 to 15 years younger. The "old" mothers were cued to be younger—and they became younger—because the concerns and experiences of their daily lives were the same as those of 20-something mothers. In a different study, she looked at the "social clocks" of much older or much younger spouses and found that the age difference resulted in what she called "age-incongruent cues." That is, the much younger spouses lived shortened lives while the older spouses, being cued young, lived longer lives than others in their age group. Each partner had taken a step closer to the other on the life line.

But the study that made me fall in love with Ellen Langer and wish I could have been one of her grad students was her famous 1988 experiment where she transported a group of old men to a carefully designed and controlled retreat where they were surrounded by cues of their younger years: magazines, newspapers, TV and radio shows, music. They were instructed to talk only about "current" events (from the 1950s), speak only in the present tense, to basically playact that they were living their 40-year-ago lives. Of course, they were subjected to a number of tests before and after. The results blew me away. After their week of living young, the men showed improvements in physical strength, manual dexterity, posture, gait, memory, taste sensitivity, hearing, and vision. Yes, you read that right. They got younger.

I'm ready to do the same. I wish I could have signed up for a neat before-and-after study—especially a weeklong retreat, perhaps in the Berkshires, where I'd get to relive my days at Camp Tamarac—but that opportunity did not present itself. Instead, I'm sitting here in the oversize pillowy recliner in Rosemarie's office. I had been prepared for her to ask me about my younger self. I'd thought that, under hypnosis, I'd maybe experience this younger self, like those old guys at the retreat, and awaken from my trance with my clock ticking backward. But Rosemarie, who's been in this business for more than 25 years, has other ideas. She smiles and says let's get started. I lean back to an almost horizontal position, put on a pair of noise-canceling headphones, and give myself over to her soft, lyrical voice and the background music she chooses, that wispy, ethereal stuff massage therapists always play. She asks me to imagine a deeply restful, safe place and asks me to go there. I'm trying, but all I can think of is whether I remembered to set my cell on vibrate and how I would be able to write about this experience later if I zoned out while actually experiencing it. But the music, her voice, the way she cues my breathing, all . . . do something. My monkey-mind keeps chattering, but now it's a distant voice I can barely hear. My breathing gets slower and deeper, and after a while I am just, well, floating: peaceful, relaxed, not exactly in the room anymore but very much aware of everything.

Rosemarie asks me to call up a strong, wise person, someone I respect and can talk to, someone, she says, "who might have something to say to you." That's when Old Oldie comes into view, a woman I have never met nor even seen a photograph of. And that's when I tell Rosemarie the Old Oldie story. In case you're wondering if you should trust my account of all this, the account of a woman under hypnosis, let me say two things: First, I actually remember, with great clarity, everything that happened during the hourlong session, and second, Rosemarie keeps wonderful notes that she gives me when we finish.

Rosemarie wonders if there's anything I want to ask Old Oldie. Of course there is! Did you really die in bed? What does it feel like to be 97 or 102 or however old you were when you died? And how did you manage to live so long? Were you happy when you were very old? Rosemarie allows me to blather. So, for that matter, does Old Oldie. Finally, Old Oldie says, "I didn't think much about my age. I just got up every morning and lived." When I say "she says," I don't mean that some conjured apparition speaks to me. It's more like the words suddenly pop into my head, but I know they're not my words. Then she says, "There was always something new every day." I tell Rosemarie this, and as soon as I say it, I realize—yes, even in whatever state I'm in, I realize—what Rosemarie is up to. She's not interested in me accessing my younger self. (What does *that kid* know anyway?) She wants me to learn about aging from someone who's done it with resounding success. She wants me to feel hope about my older self. And she wants me to feel optimism.

"There was always something new every day," Old Oldie said. Now *that's* optimism.

And optimism, according to what I'd been reading, is one of the keys, one of the "secrets" to living young.

In fact, the author of the bestseller *Learned Optimism*, a man considered to be one of the preeminent experts in what's called positive psychology, believes that optimism and pessimism affect health and well-being "almost as clearly as do physical factors." Martin Seligman, PhD, whose book I speed-read before I made the appointment with Rosemarie, maintains that there are four things we can control concerning our good health: not smoking, exercising, eating well, and cultivating optimism. Optimism, he says, is "at least as beneficial as the others."

In the book, there's a 48-question optimism test, and, of course, I take it. Regardless of my "score," I believe taking the test is prima facie evidence of my optimism. A pessimist would never have taken this test. A pessimist would never have bought the book.

That said, I am not thrilled with my results. The scoring is complicated and convoluted, with subscores that attempt to measure the permanence and pervasiveness of one's optimism or pessimism. Somehow, I manage to test both "moderately optimistic" and "moderately pessimistic," split evenly. My generic "stuff of hope" score ranks me as a somewhat tepid optimist. I don't really know what I expected. No one who knows me would accuse me of being a Pollyanna, but I certainly don't walk around with the glass half empty, a dark cloud hanging over my head. But "tepid optimist" is just not good enough. I want to be a full-fledged, card-carrying, fist-pounding optimist. It never occurred to me that optimism could be learned. I don't think I spent a lot of time pondering this, but I assumed optimism and pessimism were part of one's hardwired personality. It's eye-opening (and oh so optimistic!) to consider that optimism can be learned.

I've discovered that the scientific literature abounds with studies linking optimism and good health. The landmark MacArthur Foundation Study of Successful Aging—the research I keep coming back to—found that a key factor in health and vitality was what the researchers called self-efficacy, "a person's belief in his or her ability to solve problems, handle situations, meet challenges and otherwise influence the course of events." In a word: optimism. Seligman, the *Learned Optimism* guy, conducted a landmark study in the late 1980s that found that health at age 60 was strongly related to optimism at age 25. He was making use of a rich data set that went back to the mid-1940s. The optimists in the study experienced fewer diseases of middle age, and experienced them later (if at all) and with less severity than the pessimists. If optimism can be learned, it's intriguing to consider that (learned) optimism in midlife could translate into a much healthier, more vibrant later life. One of the lesser reported findings of the Women's Health Initiative—the massive National Institutes of Health–sponsored study of women's health issues—was that optimists were somewhat less likely to get coronary heart disease and *30 percent* less likely to die from it.

Why would that be?

The answer, like everything else about us, is wonderfully complex, a combination of the psychological, behavioral, biological, and social. Here's the way I understand it: Optimists believe good things can and do happen, and that they have significant control over that process. They have confidence that what they do (or don't do) matters. Pessimists, on the other hand, often feel helpless, like victims of circumstance. You'd think that people who expect good things to happen to them would sit back and wait for them to happen, but that's not what optimists do. The research I've been reading is pretty clear about that. Optimists seize the day. They take steps to ensure that good things will happen to them. They are far more likely to practice healthy behaviors and to seek treatment for problems than pessimists. Optimists are also far more likely to have the social support networks that researchers have found correlate with long-term good health. Learning about this makes me very happy. I am, in fact, a seize-the-day kind of person. I don't (often) suffer from victim mentality. I do believe that what I do can make a difference in my life. It's that self-efficacious attitude that has fueled my turn-back-the-clock quest. I don't know that I would ever have thought to go on this quest if I didn't believe that good things might happen.

But I never suspected that optimists might be *biochemically* different from pessimists. Feeling overwhelmed, helpless, and depressed? Feeling that way a lot of the time because you are generally pessimistic? Apparently, your brain is busy sending chemical messages to your body, and they're not love letters. One of the not-love-letters is cortisol, the so-called stress hormone. Overexposure to cortisol is like an express train to the nursing home. That's not exactly how the docs at the Mayo Clinic put it. But when they list increased risks of heart disease, obesity, memory impairment, sleep problems, and digestive disorders as potential fallout from chronic exposure to cortisol, that's pretty much what they're saying. Optimists, when stressed, produce cortisol too, but their biochemical response is muted and transient. Their cortisol levels rise, but not as much, and they fall quickly. Optimists have lower blood pressures than pessimists. Optimists have stronger immune systems than pessimists. In short: Optimism rules.

As does happiness. Hard to argue with the general notion that being happy is a more pleasant state in which to live than being sad, but there's also convincing evidence from neurobiological research that being happy protects against ill health and the risk of disease. Which is really another way of saying that being happy keeps you youthful. In one study I read, greater happiness was associated with a lower cortisol level, reduced inflammatory response, and lower heart rate. The subjects were "assessed through repeated ratings of happiness over a working day," which would make me cranky if I wasn't already, but apparently it didn't faze the happy people.

Happiness has also been linked to production of the hormone pregnenolone (dubbed, in fact, the "happiness hormone"), which contributes to better memory, greater focus, and improved concentration. You may remember that this is one of the many hormones Suzanne Somers takes as a supplement. The authors of a study published by the *Proceedings of the National Academy of Sciences of the United States* called pregnenolone, "the most potent memory enhancer yet reported." And then there is the cascade of "feel good" chemicals released when a person is happy—endorphins, dopamine, serotonin, and others—that counteract stress and pain.

A week before my session with Rosemarie I was sitting in a booth in a natural foods restaurant eating brown rice and tofu with the Guidess of Happiness, a modest (despite the moniker), soft-spoken therapist named Barb Ryan who for the past two years has been offering increasingly popular six-week, weekend, and one-day "journeys" into happiness. Her message is simple (and right in line with the latest psychological thinking): You can choose the way you feel. If that's so, she says, why *wouldn't* you choose to be happy? Although she began this work without any thoughts about the possible links between happiness and health, when I asked her how she feels these days, she paused for a moment and then said, clearly surprised, "Now that I think about it, I feel healthier, more engaged, and more energetic than I can remember." She'd be 59 in a few days.

Later, in Rosemarie's office, when I ask Old Oldie if she was "happy in her old age," she—well, she snorts. This sounds weird because, after all, this woman is an image in my mind, and her words just pop into my head. But so does this snort. I kind of like the idea that this iconic wise woman I've conjured has an attitude. "Happy?" she says, inside my head. "It's not about being happy. It's about family and useful work. Work," she repeats, to make sure I get it.

Oh, I get it. I know all about work. I don't need Old Oldie to tell me how important it is to have useful work. In fact, as I've been researching this chapter on thinking young, I've been wondering how to play more. These words, purported to be George Bernard Shaw's, haunt me: "We do not stop playing because we grow old; we grow old because we stop playing." As I am writing this—I mean right now, in real time—my daughter bursts into the room. There was an event at school, and she brought home several smiley-face balloons. She stands near the doorway and bats one of the balloons in my direction. I am about to tell her to quit bothering me, that I'm working, and then catch the irony of that. I am writing about the need to play while simultaneously eschewing the opportunity to do so. I stop writing. We bat the balloon back and forth. It gets crazy. We walk around the house, first me walking backward, then my daughter, trying to keep the balloon in the air. The cat gets in the act. The game ends suddenly and dramatically when the cat jumps up and swipes at the balloon, claws extended. He bolts, ears pasted to his head. Lizzie and I fall on the floor, laughing. I feel great. The stress I felt, deep in my body, while I was writing, is gone. My head is clear.

Yes. More play. Maybe that's not a "think young" strategy but rather an *anti*-thinking strategy that keeps you young. I wonder, are there other strategies? Here's what I cull from the research: Don't reminisce too much. Live in the present and have goals for the future. Think about what you have yet to experience, the people you have yet to meet, and, as Dr. Seuss once famously wrote, "oh, the places you'll go!" "There was always something new every day," Old Oldie had said. Hang around with people younger than you are. Be compassionate with yourself. Compassionate, eh? It turns out that people who are kind to themselves suffer less stress and anxiety, meaning less cortisol, less inflammation, maybe lower blood pressures and heart rates. Self-compassion means not being so judgmental, not engaging in critical self-talk.

I take an online self-compassion test created by an educational psychologist at the University of Texas in Austin. I fail. I am, in fact, a master of self-criticism. It begins in the morning when I scrutinize my imperfections in the mirror and ends at night when, lying in bed, I berate myself for all I didn't accomplish. And so it comes as no surprise that I have absolutely no compassion for myself for failing the self-compassion test. I'm feeling pretty bad about myself (and borderline pessimistic!) until I come across a lovely little study that links massage with a slew of turn-back-the-clock hormonal messages. Now *that* I can do.

It's near the end of the session with Rosemarie. I am deeply relaxed, my eyes closed, my breathing very slow. Rosemarie has switched gears and asked me to try to imagine my older self, my self at 90. "Tell me what you see," she says gently, her voice soft and muffled through the earphones. After a while, I see a woman up ahead, and I guess that must be me. "What does she look like?" Rosemarie prompts me again. I squint, in my mind, to make out her face. This shouldn't be difficult. I have seen a photograph of my much-older face, courtesy of the folks at the Face Aging Group and their sophisticated program. I've looked at that photo dozens of times, scores of times. But this woman I've conjured is ahead of me, and she won't look back. I can't see her face. I am trying to gain on her so I can get a close-up glimpse, but she is moving too quickly. I watch her steady, purposeful strides. I see her squared shoulders, her straight back, the rhythmic swing of her arms. She moves with confidence, with a kind of banked energy, with embodied youth. This is the image I've been looking for without knowing it. This is who I want to be, who I will be: a healthy, vital, active "longer-living" person. Expectation rules outcome.

thirteen

Starving to Be Young

I AM THREE (VERY LONG) DAYS INTO MY NEXT—AND LAST— counterclockwise experiment, CR, and I am not a happy camper. "CR" stands for "calorie restriction." No, this is not a weight-loss plan—although you do count calories, and you invariably lose weight. CR is a tightly regulated, precisely controlled dietary regimen that involves eating nutrient-dense, high-fiber, low-energy-density (aka low-cal) foods—and not a lot of them. It is purposeful, calculated *under*-eating without accompanying undernutrition, and as such, couldn't be more different from the way the majority of *over*fed, *under*nourished Americans eat. Today I am moody, grumpy, testy (not self-compassionate!), and, above all, hungry. I wake up thinking about food, go to sleep thinking about food, and in between . . . well, I think about food. I am thinking about food right now.

Logically, I should have jumped into this experiment right after detox and superfoods and eating raw, but I needed a break from all that food focus. I'd kind of had it with taking-the-joy-out-of-eating experiences. Plus, I needed time to incorporate what I'd learned into a sensible—maybe even pleasurable—eating-for-health strategy. It really wasn't that difficult to create an enjoyable everyday diet that included one or two or even three superfoods—especially if I counted dark chocolate. After my extreme eating experiences, from the ultrarestrictive hCG protocol to the three-day-prep raw lasagna, I was ready to settle into a diverse menu of judiciously chosen foods, with a focus on plants, lean protein, and whole grains. And dark chocolate. Eating had become fun again. I was feeling good. That meant I was ready to go crazy again.

To follow the CR Way—as one of the several books on the subject is titled—one must first *very* carefully calculate the number of calories the body needs and slash that number by a third or more. (I'll explain further in a moment.) It's necessary to keep the food journal to end all food journals, tracking not only calories but also protein, fat, carbohydrates, fiber, and the recommended daily amounts of all the essential vitamins and minerals in everything eaten every day. If it sounds hard to eat—and live—this way, it is. If it sounds tedious, it is. Actually, it is even more tedious than that because CR requires that one also diligently—I'd say "obsessively"—monitor the state of one's own body: daily weigh-ins, pulse takings, and body temperature readings; a battery of regularly scheduled blood tests; frequent blood pressure readings. Additional blood tests to track levels of insulin, cortisol, and DHEA are recommended, as well as body fat analyses, VO_2 max tests, an oral glucose tolerance test, DEXA scans, and several other assessments. Not just once but, for some, as often as every three months. It's like being involved in a scientific study *for the rest of your life.*

Does anyone really eat, live, and self-monitor like this? Amazingly, yes. At least a few thousand people do. Let me anticipate your next question: *Why?* Because it turns out that CR is a powerful, scientifically proven turn-back-the-clock strategy. The significant biochemical shifts caused by systemic, nutrient-appropriate under-eating have been shown to improve health and slow aging by forestalling and even reversing age-related changes. There is real science behind this, good solid research, a body of evidence so persuasive that it is impossible to ignore. So when I wrote in a previous chapter that, in terms of aging-backward strategies, exercise is It, I lied. There is this other path, perhaps an even more effective path, to prolonged youthful health and vitality. It is also a far more difficult path. More brutal than Tabata. More time-consuming than being forever in training for an Ironman competition. Harder to sustain than a five-day-a-week gym habit. That's another reason I haven't mentioned it earlier. Also, because I knew that if I mentioned it, if I presented the evidence (which I am about to), I would have to test-drive the protocol myself.

Okay. Reporting for duty. Really—the evidence is that compelling. Before I explain how the CR regimen works, let me tell you what I ate for my CR breakfast this morning: the peels of three Fuji apples, a half a cup of blueberries, and 10 raw almonds. Yes, the *peels.* Eating the entire fruit would rack up too many calories. For lunch I had an egg-white-and-spinach omelet, lightly steamed broccoli, and a whole grain, extra-fiber English muffin, dry. That was about 20 minutes ago, and I'm already watching the clock for my midafternoon snack of six ounces of plain, nonfat yogurt and a small plate of raw veggies (no carrots—they are too high in calories). For dinner it will be an unadorned three-ounce piece of salmon (that's, like, four forkfuls) or an unadorned four-ounce chicken breast. No sautéing in garlic-infused olive oil. No poaching in white wine. No sauces, no amendments. More raw veggies. Basically, after you finish eating, you feel like eating.

There are two ongoing challenges in devising the diet. The first is to keep coming up with a menu of low-fat, low-sugar, modest-protein, high-fiber, nutrient-dense meals that supply everything the body needs. (Books like *The CR Way* and Web sites like www.crsociety.org help.) The second challenge is to figure out how to accomplish this while cutting calorie intake by 30 to 40 percent. That's the "restriction" part of calorie restriction. You start by calculating your own calorie allotment so you have a baseline from which to subtract. I figure out mine two different ways. The first and simplest is estimating how many calories I usually eat (about 1,900, I think, although I've read that the average caloric intake in America is closer to 3,000) and cutting 40 percent off that. That gives me 1,140 calories a day, which is fewer calories than all but the very strictest of diets I've ever put myself on (which would be that oh-so-fleetingly successful experience with hCG). Another method is estimating my basal metabolic rate by using one of the many BMR online calculators and then applying what's known as the Harris-Benedict equation. That's the factor, determined by a person's normal weekly activity rate, by which you multiply the BMR to get the total calories your body needs to maintain itself. Then you reduce that by 40 percent. By the second calculation, my CR allotment is 1,250. So, averaging the two, I'm figuring 1,200 calories a day. Are you seeing how wonky this is? I suspect that many women put themselves on 1,200-calorie weight-loss diets, even though 1,500 to 1,800 calories is what's most often recommended. The restriction may not sound that drastic. What makes it so is that this is how one eats every day . . . forever.

Just so you know, a half a cup of almonds, which is somewhat less than a handful and can be eaten in a mindless minute while watching the opening scene of the new season of *Breaking Bad* (I can be that specific because I did exactly this last week) is just over 400 calories. A nice-size salmon fillet—the portion I was eating during my superfoods weeks—clocks in at close to 700 calories.

"Fewer calories, more life" is the adage of CR Society International, a group of like-minded, calorie-restricted, self-monitoring (lean and hungry-looking) folks who are both true believers and proselytizers who trade body stats and recipes on the society's Web site. But CR is hardly a 21st-century fad. "To lengthen life," Ben Franklin once wrote, "lessen thy meals." Franklin lived to be 84, 30-plus years beyond the life expectancy for a man born in his century. On the other hand, I've seen portraits of the man. He was a jowly, portly guy, so he may have achieved his longevity without depriving himself. (Or maybe he was the original French paradox.) A better historical example is the Okinawans, one of those long-lived and vibrantly healthy populations I've mentioned before. (They were the healthiest people on earth before the invasion of American fast-food culture around the US Marine bases there.) For generations, the Okinawans practiced CR as a way of life, consuming, on average, 40 percent fewer calories than the average American and receiving in return seemingly age-resistant health.

CR scientific research dates back to the mid-1930s when Clive McCay, PhD, a Cornell biochemist, nutritionist, and gerontologist, systematically underfed lab mice and discovered that they grew up healthier and lived up to 60 percent longer than mice given a normal diet. Since that time, more than 2,000 studies have shown that the less you eat (assuming good nutrition), the longer and healthier you live. This has proven true for such diverse species as yeasts (whose reproductive periods are extended—lucky them), worms (they become resistant to toxic proteins), mice, monkeys, and humans. Recent reports of one monkey study poke holes in the longevity claim, but still find significant health benefits.

From the 1960s through the 1990s, the CR mantle was taken up by Roy Walford, MD, an iconoclastic (to say the least) UCLA professor and researcher who, between conducting intensive laboratory research on mice and publishing more than 350 journal articles, walked across India in a loincloth measuring the rectal temperatures of holy men. His life may have been overly colorful for a scientist—he hung out with a New

York experimental theater group, wrote reviews for a Los Angeles alternative newspaper, and was an expert on the underground drug scene in Amsterdam—but his science was solid. His underfed mice had glossy coats, strong bones, and clear eyes. They were long-lived, active, and healthy. Very healthy. Researchers at Tufts and elsewhere confirmed and reconfirmed these findings. It appeared that so-called CRON (Calorie Restriction with Optimum Nutrition) protected mice against cancer, diabetes, atherosclerosis, and cardiovascular, respiratory, and autoimmune diseases while slowing the aging of their brains.

The research then moved a big step closer to us humans with a long-term study of adult rhesus monkeys—and the results were encouraging: Those on a 30 percent CR regimen had half the incidences of cancer and cardiovascular disease as the controls. None of the diet-controlled monkeys developed diabetes, while more than 40 percent of the controls did. Not only that, but the CR monkeys' immune systems and brains resisted many age-related changes. Hard on the heels of that research came reports from the Biosphere 2 experiment, where eight men and women lived in a three-acre, sealed, glass-enclosed experimental structure designed as a self-sustaining ecosystem. They had been forced by circumstance— and cajoled by their resident physician, the aforementioned Dr. Roy Walford—to adopt a CR regimen. In research subsequently published in the *Proceedings of the National Academy of Sciences*, Walford reported dramatic changes in the biomarkers of the (already healthy) Biosphere participants: Blood pressure went down to an astonishing average of 89/58; total cholesterol fell to an average of 123 (by comparison, the US average for men and women in their 40s is 200); triglycerides and fasting glucose plummeted. And, of course, they all lost weight.

Meanwhile, ordinary people—well, that might be stretching the definition of "ordinary"—were finding each other via an Internet chat group that evolved into CR Society International (Roy Walford's daughter, Lisa, was the first director). In the early 2000s, two observational studies compared these pioneering CR practitioners (they'd been on the regimen for an average of six years) with the same number of age-matched healthy people who ate a typical American diet. The CR folks had significantly lower total cholesterol, bad cholesterol, triglycerides, fasting glucose, and blood pressure. Their stats were amazing, with—in one of the studies—the triglyceride counts of the CRers (average age, 50) similar to those of the very healthiest 5 percent of 20-year-olds. Their artery walls were 40 percent thinner than the non-CR people's. (Thickness is a measure of atherosclerosis.)

Now there are even more exciting (and scientifically valid) results coming in from a multicenter, randomized, controlled trial examining the effects of two years of CR on 220 healthy, nonobese volunteers. The creators of this National Institute on Aging–sponsored study have devised an "intensive intervention" to keep the participants on the straight, narrow—and restricted—path with group and individual counseling, unique nutritional and portion-size training, and PDAs to monitor calorie intake.

As someone who has attempted to adhere to CR for now four days, seven hours, and 23 minutes (but who's counting?), I can tell you that these folks are fortunate to get outside help and support. But it's not just the special help that's making this regimen easier for the study participants to adhere to than it is for me. It's also the every-three-month feedback, the stats that tell them that what they are doing is making a difference. The participants, not to mention the researchers, must be mightily encouraged by the first round of results: bad cholesterol down; good cholesterol up; arterial plaque, inflammation, glucose levels, blood pressure, markers of DNA damage—all reduced. They see that CR works. It turns back the clock. I don't have that reinforcement. The CR Way does not make a difference in five days, or perhaps even five weeks. I would have to follow this regimen for at least 12 weeks to know how my particular body chemistry would react.

In fact, my plan has been to follow the regimen for two weeks. No, it is not enough time to see results. But it is enough time to see if living this way is possible. It's one thing to read the good-news research. It's another thing to sign on as a lifelong subject. I need to know how it feels to live in a severely portion-controlled world, to assess, measure, calculate, and compute everything I put in my mouth. I thought two weeks of CR would also give me insight into those few thousand people who have permanently adopted this lifestyle. I am several days shy of a week now, and, despite my plan, I am ready to quit. I've never been crabbier. I try to boost my mood by throwing myself into more research.

I DISCOVER THAT EVEN AFTER MORE THAN 75 YEARS OF study, exactly how calorie restriction works is still not well understood. It may be that reducing caloric intake activates a particular protein called sirtuins, which changes body chemistry in ways that help slow or neutralize or even reverse the effects of aging. Metabolism slows; body temperature decreases; the body becomes a superefficient superconserver. The natural degrading/aging processes within the body—number of cellular divisions, production of harmful free radicals, shortening of telomeres, damage to DNA—all slow down. The thought is that organisms—from yeasts to humans—have developed this complex, adaptive response to deal with periods of food scarcity. Those organisms that evolved to slow the aging process and resist degenerative diseases during adverse times had a much better chance of surviving long enough to reproduce—and thus win the evolutionary sweepstakes. It may be that the low-intensity biological stress that CR imposes on an organism elicits this evolved defensive state.

That's what I want—what we all want, right? To achieve this evolved biological state that resists disease, preserves and enhances health, and turns back the clock. I personally could do without the prolonged period of reproduction. But the rest? Who could say no to that?

At this moment, I must confess: me. It is the afternoon of my fifth CR day, and I would happily trade the promise of 20-year-old arteries for a slice of roasted red pepper, caramelized onion, chèvre pizza. Or, truthfully, a slice of *any* pizza. You know you're in trouble when Pizza Hut billboards cause excess salivation, when foods you've *never* before considered eating, junk that would normally turn your stomach—greasy ersatz panini from the corner convenience store, a Krispy Kreme doughnut, a bag of Cool Ranch Doritos—makes you swoon. It's not even that I am suffering hunger pains. It's that I've become totally obsessed with food, my senses hypersensitized to anything having to do with eating. I poach a chicken breast in fat-free, low-sodium broth and steam a plate of broccoli. I read a feature on CR in the *New York Times* and consider making this favorite recipe from a veteran calorie restrictor: Put one head of red cabbage, 2 tablespoons of caraway seeds, and 1 bay leaf in a large pot and cover with water. Boil for 6 to 10 minutes, then strain and serve the cabbage.

Wait a minute. I believe my ancestors left the old country so they didn't have to eat like this. I turn down two invitations to dinner. I make my husband crazy by limiting our restaurant choice to Baja Fresh, where I can order the ensalada with shrimp—hold the cheese and tortilla strips, and no dressing, please—and a nice glass of cold water.

But I have bigger problems with CR. For one, it goes against the basic principle I've been trying to follow throughout this quest, the gospel spread by doctors, fitness experts, advice columnists, health Web sites, and tens of linear feet of anti-aging books: Keep that metabolism revved. Now I am working to do just the opposite. And if I succeed—guess what? My job becomes even harder. If under-eating triggers the slow-everything-down response it's supposed to, then soon I will have to lower my caloric intake even more to continue to reap the anti-aging benefits. That means even smaller portions. It is odd—and disturbing—how, in such a short time, CR has transformed eating from a pleasure to a chore for me, how meal planning and cooking are now more science and math than art and culture. I read about how some CR practitioners measure their food to the tenth of a gram. Detox was downright fun next to this. My raw food week was more tolerable. It's this incessant calculation. It's these miniscule portions. It's movies without popcorn.

As extraordinary as the research results are, as amazing as the turn-back-the-clock effects seem to be, I learn that there can be significant downsides to CR. More serious than my crankiness, more unsettling than my food obsession, are the results from this old study I stumble upon. It was designed and run in the mid-1940s, with the war-torn populations of Europe in mind, to investigate the effects of calorie deprivation. Although it was called the Minnesota *Semistarvation* Experiment, really these (all-male) volunteers were just eating the CR way. Their calorie intake of 1,560 was a calculated 40 percent restriction. The results, published a few years later in a two-volume, 1,385-page work, found the 24-week regimen produced significant increases in depression, hysteria, and hypochondria. Most of the subjects experienced periods of severe emotional distress and depression, and there were a few extreme reactions, including self-mutilation. Seven decades and a couple of thousand studies later, a review of the CR literature in *Science* magazine lists amenorrhea (cessation of menstruation), infertility, osteoporosis, and immune deficiencies as negatives. Recent results from the 220-person National Institute on Aging–sponsored trial show decreases in muscle mass, aerobic capacity, and bone mineral density in the CR eaters. I am oddly buoyed by this bad news. If CR isn't the flawless route to extended youthful vitality I originally thought it was, maybe I don't have to feel so bad about not being able to embrace it. How's that for twisted thinking? Perhaps this is a sign that I am suffering from severe emotional CR-induced distress. Or maybe I'm being self-compassionate!

My mood improves when I discover that there may be ways *other* than CR to activate these wondrous age-sparing metabolic pathways. Linus Pauling Institute health-span researcher Tory Hagen, who rejects CR, calling it "impractical and unappealing" (a big "amen" to that), believes in the anti-aging power of micronutrient supplementation. It's the orthomolecular medicine approach pioneered by Pauling, who, incidentally, lived to be 93. And a half. Others, still focused on the CR idea, suggest that periodic fasting might be just as beneficial as long-term daily calorie restriction. If you fast one day a week, explains an online guide, you'll feel hungry that day. But with CR "it is not uncommon to feel hunger every day." You can also restore some pleasure to the eating experience on those nonfasting days—if you don't think ahead, that is. Then there's the thought that protein restriction, which is far easier to accomplish than calorie restriction, might mimic the effects of CR. That would be too bad for all those paleo diet folks, wouldn't it? Investigators are calling for more research in all these areas.

But the real exciting news is the search for chemical compounds that mimic CR. Yes, that's right: no draconian lifelong under-eating plan. Instead, a dietary or pharmaceutical agent that produces one or more of the principal biological effects of calorie restriction. In other words, something that fools the body into thinking it's starving while you are, in fact, eating a slice (or two) of roasted red pepper, caramelized onion, chèvre pizza. Throw in a piece of carrot cake and this is my idea of culinary heaven. But, as you might expect with something as complicated as this— that is, the human body and its multitudinous interconnected, interdependent systems—the search for a CR mimic has been tough. In the early 2000s, researchers thought they'd found a promising substance that appeared to disrupt glucose metabolism in rats. Unfortunately, it turned out to be toxic. Then all the attention turned to resveratrol, that ballyhooed substance found mostly but not exclusively in red wine. You will remember resveratrol and the work of Harvard Medical School researcher David Sinclair from earlier chapters. Although the research continues to be controversial more than a decade later, a number of anti-aging researchers believe that resveratrol works by activating sirtuins, which then activate many of the same cellular pathways triggered by CR. The problem with depending on red wine resveratrol is that you would have to drink, by one estimate, 65 bottles of pinot a day to get the "anti" effects. By then you wouldn't care how old you were. Or, for that matter, *where* you were.

Researchers like Sinclair and others at the company he founded (and then sold to GlaxoSmithKline) then got busy working on that problem, attempting to develop chemical compounds far more potent than red wine resveratrol that could be given in small doses. At one point, the company's lead drug was promising enough to merit clinical trials. But late in 2010, Glaxo halted the investigation due to adverse effects in study participants. Now researchers are investigating additional sirtuins-activating compounds as well as identifying other potential targets, like receptors for insulin, another hormone called IGF-1, and a protein called TOR.

It's not exactly back to square one. But clearly, those heady days of wine and resveratrol are over. At least as far as the scientific community is concerned. You wouldn't know that by cruising the Internet, where a search of "where to buy resveratrol" nets just under 1.25 million hits. It doesn't matter how many people are hawking it, the magic pill is not out there. Yet.

Which brings me back to CR—a *proven* strategy—and my sad admission that, on day six, I accompany my family to a Chinese restaurant, where I eat most of an egg roll, two deep-fried wontons, and a generous serving of tofu in a rich, velvety sauce that has as much relation to calorie restriction as do the fried wontons. How do I feel? Happy. Perplexed by my lack of logic.

I want to turn back the clock.

Calorie restriction is proven to turn back the clock.

I can't—I don't want to—adopt the CR Way.

It is just not a plan I can live with, even if that means I don't live as long, or as well. The superfoods approach—with generous portions, not to mention wine and chocolate—is one thing. Periodic detoxing? I can handle that. But self-imposed semistarvation? As someone said (I believe it was my bacon-loving husband), if CR doesn't actually cause you to live longer, the strain and tedium of eating this way will make you *feel* as if you're living longer.

I don't understand the few thousand true believers who have given over their lives to CR. But, for maybe the first time, I think I understand all those people who don't exercise even when faced with the incontrovertible evidence that exercise is good for just about everything that could possibly ail you. They just don't like it. Exercise seems like a chore, not a pleasure, a distasteful interruption in their day. They don't care how good it is supposed to be for you. It's just grunting and sweating to them. They hate it, like I hate CR, and they're not gonna do it. End of discussion.

It's hard, also, to not consider luck or fate or, as my fourth-grade teacher used to say, "the vicissitudes of life." There's longtime CR advocate and dedicated practitioner Roy Walford, a 138-pound dynamo, who died at age 79 of Lou Gehrig's disease. And there's my salt-everything, salami-loving father, who never met a vegetable he liked, carried an extra 30 pounds of that especially dangerous, rock-hard abdominal fat for decades—and played tennis into his eighties.

The lesson here is, of course, that we can't control everything. It's a lesson I need to be reminded of. Often. After all, I wouldn't have started this quest in the first place if I did not have something of the control freak in me. And as I've learned more about the evolving science of aging, with its new theories and its wealth of "yes, we can turn back the clock" research, I've become even more convinced of my own powers. (Just ask my daughter.) But this abbreviated experiment with CR has taught me that exerting too much control can sometimes take the gusto out of life, not to mention make you (that is, me) almost impossible to live with. The challenge, then, is to navigate a path between the supercontrolled, obsessively calculated, restricted life of someone for whom staying young is the be-all and end-all, and the path traveled by a guy like my father, who did little to help himself because, as he used to tell me all the time, "when my number is up, my number is up." I believe I'm ready to find—and to travel—that new path.

CHAPTER

fourteen

Beat the Clock

I'M CHATTING WITH A GROUP OF WOMEN, A PLASTIC CUP OF surprisingly okay white wine in my hand. It's an unpleasantly humid late-July evening in a seen-better-days New York suburb, the kind that used to be bustling with on-their-way-up young families and is now dotted with what my real estate appraiser friend euphemistically calls "deferred maintenance housing." This is where I grew up, a member of one of those on-their-way-up young families. We women are standing together in the far corner of a VFW hall, smiling at each other and squinting at the tags hanging around our necks. On them are printed not only our names, but also our photographs as they appeared in a long-ago yearbook. This is my high school reunion.

I've avoided them in the past for reasons as uncomplicated as I hated high school and have no desire to reminisce about the bad old days and as psychoanalytically complex as *Why exactly do I feel the need to present my successful adult self to all these guys I had crushes on but who never looked at me twice . . . and aren't I beyond that?* But this year I have a reason. I am an investigative reporter. I am a cultural anthropologist. I am an epidemiologist without portfolio. I am on a fact-finding mission. Where else could I be in a room with 75 people born in exactly the same year (and *no*, I am not going to tell you what year that was), 75 chronologically identical specimens? Here, in this hot and sticky hall festooned with banners and black and red (Go Panthers!) balloons, are the in-the-flesh results of everything I've been reading about all year. Here are folks who, according to the latest in scientific thinking, owe just 30 percent of who they are tonight, good or bad, to their genes. The rest is lifestyle and attitude, the circumstances they've created for themselves or had thrust upon them, maybe a touch of serendipity or, if you are a believer in such things, fate or karma.

And so, while I sip wine and work the room in a way I'd never be able to if I were not, well, *working,* I study faces. I scrutinize posture. I watch how people move. And I listen to their chosen topics of conversation, remembering Harvard University professor Ellen Langer's findings about how stage in life can trump chronological age. So there are people here talking about new career ventures, and there are people talking about grandchildren. There are people talking about health issues, and there are people talking about the trip they're taking to Greece next month. There are people talking past. There are people talking future. It is perhaps not a revelation that those in the thick of it seem animated, engaged—younger—than those who seem to have placed themselves on the sidelines.

The physical variations are quite startling, and would be even to someone who has not read the literature on differential aging. At one point, I find myself standing between a pale, slumped, gray-haired woman, her doughy features set in a permanent frown, and a slender, vivacious woman with the posture of a ballerina who, in soft light, might pass for 35. Across the room is a florid-faced bald guy with a significant gut talking to a trim, square-shouldered, curly-haired man who could be his much (much) younger cousin. They were teammates back in the day. One woman apologizes for having to sit down in mid-conversation. Her joints ache, and her doctor says she needs a second knee surgery. Another woman talks about the 10-K she ran last weekend. At one point in the evening, I stand back from the crowd and survey the scene as if I am watching a movie. I would never, ever guess that the characters onscreen are all the same age. I'd estimate that they range in age from mid-30s to early 70s. I would be not years but *decades* off. It's one thing to read about how people age at very different rates, how after 40, chronological age is the least accurate way of thinking about how old you are. It is another to experience it up close and personal.

AT THIS POINT IN MY COUNTERCLOCKWISE JOURNEY, I HAD imagined the Big Reveal. I would tell you, based on various tests and as a result of my documented yearlong efforts, how old I had become biologically. Yes, I promise I will detail some of the more interesting results, but as with anything concerning the human body, the reality is far more complicated. Just as people like my high school classmates age at very different rates, so too do body parts and systems within the same person. Just as parts of us can be healthy and other parts ill—an in-shape heart but a bad back—it seems that parts of us can be younger and parts older.

For example, for reasons neither I nor my optometrist (nor my genes) can explain, I have the eyes of a 25-year-old. Well, a nearsighted 25-year-old. I have worn glasses or contacts for faraway vision since I was in high school, but my near vision is pristine. Although presbyopia—the age-related, progressively diminishing ability to focus—is "inevitable" after age 40, my eyes continue to be able to focus on close-in objects, including that ridiculously tiny print on vitamin and supplement bottles. I don't wear reading glasses. I don't hold books at arm's length.

On the other hand, a DEXA scan—a highly reliable x-ray test that measures bone mineral density—shows that, compared with the bones of women in their 30s (the peak bone-density years), my bones are right on the borderline between normal and thinning. My T-score (reflecting something incomprehensible about standard deviations) is –1. Up to a –1, you're okay, but a score between –1 and –2.5 signals thin bones, and anywhere beyond that is considered osteoporosis. My bones, based on another score, are about average for a midlife, post-menopausal woman.

So my bones are old enough to be my eyes' mother. (You know what I mean . . .) I don't yet have osteopenia or osteoporosis, but I don't have anything to spare, either, despite the fact that I have been regularly engaging in weight-bearing exercise, eating dairy, taking calcium and vitamin D supplements, and am not a petite, small-boned person to begin with. This would be depressing and might cause me to adopt the *que sera, sera* attitude I've heard from others (like my father) if it were not for my new "think young, be optimistic" attitude and my magnificent mitochondria. You will remember from Chapter 5 that I have the mitochondria of a fit 20-something, which means my muscles use food and oxygen with youthful zest and admirable efficiency to provide considerable energy. It means I am hearty and vigorous on the inside. It means that, in this case, exercise and nutrition did make a difference.

My counterclockwise measures also made a difference—although not as dramatically—with my coronary risk panel. Although my total cholesterol went down only 13 points during my year of conscientious living, and although the number itself (216) does not look "youthful," I managed to elevate my good cholesterol by 20 points (it's now a robust 79), which means my total-cholesterol-to-good-cholesterol ratio is a youthful, heart-healthy 2.9. (Anything below 5.0 is deemed "desirable.") I'll blame the resistant-to-change, higher-than-optimal bad cholesterol on my father. I think that without my attention to fitness, food, and lifestyle, I would probably have turned out like him, on statins to bring down a cholesterol level in the mid-300s and on my way to the quadruple bypass he had in his late 60s.

There is another resistant-to-change number from my recent blood panel that I am distressed to report: my CRP, or C-reactive protein, an indicator of inflammation and a marker for future cardiovascular disease. A year ago, my CRP was higher than I wanted it to be. My doctor, noting the "moderate risk" level, recommended omega-3 supplementation. A year and 365 omega-3 horse capsules later, there's been no downward movement in that number. And remember the buzz about curcumin (turmeric) and its antiinflammatory effects? I added curcumin to the list of supplements I take more than six months ago, but those spendy bright-orange capsules seem to have made no difference. I don't want to stress over this. I could raise my cortisol levels and fast-forward my biological clock! There is a thin line between information-is-power and ignorance-is-bliss—and I'm teetering on it. Best to just stay the course and try to channel Old Oldie.

I have many other examples of my one-year-later variable biological age. A one-leg-up, hands-on-hips balance test I found in a magazine puts my current age at "less than 30." It's worth mentioning that Patrick Rabbitt, emeritus director of the aging research center at the University of Manchester University and former head of Britain's biggest ongoing study on differential aging, believes that balance could become the simplest and most reliable way of measuring a person's rate of aging. A back-of-the-hand skin pinch test says I'm in my late 40s. The Great and Powerful Oz (Dr. Oz, that is) claims that "to gauge how old your body really is, check your blood pressure." In most people, the top number rises steadily with age due to increasing stiffness of large arteries and long-term buildup of plaque. From ages 30 to 60, the top number increases from an average of 122 to 134. My number is, and has long been, between 90 and 100, depending on how stressed I am at the doctor's office. So, by blood pressure standards, I am a teenager, a teenager with low blood pressure.

As I wrote about in Chapter 4, the Web abounds with "what is your true age" self-tests, which ask many of the same questions but manage to come up with significantly different results. I have been—for brief moments in cyberspace—as young as 31 and as old as 56. Throughout this year, I have continued to find and take these tests more for entertainment value than for insight into my biological age. These tests do serve to highlight what the aging experts consider important (from nutrition to job satisfaction, exercise to education level, friendships, sleep habits, etc.), but the numbers are next to meaningless. You don't know to whom you are being compared, how these data were gathered, and how many are in the database. That also goes for in-the-flesh self-tests that ask you to—as I just did minutes ago—stand on one foot or pinch the back of your hand. What I'm saying is: Determining true biological age, arriving at a single, credible number, is impossible.

But I can make some one-year-later self-comparisons. I'm going to retake two Tufts University fitness tests I took a year ago, the comparative results of which are based on decades of rigorous research involving thousands of subjects. Then I'll repeat two other simple tests I took a year ago, an upper-body strength test and a flexibility test, and compare my before and after. I'll also retest four of the most telling biomarkers—lean body mass, percentage body fat, metabolism, and VO_2 max—to see if and how much I've managed to improve. But I do all this in a different state of mind than I was in a year ago. I do this thinking about what Ellen Langer said about being enmeshed in a culture that quantifies virtually everything: Numbers seem precise, but aren't. They may explain or confuse, reveal or obscure. Everyone is biochemically unique.

That said, it's back to the track for the walk test.

Last year I clocked a mile, walking as fast as I could, at 13.4 minutes. My pulse measured 140. According to the Tufts University charts, this put me at the low end of "good" for a 50- to 59-year-old woman, which did not please me in the least. Today I am ready, willing—and I hope able—to do better. In fact, I feel an intense sense of competition with my year-ago self. It's a lovely, cool late-summer morning. The track is empty. I lace up my almost-new Sauconys, strap on my heart rate monitor, give myself the "just do it" pep talk, and go out fast, pumping my arms and keeping my breathing as deep and regular as I can. It's four times around the track. I push it. I clock the mile at 12.58 minutes, which is better but not jump-up-and-down better. Where I see a significant difference is in my heart rate. It stays at about 120. According to the Tufts chart, this puts me squarely in the middle of the "good" range for a 40- to 49-year-old woman, a very nice improvement. I declare victory and move on to the rate of recovery test.

This test measures how quickly the heart recovers from tough, taxing exercise, which is considered a good indicator of overall cardiovascular health (which is considered a good indicator of bio age). As I wrote in Chapter 4, the test is almost as much of a math challenge as it is a physical one, but, thankfully, I did the high-level multiplication and division a year ago, so I'm all set. From the track I drive to the gym, where I jump on one of the new Spin bikes to get my heart rate up to 80 percent max and keep it there for 20 minutes. Then I stop, and two minutes later I check my heart rate. When I did this last year, the rate had gone down 68 beats, which, according to RealAge.com, made me "a lot younger" than my chronological age. This time, my heart rate decreases by 80 beats, showing increased resilience and heart health and putting me in the "outstanding" category according to one government health site. Even after reading several dozen heart recovery studies, questioning my go-to experts in exercise physiology, and checking more than 20 promising Web sites, it's impossible to find a chart that matches bio age with recovery rate. I'll have to content myself with "outstanding." Things could be worse.

The strength test is an easy redo. To keep all the conditions the same, I do my modified pushups on the floor of my writing room, as I did a year ago. I even invite my daughter to watch (and count) (and make the occasional snarky comment), as she did last year. Twenty-seven is the number to beat. Twenty-seven flies by. Okay, "flies" may be overstating it, but I am still going strong at 30, 35, 40. My daughter is making sure I don't break form, making sure the tip of my nose grazes the floor every time I go down. She is actually encouraging me! Forty-five. My biceps are burning. Forty-eight. My chest muscles are complaining. Loudly. If my daughter weren't watching and rooting for me, I'd stop right now. I collapse on the floor at 52. Not quite twice what I was able to do a year ago, but pretty damn close. Hurray for strength training! Hurray for the Sweat Chicas and those 7:00 a.m. workouts. I've turned back the clock on my upper-body strength. The chart I consulted last year now tells me I am in the "excellent" category for a woman in her 20s.

I've been working on flexibility, but maybe not as much as I should. Hot yoga was kind of a bust. Okay, a disaster. But I have attempted to incorporate at least a few minutes of stretching at the end of most of my strength workouts, and maybe once a week, twice if I am particularly virtuous, I do 15 minutes of simple yoga poses and postures. When I self-administered this test—sitting on the floor with my legs stretched out in front of me, bending at the waist and reaching forward as far as I could go—my hamstrings had screamed in revolt, and I barely touched my toes. Later, in the sports lab, my efforts encouraged by a lithe ex-gymnast, I managed to reach two inches past my toes. A minute ago, sitting on the kitchen floor, my husband, with ruler in hand, measured my reach first at five inches, then five and a half inches past my toes. The chart I referred to last year stated that a woman under 45 should be able to reach two to four inches beyond her toes. I don't know how much credit I get for going one and a half inches past the max—there's no age breakdown under 45—but I've made progress. I'm not going to give any yogini a run for her money, but clearly I am on the road to limber.

Now it's time to check back on those four benchmark biomarkers. Just about 12 months ago, my bathroom bioimpedance scale delivered the bad news that one-third of my body was fat, putting me right on the border of "overfat" (one perilous category away from, *gasp*, "obese") for a midlife woman. The scale now tells me I am a relatively svelte 27 percent fat (relative to my former self, that is, not to female athletes, who typically have body fat percentages in the mid-teens). But I'm not complaining. Twenty-seven percent is better, healthier, fitter, and "younger" than 33 percent. According to the data my Tanita scale uses, which come from National Institutes of Health and World Health Organization studies, this puts me squarely in the middle of the "healthy" category for "standard adult females" from ages 18 to 39.

The Tanita also measures muscle mass. Last year the ratio of my muscle mass to body fat earned me a disappointing 2 rating (based on Columbia University and Tanita Institute studies), which translated into "high body fat, average muscle mass." This year, having gained more than three pounds of muscle thanks to thrice-weekly strength training and dropping a bit more than 10 pounds of body fat (thank you, boot camp), my rating is a far more respectable—and youthful—6: average body fat, higher than normal muscle mass. Would I love an elite-athlete 9? You bet. Did that ship sail a long time ago? Even for a turn-back-the-clock enthusiast like me, I'm afraid so.

Still, that increased muscle mass should make a positive difference in my resting (basal) metabolic rate. Tufts' researchers say that *reduced* muscle mass is almost wholly responsible for the gradual reduction of basal metabolic rate. So my three-pound-plus *increase* in muscle mass should, theoretically, up my metabolism. A year ago, in a research lab, my RMR came in at 1,350. A few weeks ago I repeated the test, called indirect calorimetry, which involves sitting very still in a darkened room very early in the morning on an empty stomach and breathing into a tube connected to a computer that measures the oxygen you breathe and the carbon dioxide you exhale. This exchange of gases reflects how the body uses nutrients to make energy. My test this month, after adding those pounds of lean muscle and amping up my mitochondria, reveals a resting metabolic rate of 1,627. In other words, I am one chronological year older and I am 10 pounds lighter—increased age and decreased body weight both *lower* RMR—but I've managed to elevate it instead. Rather than the RMR of an average woman in her mid-50s, I now have the RMR of a fit grad-school-age woman. Increasing the RMR is excellent counterclockwise news . . . unless you are a CR devotee, in which case you'd be working hard to make the numbers go in the opposite direction.

Finally, it's on to the VO_2 max test. With all the positive news I've been getting about fat, muscle, metabolism, and mitochondria, I'm psyched to do this test. Maybe too psyched. I wake up the morning of the test with a bad case of nerves, which I interpret as performance anxiety. If I could go for a run I'd feel better, but I can't. I am supposed to arrive at the lab without having exercised for 24 hours. Also, moderately carb-loaded and very well hydrated. My appointment is not until 10:30, but at 6:00 a.m. I'm pacing the kitchen and hyperventilating. I pet the cat, which calms him but does little for me. I practice yoga breathing while telling myself *This is not a test*. But, in fact, it *is*. VO_2 max is thought to be the best single indicator of fitness, and fitness is an excellent overall indicator of biological age.

I drink four glasses of water, the final one laced with electrolytes, eat a bagel, pick up a cappuccino for a quick jolt of energy, and present myself at Andy Lovering's Cardiopulmonary and Respiratory Physiology Laboratory ready for business. A chipper grad student tapes monitors to my forehead, attaches a new mouthpiece to the hose, adjusts foot pedals, and enters my data in the computer as Andy plugs my iPod into the sound system. It's Lady Gaga, "The Edge of Glory." I'm so ready for this.

The test is much easier than I remember. When the grad student ups the resistance, I barely feel it. I am breathing hard but not out of breath. I'm damp but not full-on sweaty. I'm listening to Pat Benatar, Ke$ha . . . and then, just like that, the test is over. It doesn't feel as if more than 12 high-intensity moments have gone by. I sit on the hard, narrow bike seat, cycling slowly to cool down while the computer generates charts and graphs. I'm eager to see how I've done.

The printout shows that my VO_2 max is either two or three points higher than last year's scores (depending on which of the two tests I took last year I compare it to), which is okay and puts me in the above-average column for 36- to 45-year-old women (better than last year, when my score placed me in the 46- to 55-year-old age category). But Lovering tells me not to make too much of this. A few points one way or the other are within normal statistical variation. What he and Ty, the grad student, are more impressed with is another number, the "work" (expressed in watts) I accomplished during the test. Apparently, I did 20 percent more work at the same oxygen consumption. In other words, aerobically, I am 20 percent more efficient than I was a year ago. I'm proud of the improvement, of course, but I am downright delighted to learn the results of a recent large-scale study that focused on fitness. Even modest gains in middle age—far more modest than my 20 percent boost—translated into significantly lower incidences of eight major diseases.

This is aging backward—no doubt about it.

But, after all this, can I pinpoint my biological age? Not really. Some parts of me appear to be as young as mid-20s; other parts of me are mid-50s. Averaging the results would be meaningless. My go-to experts say I should pay the most attention to those results that measure fitness because they are measuring the health of my arteries, the strength and efficiency of my heart, and the vitality of my mitochondria, which cumulatively go a long way to define age. But how can I ignore my middle-aged bones and my less-than-youthful cholesterol panel? On the other hand, there's my elite-athlete-level blood pressure. You see the problem. Add to this my growing disenchantment with the whole "let's quantify everything" thing.

Still, I think you are expecting a proclamation at this point. So I proclaim that, biologically, I may be anywhere from a (too optimistic) late 30s to a (probably more realistic) mid-40s, neither of which ages I have seen in a while. Like, a pretty long while. How do I feel? Healthy, strong, full of energy, and if not "lithe," at least not creaky. Can I assign an age to that? I can't. I know I had less energy than this in my 20s, when I smoked a pack a day and my only exercise was walking up and down the steps of university libraries. How do I look? I don't think you'd mistake me for someone in her late 30s. But when I've had a sound night's sleep and begun the day with a few minutes of yoga and a long bike ride in the country, when my hair is looking particularly big (and not in a Country Music Awards kind of way), when I'm not standing in harsh light—and when it's not a teenage daughter making the assessment—I could pass for mid- to late 40s. When I look at lauren50.jpg, my computer-aged face as it is supposed to look at age 50, and then look at my actual face in the mirror, my mirror face is definitely younger. That would be meaningless if I wasn't biologically younger, if I didn't feel younger, if I didn't have the what's-the-next-challenge attitude of a younger person. But I am, and I do.

So have I found the Secret? The One True Path? What exactly have I learned this year? What do I, self-experimenter, human guinea pig, (mildly) intrepid reporter, (mildly) freaked-out midlifer, bring back from the frontiers of anti-aging? I thought the big lesson would come in the form of the to-do list to end all to-do lists. The Six Surefire Things You Can Do to Age Backward. The Seven Secrets of Eternal Youth. The Eight Keys to Living Counterclockwise. But what I have learned is both less grandiose and more life changing.

I've learned from the literature, especially the groundbreaking MacArthur Foundation study, that lifestyle choices trump genes. Not always. Not for all people. But to know that how and how quickly (or slowly) we age is determined 30 percent by genes and 70 percent by choices within our control is *huge*, empowering, energizing news for everyone—but especially for someone like me whose mother died of Alzheimer's and whose father suffered from coronary artery disease.

I've learned that the healthy, youth-promoting lifestyle advice that is so frequently and ubiquitously given and now seems so obvious that it's not worth mentioning anymore is not obvious to more than 90 percent of us and is very much worth mentioning. I was floored by the findings of a retrospective study published in the *American Journal of Medicine* that looked at midlife and older adults' adherence to the five behaviors most associated with vitality and health: eating a diet rich in fruits and vegetables, engaging in regular exercise, not smoking, maintaining a healthy weight, and consuming only moderate amounts of alcohol. Nothing earthshaking there, no medical breakthroughs, just the ho-hum we know so well, right? The study found that in 1988, 15 percent of adults ages 40 to 75 followed all five behaviors. *Fifteen*. Catch your breath, because in 2006, according to the study, only 8 percent were following those behaviors. Astonishingly, amid the backyard-farmer, farmers' market, locavore, and organic movements—not to mention the medical-media juggernaut touting a healthy diet—those who regularly ate five servings of fruits and vegetables a day decreased from 42 percent in 1988 to 26 percent by the mid-2000s. (During the same period, and undoubtedly related to it, the rate of adult obesity went from 28 to 36 percent.) The lesson I take from this is that many of us, far too many of us, are making our own beds and will be lying—permanently—in them. As in eternal rest. And too soon. It is the underside of having all this control over our own health and aging.

I've also learned a thing or two about these "behaviors" that can keep us youthful. I've learned, both from the literature and from the lives of real people (their successes and cautionary tales), that it is the *long-term* accumulation of *small* decisions and *daily* actions that lead to a vigorous and healthy life, not some drastic change (raw foods, anyone?) or some overarching New Year's resolution that is just a recipe for failure and self-recrimination (been there) or the newest get-young-quick scheme. In fact, as all my reading and interviewing have impressed upon me, aging is an enormously complex, interdependent, and interwoven biochemical and psychosocial process. Interceding with one action, from upping the level of a certain hormone to supplementing with a promising-in-the-lab substance, is often ineffective or even harmful. It is, as the authors of *The Longevity Project* say, a "constellation of habits and patterns of living" that are associated with a healthy, vital (and long) life. It is happy relationships as well as healthy foods, job satisfaction as well as gym time, optimism about the future and an ability to express feelings as well as omega-3s and sunscreen.

And maybe more. It was eye-opening to read about the healthiest, longest-lived cultures on earth, cultures extensively studied by both medical researchers and anthropologists. Much has been written about the pristine dietary habits and exemplary levels of physical activity that are part of the everyday lives of these people, but for me the aha moment came when I learned about the attitudes these cultures hold concerning aging and older people. It's worth repeating what I've written about this: These are societies where our Western concept of "old" never took root. Aging in these cultures is not associated with diminution of vigor or, more important, of usefulness. Rather, activity, involvement, and engagement continue unabated throughout life. Older people are as integral to the health and welfare of these societies as younger people, and it may be that this belief even more than healthy behaviors keeps those older people demonstrably, verifiably biologically young. Attitude, feelings of self-efficacy, and age cues from the environment seem to play discernible roles in how we age. That, in itself, is a huge lesson.

Could this positive (or at least neutral) attitude about aging and older people ever be part of our culture? It would require extraordinary, dare I say *mind-blowing*, change politically, culturally, economically, and every other way imaginable. Because I am trying hard to make "optimism about the future" a part of my constellation of youthful habits, and because this applies not only to my personal future but also to The Future, I am going to say that such change is possible. And I am going to say that right now, at this moment in time, this change may be the most possible it will ever be. Why? Because of the frequently ridiculed and more-often-than-not dismissed generational cohort of which I am a part. Yes, I am talking about the baby boomers, the pig-in-the-python generation, the unique-in-history demographic bulge that has—for both good and ill—remodeled society as it has passed through it. Perhaps, 76 million strong and currently in control of more than 80 percent of personal financial assets and 50 percent of discretionary buying power, this generation can effect such change. It can effect it by example, by continuing to actively contribute to and engage with the culture, by choosing not to live in isolated, gated, same-age communities, by embracing change, by staying both physically and intellectually resilient. By using our added years of youthful good health to be useful and do good.

If this sounds like a call to arms, it is. I am calling *myself* to arms too. These are *my* marching orders. And they directly relate to why someone, anyone, me, would want to turn back the clock. It's not—or shouldn't be—because our culture idolizes youth and we want to be "forever young." It can't be because we deny aging. To deny aging is to deny life. To make youth the goal or the destination is to set off on a journey that will always, always end in failure. That's what I've learned this year.

Amid all these forays into the hope and hype of aging backward, amid the rigors I've subjected myself to, and the tests I've taken, and the measurements I've gathered while striving for some definitive (but, alas, elusive) youthful bio age, it's come as a revelation that youthfulness is not the destination. It's the path. I know that sounds like a cross between a cut-rate Zen master and a cheesy bumper sticker, but I offer it with the greatest sincerity. It is, I am now convinced, the ongoing act of living "younger" that is itself *being* younger. I'm not adopting behaviors so that I can arrive at a younger me. I am embodying the younger me as I adopt (and live) the behaviors.

But really it's not about being young at all—as in 35 or 46 or some other number. It's about high-level wellness. It's about having an abundance of energy—physical, intellectual, and creative. It's about continuing to feel in the thick of things, seek out new experiences, make plans, embrace change, stay flexible and resilient. It's about remaining curious, remaining open to—*welcoming* of—surprise. It's about choosing to *do* something with this prolonged health span, about making *use* of a fit body and an agile mind.

But it is also, I admit, about this—because, high-minded, life-changing thoughts notwithstanding, there is, *sigh*, this:

I AM STANDING AT THE COUNTER DRINKING A CAPPUCCINO at a local espresso joint and bakery. My son Zane is a part-time barista here. I've just bicycled into town, 6.6 miles on a challengingly serpentine and hilly country road. I'm all decked out: helmet and sunglasses, bike gloves and hydration pack, heart rate monitor, bike shorts. When I left the house, my husband said I looked like I was ready to explore another planet, like Dune.

Zane and I have been joking around as he grabs bread off the shelves for customers, makes drinks, heats slices of pizza. There's another guy behind the counter, college age, whom I don't recognize. My son grabs a tub of dishes and disappears back into the kitchen. The young guy moves toward the end of the counter where I'm standing.

"Hi," he says, stretching out his hand, "I'm Alex, Zane's new protégé." I smile at him.

"Hi," I say, shaking his hand, "I'm Lauren, Zane's old mother." He gives me the once-over. Not a snarky once-over, but a kind of interested-assessment once-over.

"Oh," he says, "I wouldn't say 'old.'"

A Note on Sources

IF YOU WANT TO READ ALL THE GET YOUNG/STAY YOUNG books out there, you'll have to, well, stay young. For a *really* long time. If you read at the rate of a book a week, you can get through the current list—from *Treat Your Face Like a Salad* (the imagination runs wild) to *Anti-Aging Herbs* (sprinkled on the face/salad?) to *77 Outrageously Effective Anti-Aging Tips and Secrets* (which might involve treating your face like a salad)—in 159 years and 46 weeks.

Obviously, I didn't read all the books out there to prepare for writing mine. My research—I am referring to the reading, not the interviewing, observing, and participating—primarily involved reviewing and working hard to make sense of original studies published in credible, peer-reviewed medical and scientific journals. I located these published studies through PubMed and Google Scholar searches and by following the suggestions of the various experts I interviewed and spent time with. I try to give enough hints in the text (a searchable keyword, the year of the study, the academic homes of the scientists) so that you can easily find the research if you are so inclined.

I do want to say a word about the books I found to be most helpful. There's a big difference between the amped-up bestsellers packed with recycled advice and the thoughtful, research-based books that investigate and explain the mysteries of aging. Among the latter, I found two older books to be the most helpful. John W. Rowe and Robert L. Kahn's *Successful Aging*, clear and authoritative, outlines the (still, after almost two decades) groundbreaking work undertaken by the MacArthur Foundation Study of Successful Aging in America. Equally as instructive is *Biomarkers* by William Evans and Irwin H. Rosenberg, then professors of nutrition and medicine, respectively, and both research heavyweights at the USDA Human Nutrition Research Center on Aging at Tufts University. *The Longevity Project* by Howard S. Friedman and Leslie R. Martin, based on one of the most extensive studies of long life ever conducted, makes fascinating reading. Sally Beare's *50 Secrets of the World's Longest Living People* popularizes the extensive research conducted on cultures where long life and good health go hand in hand.

Of the other books I found helpful for their summaries of the best of anti-aging research, I found two to be noteworthy: John Robbins's *Healthy at 100* and Elizabeth Somer's *Age-Proof Your Body*. And it's hard not to give a nod to Deepak Chopra's *Ageless Body, Timeless Mind* for its focus on the now scientifically verified connection between mind and body when it comes to health and well-being. It was good to read Chopra in concert with Martin Seligman's eminently practical *Learned Optimism*, Lionel Tiger's (yes, his real name) venerable *Optimism: The Biology of Hope*, and Ellen Langer's many published studies.

I want to mention the two big books from the two big players in the anti-aging arena: *The Official Anti-Aging Revolution* (by the founders of the American Academy of Anti-Aging Medicine—the folks who put on the Las Vegas conference I reported on in Chapter 1) and *Life Extension Revolution* (from the Life Extension Foundation, one of the first and largest organizations dedicated to longevity and health). Here you will find the most optimistic take on our ability to control the aging process, including strong arguments for hormone replacement therapy (including human growth hormone, DHEA, and testosterone), as well as strong endorsements of a pharmacopoeia of vitamins, minerals, amino acids, and other anti-aging nutrients yet to be subjected to rigorous testing. These books are unabashed cheerleaders for the anti-aging movement and the multibillion-dollar industry it has spawned, and are instructive, if only for that reason.

It's important to give the critics their due. There are those who argue quite persuasively that we are being sold a bill of goods—and at a very high price. Aging is not a disease to be cured, they say, but a natural stage of life. The new Old Age (the "80 is the new 60" approach) is a myth, and a dangerous one at that. It makes it possible for us to ignore deep and troubling problems in health care and eldercare. Three smart, angry—and more than occasionally sharp-tongued—authors are worth reading on this subject: Muriel R. Gillick (*The Denial of Aging*), Susan Jacoby (*Never Say Die*), and Arlene Weintraub (*Selling the Fountain of Youth*).

Finally, I want to mention two beautiful, important, and truly transcendent books that opened my eyes to the messy miracle of the human body, Sherwin Nuland's *The Wisdom of the Body* and Lewis Thomas's *The Lives of a Cell*.

Acknowledgments

I LOVE NARRATIVE NONFICTION BECAUSE IT IS ABOUT BOTH the power of fact and the resonance of story. It gives me the opportunity to be reporter, researcher, and shirttail cultural anthropologist as well as teller of tales and crafter of narrative. I love it because it gives me the opportunity to go out into the world, into many different worlds, and meet people I'd never meet in my nonwriting life, watch them, pepper them with questions, immerse myself in their universes, and learn from them. In truth, I feed off their energy and passion. The thanks I owe to many of the people I will mention here is therefore deeper and more elemental than simply acknowledging those who guided (or accompanied) me on this counterclockwise journey. I have built my career on—and greatly enriched my life with—the intellectual ardor of people who help satisfy my curiosity and fill me with stories.

I thank the ebullient Karl Ricanek, director of the Face Aging Group, and his terrific colleagues Midori Albert, Amrutha Sethuram, Tracy Chen, Yishi Wang, Yaw Chang, and Eric Patterson. I thank plastic surgeon Mark Jewell for sharing his expertise so generously and skin maven Sherry Lavelle for those rejuvenating (albeit painful) treatments. I thank Jan Stafl, MD, and Andrew Elliott, ND, my go-to medical experts, and the following researchers who took the time to share their work with me, help me untangle some of the mysteries of aging, and, in some cases, aid and abet my guinea pig proclivities: Douglas Seals, George Merriam, David Cook, Hans Dreyer, Tory Hagen, Andrew Lovering, John Halliwell, Christopher Minson, Melissa Gergel, and the Bowerman Sports Science Clinic crew. I thank detox expert Ellen Syverson, nutritionist Beth Naylor, health instructors Stacie Steinbock and Sharrie Herbold, happiness "guidess" Barb Ryan, hypnotherapist Rosemarie Eisenberg, life coach Jen Morton, and raw foodist Jill Devine (and Ann Best for helping me find her). Special thanks to Lisa Heyamoto for research assistance early on.

I owe an enormous debt to the trainers and fitness professionals who shared their knowledge, worked with me, inspired me, and assumed (sometimes but not always correctly) that I could do just about anything: Kirkland Sale, Cathy Grierson, Janice Poloway, Katya Hayes, Tiffany Yeates Gust, Robin Evans Walden, Sharon Read, Anna Marie Smith, Stretchin' Gretchen Raddatz, Jay Martin, Anita Horsley, Roma "Panther" Pawelek, and most especially the amazing Randy Davis.

And where would I be without the support, encouragement, and occasional heckling of Linda Fontes Brunson, Tony Coslet, Patricia Dant, Cher Donnel, Morgaine Hager, Mark Matassa, Perrie Patterson, Jan Ryan, Evelyn Sharenov, Leslie Steeves, Lizzie Reis, Jane Scheidecker, and Mike Welsh? Thanks for rooting me on. Special thanks to the always-strategic communicator and social media savant, Kim Sheehan, my loyal buddy, coconspirator, and pro bono brand manager.

And where would I be if I hadn't met 'n' sweated with the likes of Audrey Adams, Laura Ashworth, Tracey Ellerson, Lorraine Gutierrez, Brady Mitchell, Michelle Riklan, Maria Saddler, Cindy Spires, Karin Langwasser, and especially Natasha Dyer (who should be cloned so that everyone can have a Natasha Dyer in her life). A very big thank-you to the kick-ass women of the Big Climbers, the Pretty in Stinkers, the Pisgahpalians, the Bike Chicas, and the Sweat Chicas. To my dear friends and sweat sisters Shelli Robertson, Beth Machamer, and Ellen Chamberlain, thank you for keeping the bar high and the humor low.

I thank (and so very much appreciate) my hardheaded, softhearted agent, David Black, for caring about both me and my work. And I am deeply indebted to all the folks at Rodale who care so much about health and wellness, and understood what I was doing and why. A big thanks to Trisha Calvo for striking the balance between trusting me and challenging me. You are the editor every writer hopes to work with. My thanks also to Nancy Elgin, copy editor extraordinaire, to designers George Karabotsos and Laura White, and to Aly Mostel and Brent Gallenberger for their enthusiasm and hard work in promoting and marketing the book.

And finally and most lovingly, *grazie mille, mia famiglia*: To Jackson for helping me plot the superfoods chapter, and for his design genius and digital chops (he designed my blog, Counterclockwisebook.com, and shot and edited the book trailer—and is available for hire!). To Zane, who created an extraordinary, from-scratch, 20-item, 100 percent superfoods dinner for Mother's Day and whose love of cycling reignited mine. To Lizzie for spending two solid weeks hiking hard with me and almost never complaining. To Tom, for continuing to be surprised and occasionally amused after all these years, and for supporting what I do even when—especially when—he doesn't have a clue why I do it.

Index